Dow   02/03   £18·95

D0490463

The Earthscan Reader in Sustainable Tourism

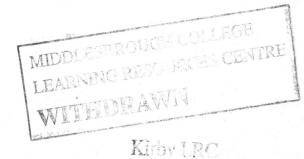

The Earthscan Reader in Sustainable Tourism

Edited by Lesley France

Earthscan Publications Ltd

First published in the UK in 1997 by
Earthscan Publications Limited

Copyright © ETC UK Ltd, 1997

Reprinted 1999, 2002

A catalogue record for this book is available from the British Library

ISBN: paperback 1 85383 408 4   hardback 1 85383 409 2

Typesetting and page design by PCS Mapping & DTP, Newcastle upon Tyne

Printed and bound by Biddles Ltd, *www.biddles.co.uk*

Cover design by Andrew Corbett

For a full list of publications, please contact:
Earthscan Publications Ltd
120 Pentonville Road
London N1 9JN
Tel: +44 (0)20 7278 0433
Fax: +44 (0)20 7278 1142
email: earthinfo@earthscan.co.uk
WWW: http://www.earthscan.co.uk

Earthscan is an editorially independent subsidiary of Kogan Page Limited
and publishes in association with WWF-UK and the International Institute
for Environment and Development.

Contents

Acronyms

BTA	British Tourist Association
CAMPFIRE	The Communal Areas Management Programme
CTO	Caribbean Tourism Organization
CTRC	Caribbean Tourism Research and Development Centre
DWC	District Wildlife Committee (CAMPFIRE)
ECTWT	Ecumenical Coalition on Third World Tourism
ETB	English Tourist Board
GDP	Gross Domestic Product
IUCN	International Union for the Conservation of Nature
MTO	Maasai Tourism Organization
NPD	National Parks Division (Thailand)
OAS	Organization of American States
PATA	Pacific Asia Travel Association
PKF	Panel Kerr Forster
TAP	Tourist Action Plan (Jamaica)
TAT	Tourist Authority of Thailand
TDAP	Tourism Development Action Programme (Bermuda)
UNCED	United Nations Conference on Environment and Sustainability
USAID	United States Aid in Development
VWC	Village Wildlife Committee (CAMPFIRE)
WCED	World Commission on Environment and Development
WCS	World Conservation Strategy
WTO	World Tourism Organization
WWC	World Wildlife Committee (CAMPFIRE)
WWF	World Wide Fund for Nature

Acknowledgements

The editor would like to thank Donna Porter and Ann Smith at ETC UK for their unfailingly cheerful administrative support. Thanks are also due to ETC members, including John Kirkby, Phil O'Keefe and, above all, Mike Sill, for their helpful comments on the text and their encouragement. Generations of undergraduate and graduate students of tourism at the University of Northumbria have joined in discussions of many of the ideas advanced in this Reader and to them may be attributed its inspiration. Finally I would like to thank Jonathan Sinclair Wilson and his colleagues at Earthscan.

NOTE TO READERS

Unless otherwise indicated, all references within the extracts refer to the original publications from which the extracts have been taken.

The sequence [...] indicates that text has been omitted.

Chapter 1

Introduction

This reader is an attempt to draw together material that explains how and why tourism has emerged as a major international industry, the problems it has generated and, above all, the search for solutions that try to introduce a measure of sustainability. The meaning and reality of sustainability within tourism are explored through theoretical readings and case studies. Grouped under headings that are clearly related to Agenda 21, one of the outcomes of the United Nations Conference on Environment and Development (UNCED) held at Rio de Janeiro in 1992, each set of extracts has its own introduction. An overview of tourism in this general introduction sets the context and provides a framework for the readings. Inevitably these are selective; space prevents the inclusion of many interesting and valuable items. Nevertheless, the extracts chosen should give all those interested in this increasingly important approach an insight into the relevant literature.

THE SCALE AND IMPORTANCE OF TOURISM

The number of people who travel for pleasure is believed to comprise between two-thirds and three-quarters of all travellers (Elliott 1991). Inevitably they are not spread evenly across the world. This is as true for international movements as it is for domestic travel, which has been estimated to generate ten times the numbers of tourists and seven times the expenditure (World Tourism Organization (WTO) quoted in Elliott 1991, 4). In large countries, like the US, domestic tourism is of considerable significance. However, where many small countries are juxtaposed and travel among them is relatively easy, as in Europe, which recorded 60 per cent of all international arrivals in 1995 (WTO 1996), international tourism is proportionately more important. A similar situation exists where individuals choose to flee inclement climates in search of the sun, like many who travel from Canada to the Caribbean or from the UK to countries bordering the Mediterranean. There are exceptions, like the French, who often prefer to take their holidays within their own territories (Elliott 1991), partly because there is a degree of climatic and environmental variety within the country; but also because of socio-economic factors, like the high incidence of second home ownership and the distinctive quality of life; and psychological factors, that include an element of chauvinism.

Despite the enormous scale of domestic tourism the industry is fragmented, independently organized, and almost impossible to estimate accurately. However, it is upon the international tourism industry that most of the readings within this book focus. Nevertheless, the principles underlying both the theory and the selected case studies are, in general, applicable to domestic as well as to international tourism. While statistics are more readily available for international tourism than

Table 1.1 *International World Tourist Arrivals*

Year	Number of arrivals (millions)
1950	25.3
1960	69.3
1965	112.9
1970	165.8
1975	222.3
1980	284.3
1985	327.6
1990	455.7
1995	561.0

Source: WTO 1995; WTO 1996.

for the domestic industry, they remain far from standardized or accurate (Callaghan, Long and Robinson 1994). With this proviso, a measure of the importance of international tourism can be obtained from figures produced by the WTO (1996).

International world tourism arrivals reached 561 millions in 1995, a dramatic increase from the early post-war figure of 25 millions, and even from the period of boom in the industry during the 1970s and mid-1980s (see Table 1.1). Long-haul tourism destinations especially have shown increased growth in recent years, with Africa experiencing a modest increase in the number of arrivals, while the Middle East, East Asia and the Pacific, and South Asia have demonstrated buoyant tourist activity (Table 1.2). The Caribbean has also registered a relatively sustained growth of inward tourism, especially in the cruise market (WTO 1996).

The size and importance of the tourist industry is not just reflected in the numbers of arrivals, but also in terms of its value. In 1995 tourism receipts accounted for 30 per cent of the value of world trade in the service sector and almost 8 per cent of the total value of world trade (WTO 1996). Tourism is particularly important as a source of foreign exchange and employment in developing countries, representing more than 10 per cent of their total trade in 1994. Continued growth occurred in 1995, especially in East Asia and the Pacific, in South Asia, and in the Caribbean (WTO 1996). Nevertheless, in spite of a loss of

Table 1.2 *International Tourist Arrivals by Region (millions)*

Region	1985	1990	1995
Africa	9.7	15.1	18.7
Americas	66.4	93.6	110.6
East Asia/Pacific	30.8	53.1	83.0
Europe	213.8	286.7	333.3
Middle East	6.2	7.6	11.1
South Asia	2.5	3.2	4.3

Source: WTO 1996

market share to Asian countries as world tourism diversified and new destinations emerged, Europe and the Americas have maintained their traditional positions of dominance in international tourism. Together they accounted for almost 80 per cent of tourist arrivals in 1995 and 71 per cent of receipts.

DEFINITIONS AND THE EVOLUTION OF TOURISM

The concept of leisure has assumed increasing importance in the lives of many in western society during the last century. Today it is perceived as the antithesis of work rather than as an integral part of daily living, as it was in the past and as it still is in some other cultures.

There is a great deal of overlap between the various components of the whole set of ideas relating to leisure, but the emphasis is frequently on enjoyment. Samuel Johnson's definition of 'play', one of the components of the concept, set the context when he described it as 'to do something not as a task but for pleasure' (Armitage 1977, 11). Indulgence in an activity that 'comforts or consoles' (OED 1989) is common to both play *and* recreation. They are carried out in leisure, which provides 'freedom or opportunity' to spend time 'as one pleases' (OED 1989). Leisure is not always narrowly interpreted as residual time, ie that which is not devoted to work or other commitments, but also as the activities that take place in such time, when it overlaps with recreation and with play (Shaw and Williams 1994). These activities denote an attitude of mind and are usually enjoyable and revitalizing (Shaw and Williams 1994, Urry 1990), in direct contrast to the experiences of many people who are engaged in boring and repetitive work.

The separation of work and leisure is a fairly modern phenomenon. In the Middle Ages in Europe, and in more traditional – especially agricultural – societies even today, people have often had more leisure (Pimlott 1968). The loss of opportunities for enjoyment built into the daily and seasonal rhythm of life in the past is not hard to explain. In part it was a result of the widespread adoption of puritanical ideas as a reaction to the profligacy and vice of the early seventeenth century. More fundamental were the contemporaneous economic and social changes that led, among other things, to the rise of industry, the extension of the monetary economy, agricultural depopulation and the growth of the cities (Pimlott 1968). The significance of these factors is that they altered working patterns so that those labouring in the new manufacturing industries operated in shifts, their lives dominated by machines. This contrasts starkly with traditional, seasonal patterns of work. Another important influence in the emergence of new attitudes to work and life, that were to alter our approach to leisure, was undoubtedly the early twentieth century development of paid holidays (Urry 1990).

Expanding horizons, resulting from increased leisure time, wealth and technological advances like the railway, allowed more people to travel further afield in search of pleasurable experiences as the nineteenth century progressed. Nineteenth century travellers became twentieth century tourists, following prescribed programmes to see new places for their 'interest, scenery or the like' (OED 1989). A tourist, it was said, is 'on holiday from his normal life' (Feifer 1985, 2). Yet, in spite of the changing nature of the concept of leisure through history, certain characteristics remain the same. These are rooted in human behaviour, with people from different social classes and with different psychological profiles perpetuating traditions and attitudes over 1000 years old. Ancient Roman customs such as Saturnalia, when slaves and their masters exchanged places, are echoed in the middle class tourists of the late twentieth century who seek to be 'king/queen for a day' (Urry 1990, 11). These tourists rarely favour the label they are given. Most prefer to be called 'travellers', who are seen as journeying to strange places in foreign countries in a spirit of independence (OED 1989, Feifer 1985), like their counterparts in the past. They are in search of the faraway rather than the familiar (Urry 1990) and although many do wish to remain within their own 'environment bubble' and so concentrate into tourist enclaves (Lea 1988, Pearce 1989), where they are often provided with the 'imaginative hedonism' (Urry 1990, 13) they seek, there are still those who 'travel widely to different sorts of places seeking different distractions because they are fickle, tired of soft living, and always seek after something which eludes them' (Seneca quoted in Feifer 1985, 9). The existence of travel with such unpredictable characteristics, lacking homogeneity and in search of a self-directed, highly individual approach obviously, therefore, has its roots embedded firmly within history. It surfaces not simply in the 'new tourists' described by Poon (1993), but in all those whose motivations differ from the majority of the population. Before the nineteenth century most travellers came into this category and so constituted the 'mass'. They wanted, as Seneca said (ibid), to 'experience something different', a phrase Poon also used to describe the 'new tourists' (1993, 10). Nonetheless, the analogy cannot be pushed too far. Many travellers in the past used highly organized structures: the splendid roads and post houses of the Roman Empire; the network of medieval monasteries that provided accommodation throughout Western Europe; and the stagecoach system and inns of the sixteenth, seventeenth and eighteenth centuries all facilitated the movement of those who were able to travel and directed them along formalized channels.

TYPES OF TOURIST

The various types of tourists influence the nature of the holiday experience they demand and the opportunities available for the provision of more sustainable forms of tourism. Relatively simple classifications devised by Cohen (1972) and Plog (1972) are determined by the attitude of individuals towards their trip, their expectations and the role of such an experience within their lives. Table 1.3 shows the whole spectrum. At one extreme is the small number of allocentrics or drifters and explorers who are prepared to try new, exotic and challenging situations in which there is a degree of risk, in order to obtain a novel and more authentic travel experience. Such people are absorbed into different cultures with minimum impact. They are travellers who journey independently and eschew organized forms of travel. In contrast, psychocentrics or organized mass tourists prefer the security of a familiar environment from which risk has largely been eliminated. Their experience is created for them by the holiday industry and the perceived reality of their destination is rarely a true reflection of local life, but one which has been tamed and packaged to reduce contact with the indigenous population. Between these extremes is a range of tourist types that varies according to a preference for novelty and risk rather than security and familiarity, and for organized travel in contrast to independent journeying.

It is perhaps here that Poon's 'old' and 'new' tourists (1993) fit most appropriately. 'Old' tourists, with their desire to escape from work and home to a sunny

Table 1.3 *Types of Tourist*

	Cohen (1972)	*Plog (1972)*	
Non-institutionalized traveller	Drifter Explorer	Allocentric	Adventurer in search of new travel experiences
Institutionalized traveller	Individual mass tourist	Mid-centric	Individual travel arrangements made to increasingly well-known destinations
	Organised mass tourist	Psychocentric	Package holiday-makers in search of familiarity at their destination

destination about which they can later boast to friends and relatives (Poon 1993), equate with psychocentrics, who Cohen (1972) and Plog (1972) also designate 'mass tourists'. 'New' tourists, whose search is for novel experiences and who wish to be independent (Poon 1993), are more akin to allocentric travellers. Cohen and Plog affirm the relatively small numbers of allocentrics whose psychology dictates an adoption of Poon's 'new tourism', while Poon asserts that, ultimately, 'new tourists' will become the norm and outnumber those who travel to traditional destinations for motivations of escape in risk-free surroundings. However she does acknowledge (Poon 1993) that, in the short term, demand for traditional holidays from new markets in eastern Europe, Asia, the Pacific and Africa, could well delay the realization of the widespread introduction of new patterns.

Alternative, more adventurous forms of tourism, like ecotourism, are favoured by people whose characteristics place them towards the allocentric end of the tourist spectrum, and who have come to be described as the 'new tourists' (Poon 1993). It is often suggested (Shaw and Williams 1994, Jarviluoma 1992, Millman and Januarius 1989) that it is precisely these forms of tourism that provide greater opportunities for sustainable development. The supposition is generally made that traditional forms of mass tourism are inherently unsustainable (Millman 1989, Lane 1990, Ferguson 1991, Shaw and Williams 1994). Unfortunately the rapid growth of a global tourism industry, in which the number of allocentric tourists remains relatively low and those of mass tourists is still high, implies an inability to achieve sustainability in tourism. The discussion and illustration of this dilemma is an important focus of this reader.

THE IMPACTS OF TOURISM

Since the Second World War increasing numbers of people have come to expect a holiday as an integral and necessary part of their life. So the pressures placed upon destination areas have risen and the consequent effects are only too apparent. The search for holiday destinations that offer a different perspective from that of mundane daily life in the urban and industrialized countries, where the majority of international tourists originate, has tended to focus on peripheral areas. Transport improvements and the economies of scale associated with them, and with the 'packaging' of destinations during the last half century, have led to significant cost savings in real terms that have been passed on to consumers. These have allowed wealthier and more adventurous people to extend their searches for new experiences to more distant countries.

Models

As early as the 1960s Christaller (1964) was talking about expanding peripheries as holidaymakers began to travel further afield. This, and related concepts, have been formalized in a number of models that seek to provide a theoretical framework for tourism studies. Those most commonly applied are classified in Table 1.4 according to their major characteristics. They tend to focus on the supply side, ie on aspects of tourism in the destination area, and generally choose to examine a restricted number of factors, thereby permitting them to be arranged into sub-groups.

Miossec (1976) and Gormsen (1981) considered the evolution of tourism at the destination in a spatial and dynamic framework that linked the behaviour and style of tourists to the geographical pattern of their distribution. Thurot (1973) perceived this evolution in terms of class succession, while Butler's widely quoted model (Mathieson and Wall 1982, Pearce 1989, Cooper and Jackson 1989 etc) summarizes the life cycle of tourism development in a destination area. He uses the types and numbers of tourists, and the level and nature of local involvement, as major factors in establishing the position of such an area in his life cycle.

Lungren (1973) introduced the notion of linkages within the tourism sector and this was also a theme in Britton's (1980) model, which focused on the degree of local involvement in the context of Fijian tourism. His model stressed the dependency of the periphery on the core, not just for tourists themselves, but also for capital, entrepreneurial ability, skilled labour and technology. Profits, it was suggested, are repatriated from the periphery to the core. Although originally set in a developing world context, this model is equally applicable to peripheral areas in more developed continents and/or countries.

Only Britton's model is relatively comprehensive and even that has a distinctive perspective. The relationship between ownership patterns and local participation is highlighted by a large sub-group of models that use these factors to explain the dynamic pattern of tourism development. They are frequently set within a spatial context. Work by Butler and Britton is especially widely acknowledged and applied, and demonstrates some links with earlier models by Lungren, Thurot, Peck and Lepie. Doxey attempts to explain the links between tourism development and behaviour in which a change of attitude over time can be seen by host communities as tourism fatigue develops.

To complete the picture, sub-groups can also be identified on the demand side of tourism, with Cohen, Plog and Smith detailing the nature and motivation of various types of tourist/traveller.

6

Table 1.4 *Classification of Some Common Tourism Models*

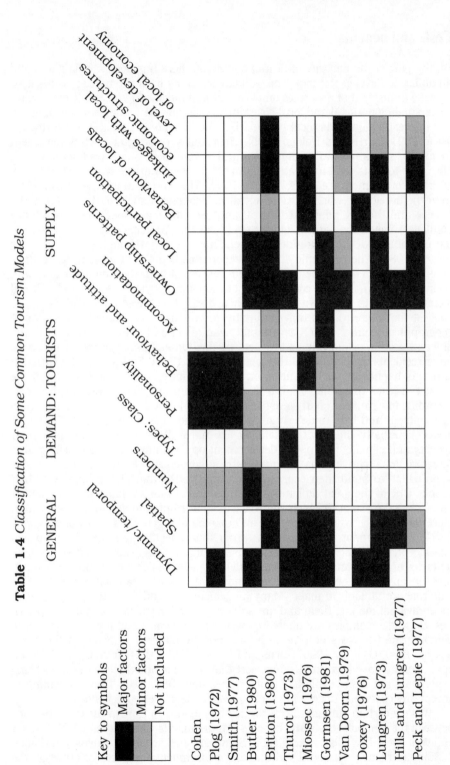

Costs and benefits

On the part of the majority of destination areas there has been a willingness and an ability to develop tourism. The willingness stems from the nature of this fast-growing industry that generates employment and income in vulnerable economies, so persuading national and local governments, landowners, hoteliers and commercial interests, as well as local people, that the benefits it confers are worthwhile (Ryan 1991, Burns and Holden 1995). Their ability to promote such development frequently stems from an 'unspoilt' natural environment and a traditional way of life, since tourists tend to be attracted to fragile environments which exhibit signs of underdevelopment (Lea 1988, Pearce 1989). This is true in a range of countries, from the developing world to more advanced economies such as those of Austria, Greece and the UK, where structural and geographical aspects of dependency highlight some of the dangers of tourism (Shaw and Williams 1994), in addition to its advantages of spreading development more widely throughout the country (Pearce 1989). The economic and socio-economic benefits of tourism to destinations have thus come to be questioned in respect of both their limited extent and their transitory nature. A complex mix of economic, physical, social and cultural factors, each with their own costs and benefits, led Mathieson and Wall (1982) to suggest that there was no universal pattern, but that areas differed according to geographical location. Such a variability can also be identified in respect of the different groups or individuals involved, be they promoters, operators, employees, other residents or the tourists themselves (Pearce 1989). Fortunately the situation is not as haphazard as this initial impression suggests. It is the *intensity* of the impacts rather than their *nature* that alters from one destination to the next, according to a range of characteristics (see Box 1.1) that set the context for tourism development and help to determine whether or not it is 'a good thing'. For many areas, especially those with relatively few natural resources other than their scenery and climate, alternative development opportunities are often lacking. It is therefore not surprising that many countries have chosen tourism as the industry upon which to build their economy and improve the material wellbeing of their people. One of the great difficulties in any study of tourism impacts is to identify and isolate the extent to which changes can be attributed to man or to nature and, more particularly, whether they are an outcome of a general process of economic development and/or westernization rather than specifically induced by tourism (Mathieson and Wall 1982). Since tourism is not a single sector, but spreads its tentacles across a range of economic activities as well as demonstrating an involvement in physical, social and cultural modifications, accurate assessments of its true role are difficult to make. Many judgements depend upon the perspective of the individual making them and are subject to their particular agenda and priorities. So while examples are quoted by western academics and pressure groups to demonstrate the costs of tourism in some of the poorest countries of the world (Pearce 1989, O'Grady 1990, Burns and Holden 1995), those from the least developed nations have been known to assert that 'There is one thing worse than being exploited – not being exploited' (quoted in Cater 1987, 210). They are willing to accept any costs that accrue in order to realize the perceived benefits.

While a certain amount of controversy has tended to exist in the exact balance between the economic costs and benefits of tourism, it is widely accepted (Mathieson and Wall 1982, Lea 1988, Pearce 1989, Shaw and Williams 1994, Burns and Holden 1985) that the negative social, cultural and environmental impacts far outweigh the

---

BOX 1.1 DESTINATION CHARACTERISTICS INFLUENCING THE INTENSITY OF TOURISM IMPACTS

1. Size of the destination country or area
2. Scale and rate of tourism development and numbers of tourists
3. Fragility and sensitivity of the landscape, flora and fauna
4. Political environment of development
5. Sensitivity of development in relation to the local environment and culture
6. Development incentives
7. Social and cultural attitudes of the local people
8. Types of tourists
9. Competition from other areas
10. Accessibility from the main generating regions: both physical and economic accessibility
11. Degree of foreign ownership
12. Employment of non-indigenous labour
13. Government provision of infrastructure
14. Nature and attractiveness of tourist facilities
15. Level of economic development of the area
16. Whether the area is rural or urban

Sources: Ryan 1991, Shaw and Williams 1994, Burns and Holden 1995

---

positive ones. Inevitably these are exacerbated as tourist numbers rise and destinations become more popular. Doxey (1976) codified them for the social effects of tourism in his index of irritation, which describes the reaction of the host community to tourism and covers a spectrum from euphoria to antagonism.

Since sustainable approaches to tourism are among attempts to manage the deleterious impacts, a brief review of the costs and benefits is appropriate and occurs in the introductions to the readings in chapters Four, Five, Six and Seven. Traditionally these impacts are divided into: physical/ecological/environmental; economic; and social and cultural. Political issues, although important, have rarely been considered separately in the literature, tending to be subsumed within the other categories. There are two stages in the study of each of these categories. The first involves the identification of the broad range of costs and benefits, while the second focuses on the more precise measurement of these impacts. The latter can introduce a range of detailed techniques that can be both qualitative and quantitative, and which are better presented in a technical volume rather than in a reader of this type.

DEVELOPMENT THEORY AND TOURISM

The notion of different paradigms or styles of development can be applied to tourism. Common strands within the various paradigms and theories can be useful ways to describe and explain the evolution of tourism and provide pointers towards potential new directions.

The classic approach, which is top–down, state instigated and expert-led, usually involves a three stage process: problems and opportunities are identified by external agents; technical measures are developed and selected by the state, with the cooperation of the community; and plans are implemented through a mixture of encouragement and coercion (Blaikie 1996). Consequent failures are partly technical, as a result of inadequate research; partly a result of a lack of fit between techniques adopted and local lifestyles; and partly a result of the inadequacies of state bureaucracies (Blaikie 1996). Aspects of modernization theory and underdevelopment theory as applied to tourism show some similarities with these ideas. The top–down, expert-led approach is evident in the control exerted by multinational companies, with their external capital, expertise, technology and ideas. Frequently operating in a neo-colonial role, they either disregard local tradition and culture (underdevelopment theory) or consider it antithetical (modernization theory); one of the failures clearly identified in relation to the classic approach. The entrepreneurial role of elites and the lack of planning control over large-scale package tourism that is usually aimed at foreigners reflects the inadequacy of the state, which rarely has the desire or the ability to limit development without losing what are perceived as valuable jobs and revenue.

The neo-liberal paradigm is dominated by market forces. In fact it typifies the mass tourism industry, in which multinational companies based in the developed nations shape and direct largely developed world demand, whether the destinations are in developed or less developed areas or nations. Profit margins per tourist may be small, but total financial returns to these companies are generally large. Other associated characteristics include the limited or negligible role both of local lifestyles and of the majority of local people involved in low-income, low-status occupations. These realities are often hidden behind glossy advertising which highlights distinctive traditions and customs as attractions for visitors. The much vaunted jobs and revenue are equally deceptive. The former are frequently perceived by western academics, and even by the tourists themselves, as low-income and low-status. This, however, may *not* be the attitude of many of those engaged in such jobs within relatively poor destination countries, where alternatives may be even less financially rewarding, less secure and more distasteful. A considerable amount of the revenue fails to accrue to local people: it is leaked out of the local, the regional and the national economy.

There are a number of convergent ideas within neo-populist development, with its focus on a bottom–up approach involving local people from the beginning, and post-modernism. Some of these can be traced to sustainable forms of development and related to tourism. Alternative approaches that stem from grassroots development, including certain types of ecotourism and community-based tourism, such as the Campfire project in Zimbabwe and the Casamance scheme in Senegal, exhibit more sustainable characteristics than does mass package tourism. These examples also illustrate the desire to generate small-scale enterprises, like the increasing use of local agricultural produce in islands like St Lucia and Barbados in the Caribbean. An aspiration to return to traditional values and skills can result in cultural and craft revivals that can act as important tourist attractions, as well as increase local pride and self-confidence *and* boost the local economy. It is not only through cultural events like carnivals and local craft production that participation in tourism can emerge, but also through agricultural diversification, mentioned earlier, that important linkages may develop with other sectors of the economy. Over time education, training and government support can move local people into managerial roles within the tourism industry and, as knowledge and experience are diffused, so their role in decision making, and hence in more active participation, increases. This can then be extended to embrace a degree of empowerment. However, the multinational nature of tourism makes it an activity within which the full empowerment of local people is unlikely to occur. It is perhaps better to envisage a spectrum, from neo-colonial paternalism to empowerment, along which attempts should be made to move away from the more extreme aspects of paternalism towards empowerment.

THE THEORETICAL BACKGROUND TO SUSTAINABLE TOURISM

The assertion that 'in reality, we all know what it [sustainability] means' (Porritt in the forward to Croall 1995) is manifestly untrue in terms of both the literature and the perspectives of various actors involved in tourism, as Croall himself points out (1995). In order to understand the implications of sustainable tourism then it *is* worth considering the origins of the concept. The evolution of the concept of sustainable development, which lies behind its application to tourism, is clearly described by Kirkby (1995) and outlined in Box 1.2.

Sustainable development has traditionally been defined (WCED 1987) as development which involves the use of renewable natural resources in a way that does not degrade them. Redclift (1987) suggested the term assumed that lessons learned from ecology could be applied to economic processes. As a result, not only should such development preserve environmental quality in the long run, but it should also maintain or increase productivity (Tolba, quoted in Elliott 1994, 3). This implies the management of economic systems in a way that achieves a rate of growth in per capita real incomes with minimum levels of depletion of environmental assets (Turner 1988). It is therefore resource-based or asset-led development, rather than that controlled by purely market forces, that is one of the cornerstones of sustainable development in general and sustainable tourism development in particular (Owen 1991). Growth is inevitable as a goal for most economies and is required to alleviate poverty. The difficulty is to promote economic growth whilst avoiding the consumption of natural resources at an unsustainable rate.

It was Krippendorf's seminal book *The Holiday Makers* (1984) that introduced to tourism some of the basic ideas inherent in sustainable development (Croall 1995), first presented in the World Conservation Strategy (IUCN 1980). However, it was not until 1987 that the Brundtland Report (WCED 1987) began to stimulate increasing concern and initiate change designed to mitigate some of the growing negative impacts of tourism (Croall 1995). The subsequent Rio Conference in 1992 led to a wider dissemination of the concept of sustainable *tourism* development. Of particular importance were the principles and recommendations presented in the Rio Declaration on the Environment and Development and in Agenda 21. These guided the World Conference on Sustainable Tourism held in Lanzarote, Canary Islands, Spain in 1995 (whose principles and objectives are listed in Box 1.3) and are used in this reader as an outline structure within which appropriate extracts have been selected and grouped.

Tourism can use renewable resources, provided it is carefully managed, and Table 1.5 provides a summary of appropriate strategies and tactics for the main actors involved in the industry. Indeed, tourism is often quoted as a justification

BOX 1.2 THE EVOLUTION OF THE CONCEPT OF SUSTAINABLE DEVELOPMENT

The World Commission on Environment and Development (WCED 1987) Report, (commonly known as the Brundtland Report after its chairwoman) ... is the key statement of sustainable development. It marked the concept's political coming of age and established the content and structure of the present debate. The United Nations Conference on Environment and Development (UNCED) commonly known as the Rio Conference of 1992 was the follow up to Brundtland and sought to move towards the achievement of Brundtland's aims.

... the main components of sustainability as interpreted by Brundtland:

- Revive growth
- Change quality of growth
- Meet basic needs
- Stabilise population
- Conserve and enhance resources
- Reorient technology and manage risk
- Put environment into economics

Clearly the Brundtland statement has a strong people-centred ethical stance, concentrating on the satisfaction of human needs, rather than, for example, on protection of the environment in general as WCS (World Conservation Strategy (IUCN 1980) in which the concept of sustainable development first appeared).

... the United Nations General Assembly asked for a report back on progress in sustainability after five years. This report back was known as the United Nations Conference on Environment and Development (UNCED) which was held in Rio de Janeiro, Brazil in 1992.....

The intention was to build on Brundtland's hopes and achievements to respond to pressing global environmental problems, ... and to achieve agreement on principles and actions for sustainable development.

Among the outcomes were *Agenda 21* and the *Rio Declaration on Environmental Development.*

Four groups of topics are considered (in Agenda 21):

1. *Social and economic development,* including: international cooperation, poverty, sustainable consumption, population, health, settlements, and integration of environment with development.
2. *Resource management,* including: atmosphere, land resource planning, deforestation, fragile ecosystems, mountains, rural development, biodiversity, biotechnologies, oceans, freshwater, toxic waste, hazardous waste, solid wastes and sewage and radio active wastes
3. *Strengthening the participation of major groups.* This includes virtually everyone: women, children, indigenous people and NGOs are among groups specified.
4. *Means of implementation* includes finance, institutions, technology, transfer, sciences, education, capacity building, international institutions, law and information for decision making.

.....The *Rio Declaration on Environmental Development* comprises 27 principles for the achievement of sustainable development. On the surface they appear bland and uncontroversial: they were in fact bitterly contested. Many stress development issues. The first and presumably most important is 'human beings are at the centre of concerns for sustainable development. They are entitled to a healthy and productive life in harmony with nature'. On the surface at least, it appears that Brundtland's equity cornerstone has been incorporated in Rio.

Source: Kirkby et al 1995, pp1–12

BOX 1.3 CHARTER FOR SUSTAINABLE TOURISM
OUTLINE OF PRINCIPLES AND OBJECTIVES

1. Tourism development should be based on the criteria of sustainability. It should be: ecologically bearable; economically viable; and ethically and socially equitable for local communities.
2. Tourism should contribute to sustainable development and be integrated with all aspects of the environment, respecting fragile areas and promoting the assimilation of impacts so that these lie within capacity limits.
3. Tourism must consider its effects on the cultural heritage and traditions of local communities.
4. Participation of all actors in the process is essential.
5. Conservation of the natural and cultural heritage involves cooperation, planning and management.
6. The satisfaction of tourists and preservation of destinations should be determined together with local communities and informed by sustainable principles.
7. Tourism should be integrated into local economic development.
8. Tourism development should improve the quality of life.
9. Planning tourism is important.
10. Equity of the benefits and burdens of tourism should be sought.
11. Special priority should be given to environmentally and culturally vulnerable areas and areas already degraded.
12. Alternative forms of tourism compatible with sustainable principles should be promoted.
13. Research should be promoted.
14. Environmentally compatible management systems should facilitate a sustainable tourism policy.
15. The travel industry should promote sustainable development, exchange experiences etc.
16. Particular attention should be paid to transportation and the use of non-renewable energy.
17. Codes of conduct should be established for the main actors.
18. All necessary measures should be implemented to promote awareness of sustainable tourism among all involved in tourism.

Source: Martin 1995

---

for the existence of national parks in East Africa (Mathieson and Wall 1982), while in some countries it is the most feasible of the few options for development – from small tropical islands in the Caribbean and in the Pacific and Indian Oceans, to mountain states like Nepal. A significant issue here is the quality of growth. Large numbers of people who demand access to game and to relatively luxurious travel and accommodation facilities have caused problems such as overcrowding, leading to the disturbance of animal lifestyles, the trampling of the vegetation and soil compaction, and the production of waste within the game parks of Kenya (Lea 1988, Olindo 1991). The distribution of benefits is also a problem, typified by the protests in Goa that few Goan people profit from tourism (O'Grady 1990).

Societies striving for a measure of sustainability do not necessarily eschew growth, but recognize limits and look to alternative, less capital-intensive and western-oriented approaches (Coomer, quoted in Elliott 1994, 3). One of the

Table 1.5 *Sustainable Tourism: Strategies and Tactics*

Actors	Strategies		Tactics	
Host Area	1	Tourism as part of a diverse economy	1(a)	Planning and management
			1(b)	Encouragement of alternative economic activities through policy measures
	2	The provision of both unskilled and skilled employment for local people	2(a)	Education and training for local people
			2(b)	Restrictions on expatriate labour
	3	Conservation of the natural environment	3(a)	Planning to agreed capacity levels
			3(b)	Education of all actors
	4	Harmonious architecture	4	Appropriateness of development regulated by planning measures
	5	Equity, including local decision making	5(a)	Education of local people
			5(b)	Drawing together different interests and establishing continuing dialogue
	6	Maintenance of traditional values	6	Education of tourists
	7	Benefits diffused through communities	7(a)	Tactics agreed by those on the ground from all sectors: public, private, local
			7(b)	Optimisation not maximisation
	8	Limits to growth	8	Effective planning involving public, private and local sectors
Tourists		A satisfying holiday	a)	Provision of an environment suited to the psychographic profile of the individual
			b)	A good value holiday with no evident over-exploitation by the host area or the tour operator
			c)	Education to facilitate: (i) choice of the most suitable holiday (ii) maximum knowledge of and therefore a more accurate expectation of the destination so maximum enjoyment can be achieved with limited stress/uncertainty/risk
Tour Operator		Brand loyalty through repeat business that leads to economic success and profitability	a)	Provision of a good value holiday
			b)	Education of the consumer, especially the provision of adequate and accurate information about the holiday and the destination prior to the visit so the most appropriate choice can be made
			c)	Agreeing structures for development with all interests at the destination to provide a harmonious and appropriate product

concepts at the heart of sustainable development is that of equity (Kirkby et al 1995), which can only be achieved when participation occurs and local people become involved in decision making. Among the limited number of tourism projects with these characteristics are the Casamance in Senegal (Inskeep 1994) and the Zimbabwe Campfire Scheme (Chalker 1994).

THE EMERGENCE OF NEW FORMS OF TOURISM

It is evident that not only has tourism grown rapidly worldwide, but that many of those concerned about its negative impacts at the destination assume that mass forms of tourism are largely responsible for these problems (Cooper and Ozdil 1992). Although the notion that mass tourism is 'a bad thing' is perhaps rather simplistic (Cooper and Ozdil 1992), it has been suggested that controlling the volume of tourism might alleviate the situation (Wheeller 1990), especially since tourism is typically found in locations with fragile environments, such as mountains and coasts, many of which are peripheral to the world economy (May 1991). Increased interest in alternative forms of tourism is perceived as a response to the emphasis placed on exploitation associated with mass tourism, especially in developing countries (Fennell and Smale 1992). The search for a different holiday experience is not a new phenomenon. It has been codified by writers such as Christaller (1964), Turner and Ash (1975), Cohen (1972) and Plog (1972). But there has been a renewed concern with environmental ethics, which has focused on the deleterious effect of mass tourism as it impinges on important and fragile natural environments (Fennell and Smale 1992). This led to the emergence of a more sensitive form of tourism, in which the aim is to minimize the environmental (and also the social, cultural and economic) costs and maximize the benefits. It has been given a number of different labels – appropriate, responsible, soft, green – but perhaps the most useful is 'alternative' tourism, since it is pursued as an alternative to mass tourism and its associated negative impacts (Wheeller 1991, Cater 1993). The major characteristics of alternative tourism are shown in Table 1.6 and contrasted with those of mass tourism. Small numbers of individual travellers are preferred to multitudinous tourists, who are often in groups. Locally provided accommodation and decision making encourage slow, controlled growth that lies well within the capacity of the host area to absorb, without damage to its culture or the natural environment. These factors contrast with the rapid pace of the large-scale development often favoured by multinational companies, which overwhelms any destination and frequently leads to soaring costs (Lane 1990, Wheeller 1990, Heritage Coast 1992). Inevitably this polarization masks a continuum in reality, along which a range of variants and sub-types can be identified. The nomenclature is confusing and clear definitions can be difficult to find. In addition there is overlap among the categories. This is compounded by an assumption sometimes made (Wheeller 1990, Mowforth 1993) that sustainable tourism is simply another *type* of tourism, synonymous with alternative and the antithesis of mass tourism. An attempt to clarify this situation is made diagrammatically in Figure 1.1, which shows the major types of tourism and their variants. Descriptions of some of these sub-types are summarized in Table 1.7, which illustrates their breadth with a range of examples from mass to alternative, and which have different levels of sustainability regardless of their avowed intentions. Ecotourism, as a variant of adventure tourism (Cater 1993) rather than as a sub-

Table 1.6 *Th Major Characteristics of Alternative Tourism*

Mass	Alternative	Sustainable
Tourist	Traveller	
Large Firms	Independent, specific operators	
Large-scale	Small-scale	Appropriate scale
Multinational hotel chains	Small-scale accommodation	
Rapid development often without planning	Slow and controlled development	Planned – pace may not matter
Multinational decision making	Local decision making	Local decision making
Effects ignored, ie impacts	Minimizes negative effects	Growth at agreed price
Fuel effective transport Resorts space-efficient	Often ineffective fuel-wise	

Sources: Lane 1990, Wheeller 1990, Heritage Coast 1992

Table 1.7 *Variants of Alternative Tourism and their Characteristics*

	Characteristics
Adventure tourism	Attracts mainly allocentric and mid-centric tourists. Usually resource-based. Involves physical challenge, education and contact with nature. Can be small-scale with many ecotourism characteristics, eg bird-watching or scuba-diving in Dominica; medium-scale and sports oriented, eg canoeing and rafting along Colorado River; or large-scale and an aspect of mass tourism, eg safaris in East Africa.
Nature tourism	An aspect of adventure tourism where the focus is upon the study and/or observation of flora, fauna and/or landscape. It tends towards the small-scale, but it can become mass or incipient mass tourism in many national parks, eg Yosemite. It is sometimes perceived as synonymous with ecotourism since one of its aims is to protect natural areas.
Community tourism	A type of tourism run by and for the local community. It may be alternative in character like the Casamance scheme in Senegal or may cater for larger numbers and have more in common with aspects of mass tourism as in some heritage museums like Beamish in County Durham and colonial Williamsburgh, Virginia and farm tourism in New Zealand which can be associated with organised packages and even coach travel.

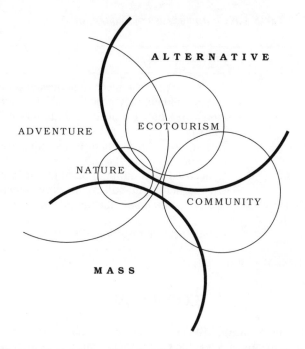

Figure 1.1 *Major Types of Tourism and their Variants*

type of equal status (Ruschmann 1992), has been accorded so much attention in the literature (Cater 1993, Moore and Cater 1993, Smeding 1993, Cater and Lowman 1994) and in the popular press (Powell 1993) that it is worth separate consideration. The complexities of definition in print are compounded by perception on the part of the consumer, and by temporal changes that can result in the movement of a host area within the boundaries of a category or from one type or sub-type of tourism to another, often with amazing rapidity. This is most clearly exemplified by the changing patterns of travel in inland Andalusia, southern Spain. In the 1930s Laurie Lee (1971) walked through Andalusia, while during the early 1960s Penelope Chetwode (1963) travelled around the area on horseback – travellers and adventurers both in a region hitherto relatively unfrequented by foreigners. Those touring the same area by motor vehicle in the 1990s may still find quiet backwaters and see themselves as explorers indulging in an adventurous holiday. From a totally different perspective travellers on the 'Andalus Express', the luxury train that traverses Andalusia, may perceive their journey as an adventure. Yet this highly structured experience in an environmental bubble whose conditions are totally at variance with those of the surrounding countryside, can clearly be described as a form of wealthy mass tourism. Still further along the postulated spectrum are the coach tours of Andalusia offered by a number of multinational companies, bringing typical mass package tourism activities to the region.

Table 1.8 *Characteristics of Ecotourism Actors*

Actors	*Characteristics*
Tourists	A tolerance for the inconveniences of remote travel
Tour Operators	Focus holidays they provide on flora, fauna, landscape, native culture and archaeology, and sport
Host Communities	Require local involvement in planning and operating tourism
Host Governments	Concerned with national planning to exploit natural environments and culture for development
International Conservation Groups	See ecotourism as a means to ensure conservation
Academics	Debate precise meaning of ecotourism

Sources: Kallen 1990, Mowforth 1993

ECOTOURISM

The World Wild Fund for Nature (WWF) defines ecotourism as 'tourism to protected natural areas, as a means of economic gain through natural resource preservation. A merger of recreation and responsibility' (quoted in Kallen 1990, 37). A useful starting point, this is rather general and masks a complex situation for, as Mowforth (1993) suggests, there is no single perspective on ecotourism. Instead the various actors involved each have their own distinctive definition and they fail to provide a consensus (see Table 1.18). A further layer can be added as a result of a lack of homogeneity within each group of actors. This is demonstrated in Table 1.9, which shows a range of tourist types who are likely to perceive themselves as ecotourists, classified according to their major characteristics. Such listings are not without controversy, as there are those (Ruschmann 1992) who, unlike Kallen (1990), Moore and Carter (1993) and Mowforth (1993), would place the 'rough' type of ecotourist, whose activities are focused on sport and adventure provided by specialist companies, within the separate and distinctive category of 'adventure tourism' (Table 1.7). It is also likely that some of those tourists undertaking safaris, described here as 'smooth' ecotourists, might more appropriately be re-classified as mass tourists rather than as those who seek the ecotourism variant of alternative tourism. In spite of a realistic acknowledgement that even this ecotourism variant of tourist and tourism is far from simple and straightforward, it is possible to identify a number of criteria by which such a variant can be described.

The aims of ecotourism include 'ecological and socio-cultural integrity, responsibility and sustainability' (Cater 1994, 3) and its major characteristics, outlined in Table 1.8, reveal that it is soundly grounded in alternative tourism. Its emergence in specific destination areas depends on a number of factors, such as: the political stability of the area; the commitment of host governments and communities to ecotourism; the degree of promotion by governments and tour operators; the amount of controversy associated with the area; the range of accommodation, infrastructure and other facilities available; and the continued demand

Table 1.9 *Types of Ecotourists and their Characteristics*

Types	Age	Travel Arrangements	Accommodation	Food	Activities
Rough	Young – Middle aged	Travel as individuals and small groups. Independent arrangements. Often use buses at the destination	Cheap – often locally owned	Local	Sport and adventure
Smooth	Middle aged	Travel in groups, often on tours. Tend to use taxis at the destination	3–5 Star hotels that may be multinationally owned	Luxury restaurants used. Often imported food and beverages consumed	Nature oriented and safari
Specialist	Young – Old	Travel individually or on specialized tours. Arrangements often independent. Wide range of transport types used at the destination	Wide range used	Wide range used	Scientific or specialist interest

Source: Mowforth 1993

for this increasingly popular and 'politically correct' form of tourism (Kallen 1990, Moore and Carter 1993, Smeding 1993). Evidence exists to show that ecotourism can provide benefits to the destination areas. In the 1980s, before civil war tore the country apart, ecotourism generated sufficient income to protect habitats and prevent poaching in the Parc National de Volcans in Rwanda, as well as making tourism the second largest source of foreign exchange (Warner 1989). The Annapurna Conservation Area Project believes that this form of tourism could bring great benefits to parts of Nepal (Gurung and de Coursey 1994). Often, such tourists are even prepared to fund conservation, as in the case of the Galapagos Islands, where an appeal to those who had signed the Darwin Research Station visitors' book raised US$150,000 (Warner 1989). Eco-tour kits with biodegradable ballpoint pens, and demands from potential tourists that companies demonstrate that they recycle money back into host communities, reinforce the role and importance of consumer demand. US travellers have even been known to sue if the environmental policy of their specialist ecotourism operator fails to live up to expectations (Powell 1993). But there is a danger that, because of its very popularity, ecotourism could degenerate into a marketing mechanism that merely brings profits to tour operators and lucrative foreign exchange to developing countries like Nepal and Kenya, engendering many of the negative effects of traditional tourism it was intended to avoid (Kallen 1990). This is a risk these countries should guard against.

REFERENCES

Armitage, J (1977) *Man at Play*, Frederick Warne and Co Ltd, London

Blaikie, P (1996) 'New knowledge and rural development: A review of views and practicalities'. A paper for the 28th International Geographical Congress at the Hague, August 5–10 1996. A state- of-the-art lecture for the Third World Commission registered under No 5590

Britton, S G (1980) 'The spatial organisation of tourism in a neo-colonial economy: A Fiji case study', *Pacific Viewpoint*, 21(2) pp144–65

Brook, E (1988) 'Through Sherpa eyes' *Geographical Magazine*, August LX(8) pp28–34

Burns, P H and Holden, A (1995) *Tourism. A New Perspective*, Prentice Hall International (UK) Limited, Hemel Hempstead

Butler, R W (1980) 'The concept of a tourist area cycle of evolution; implications for management of resources', *Canadian Geographer*, 24(1) pp5–12

Callaghan, P, Long, P and Robinson, M (eds) (1994) *Travel and Tourism* 2nd ed Business Education Publishers Ltd, Sunderland

Cater, E (1987) 'Tourism in the least developed countries', *Annals of Tourism Research*, 14, pp202–26

Cater, E (1993) 'Ecotourism in the Third World: Problems for sustainable tourism development', *Tourism Management*, April 14 (2) pp85–90

Cater, E (1994) 'Ecotourism in the Third World – Problems and Prospects for Sustainability', Chapter 5 in E Cater and G Lowman (eds) *Ecotourism. A Sustainable Option?* Wiley, Chichester

Cater, E and Lowman, G (eds)(1994) *Ecotourism. A Sustainable Option?* Wiley, Chichester

Chalker, Baroness L (1994) 'Ecotourism: on the Trail of Destruction or Sustainability? A Minister's View', chapter 6 in E Cater and G Lowman (eds) *Ecotourism. A Sustainable Option?* Wiley, Chichester:

Chetwode, P (1963) *Two Middle-Aged Ladies in Andalusia*, Century Publishing, London

Christaller, W (1964) 'Some considerations of tourism location in Europe', *Papers and Proceedings of Regional Science Association* 12, pp95–105

Cohen, E (1972) 'Towards a sociology of international tourism', *Social Research* 39, pp164–182

Cooper, C and Jackson, S (1989) 'Destination life cycle. The Isle of Man Study', *Annals of Tourism Research* 16, pp377–98

Cooper, C P and Odzil, I (1992) 'From mass to responsible tourism: the Turkish experience', *Tourism Management*, December 13(4) 377- 386

Croall, J (1995) *Preserve or Destroy. Tourism and the Environment*, Calouste Gulbenkian Foundation, London

Doxey, G V (1976) 'When enough's enough: the natives are restless in Old Niagara', *Heritage Canada* 2, pp26–7

Elliott, J A (1994) *An Introduction to Sustainable Development*, Routledge, London

Elliott, M (1991) 'Travel and Tourism', *The Economist*, 23 March, pp3–26

Feifer, M (1985) *Going Places*, Macmillan, London

Fennell, D A and Smale, B J A (1992) 'Ecotourism and natural resource protection. Implications of an alternative form of tourism for host nations', *Tourism Recreation Research* 17(1) pp21–32

Ferguson, J (1991) 'Unsustainable development', *In Focus* Summer (1) 4–5

Gormsen, E (1981) 'The spatio-temporal development of international tourism: attempt at a centre-periphery model', pp150–70 in *La Consommation D'espace Par le Tourism et sa Preservation, Chet,* Aix-en-Provence

Gurung, C P and de Coursey, M (1994) 'The Annapurna Conservation Area Project: a Pioneering Example of Sustainable Tourism?', Chapter 11 in E Cater and G Lowman (eds) *Ecotourism. A Sustainable Option?* Wiley, Chichester

Hailes, J (1991) 'Ecotourism: A Load of Rubbish?', *The Independent on Sunday* 28 April p39

Heritage Coast (1992) 'But what does it mean?', *The Bulletin of the Heritage Coast Forum* Issue 8: 'Tourism', September

Hills, T L and Lundgren, J (1977) 'The impact of tourism in the Caribbean: A methodological study', *Annals of Tourism Research* 4(5) pp248–67

Inskeep, E (1994) *National and Regional Tourism Planning. Methodologies and Case Studies,* Routledge, London

IUCN (1980) 'World Conservation Strategy: Living Resource Conservation for Sustainable Development', IUCN, UNEP and WWF, Gland, Switzerland

Jarviluoma, J (1992) 'Alternative tourism and the evolution of tourist areas', *Tourism Management* March pp118–120

Kallen, C (1990) 'Eco-tourism: The light at the end of the terminal', *E Magazine* July–August, pp37–41

Kirkby, S J (1995) 'Introduction', pp1–14 in J Kirkby, P O'Keefe and L Timberlake (eds) *The Earthscan Reader in Sustainable Development,* Earthscan, London

Lane, B (1990) 'Sustaining host areas, holiday makers and operators alike', Paper to The Sustainable Tourism Development Conference, Queen Margaret College, November

Lea, J (1988) *Tourism and Development in the Third World,* Routledge, London

Lee, L (1971) *As I Walked Out One Midsummer Morning,* Routledge, London

Lungren, J O J (1973) 'Tourist impact/island entrepreneurship in the Caribbean', Conference paper quoted in Mathieson and Wall (1982)

Martin, C (1995) *Charter for Sustainable Tourism,* World Conference on Sustainable Tourism 27–28 April 1995 Lanzarote, Canary Islands

Mathieson, A and Wall, G (1982) *Tourism. Economic, Physical and Social Impacts,* Longman, Harlow

May, V (1991) 'Tourism, environment and development. Values, sustainability and stewardship', *Tourism Management* June pp112–18

Millman, R (1989) 'Pleasure seeking v the "greening" of world tourism', *Tourism Management* December pp275–77

Millman, R and Januarius, M (1989) 'Tourists or Travellers?', *Leisure Management* 9(3) pp68–71

Miossec, J M (1976) 'Eléments pour une Théorie de l'Espace Touristique', *Les Cahiers Du Tourisme,* C–36, CHET, Aix-en-Provence Quoted in Pearce (1989)

Moore, S and Carter, B (1993) 'Ecotourism in the 21st century', *Tourism Management* April 14(2) pp123–30

Mowforth, M (1993) 'In search of an eco-tourist', *In Focus* Autumn, 9, pp2–3

OED (1989) The Oxford English Dictionary 2nd edition. Prepared by J A Simpson and E S C Weiner, Clarendon, Oxford

O'Grady, A (ed)(1990) *The Challenge of Tourism,* Bangkok: Ecumenical Coalition on Third World Tourism

Olindo, P (1991) 'The Old Man of Nature Tourism', Chapter 2 in T Whelan (ed) *Nature Tourism Managing for the Environment,* Island Press, Washington DC

Owen, R E (1991) 'Strategy for Sustainable Tourism, the Theory and the Practice', Paper to the International Conference on Tourism: Development Trends and Prospects in the 90s, Kuala Lumpur, 16–18 September

Pearce, D (1989) *Tourist Development,* 2nd edition, Longman, Harlow

Peck, J G and Lepie, A S (1977) 'Tourism and development in three North Caroline coastal towns', in V L Smith (ed) *Hosts and Guests: An Anthropology of Tourism,* University of Pennsylvania Press, Philadelphia

Pimlott, J A R (1968) *Recreations,* Studio Vista, London

Plog, S C (1972) 'Why destination areas rise and fall in popularity', quoted in P E Murphy (1985) *Tourism. A Community Approach,* Methuen, London

Poon, A (1993) *Tourism, Technology and Competitive Strategies* CAB International, Wallingford

Powell, B (1993) 'Eco and the funny men', *The Guardian Weekend* 16 October pp57–8

Redclift, M (1987) *Sustainable Development: Exploring the Contradictions,* Methuen, London

Ruschmann, D (1992) 'Ecological tourism in Brazil', *Tourism Management* March pp125–28

Ryan, C (1991) *Recreational Tourism,* Routledge, London

Shaw, G and Williams, A M (1994) *Critical Issues in Tourism. A Geographical Perspective,* Blackwell, Oxford

Smeding, S S A (1993) 'Low impact eco-tourism – clarion call or reality? – the challenge of Botswana', *The Tourist Revue* 3, pp25–7

Smith, V L (ed)(1977) *Hosts and Guests: An Anthropology of Tourism,* University of Pennsylvania Press, Philadelphia

Thurot, J M (1973) 'Le Tourisme Tropical Balnéaire: Le Modèle Caraibe et ses Extensions', Thesis, Centre d'Études du Tourisme, Aix-en-Provence. Quoted in Pearce (1989)

Turner, R K (1988) *Sustainable Environmental Management,* Belhaven, London

Turner, L and Ash, J (1975) *The Golden Hordes: International Tourism and the Pleasure Periphery,* Constable, London

Urry, J (1990) *The Tourist Gaze: Leusure and Travel in Contemporary Societies,* Sage Publications, London

Van Doorn, J W M (1979) 'The Developing Countries: Are they Really Affected by Tourism? Some Critical Notes on Socio-cultural Impact Studies', Paper presented at Seminar on Leisure Studies and Tourism, 7–8 December, Warsaw (Mimeo). Quoted in Pearce (1989)

Warner, E (1989) 'Ecotourism!', *Environmental Action* September/October 21(2) 18–21

WCED (1987) *Our Common Future,* Oxford University Press, Oxford

Wheeller, B (1990) 'Responsible tourism', *Tourism Management* 11 (3) pp262–63

Wheeller, B (1991) 'Tourism's troubled times. Responsible tourism is not the answer', *Tourism Management* June 12(2) pp91–6

WTO (World Tourism Organization) (1995) *Compendium of Tourism Statistics 1989-93,* 15th Edition, World Tourism Organization, Madrid

WTO (World Tourism Organization) (1996) *Tourism Market Trends,* World Tourism Organization, Madrid

Chapter 2

Principles of Sustainable Tourism

INTRODUCTION

Sustainability as a concept involves a number of different strands. Environmental, ecological and economic factors assume that it is applicable in the technical sciences, whereas social and political factors relate to power and values. Within these strands, questions of scale: family, community, region; and timescale: project life, indefinite and so on, are critical elements. These ideas are illustrated most clearly using examples that gradually bring them closer to tourism applications.

In a very narrow sense *ecological sustainability* can be achieved by excluding or restricting people from particularly vulnerable areas, such as a designated wilderness. In development or social terms, however, such an approach could be catastrophic. A less extreme possibility would be to permit a small group of people to benefit, while still achieving a relatively high degree of ecological sustainability. Such a group could be an elite connected with a specific development project. This might involve a visit by tourists to a luxurious hotel, as in Costa Rica, or a luxury safari, like the gorilla safaris in central Africa. These examples have changed the surrounding area very little but have brought satisfaction and financial rewards to small numbers of wealthy tourists and elite owners. These beneficiaries have access to power and/or money which enables them to gain access to resources such as land.

A different view of sustainability, with a *political and economic* stance, can set notions like equity and the reduction of poverty alongside ecological maintenance. This balance is difficult to achieve because it contains contradictions. The challenge is to compromise between ecological sustainability and sustainable lifestyles for the majority of the population, including underprivileged groups such as the poor, the elderly, women and ethnic and religious minorities. Some of these dilemmas exist in the national parks in which tourism, conservation and benefits and costs to local people create immense planning and management difficulties, as is highlighted in the national parks of East Africa, where pastoralists can clash with those who run the game parks mainly for tourism.

The only realistic approach is to agree priorities. If the main aim is agreed to be to satisfy the needs of tourists, then the needs of others are of lesser importance. If conservation of the physical environment is of paramount concern, then the needs of people – both tourists and local inhabitants at the destination – are relatively unimportant. Conversely the principal focus could be the improvement of the circumstances of the disadvantaged and powerless, who are likely to lose through the actions of market forces. It is likely that at different stages destina-

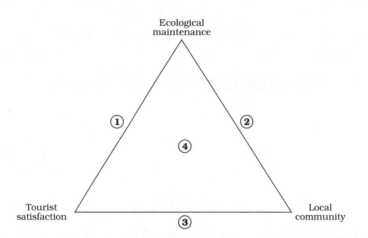

Figure 2.1 *Strategic approaches to sustainable tourism*

tion countries and/or areas may vary their priorities. Figure 2.1 shows a number of possible strategic approaches in the search for sustainable tourism.

Situation (1) could be demonstrated by small numbers of tourists who visit a relatively remote area, thereby gaining a high level of satisfaction from their visit and leaving their destination relatively unchanged. If such a visit is organized and operated by an external company, perhaps a multinational, or by one or more members of a local elite, benefits are unlikely to filter down to the local community and therefore will not improve the quality of life of those in most need. Expeditions and specialized package holidays, like small-scale safaris, typically satisfy these criteria.

A small-scale local guest house could illustrate situation (2). It would provide accommodation within a physical and social environment that has been modified relatively little. The standard of comfort provided for tourists is likely to be low, however, rendering demand minimal. Nevertheless, the original environment is preserved and any economic benefits that do accrue will go directly to the local community.

Situation (3) can occur when a large tourism enterprise employs many local people. Not all members of the local community will obtain jobs and the majority of the employment provided is likely to be unskilled, but work *is* made available to those who may otherwise be unemployed. A large enterprise such as this may well satisfy certain types of tourists but, in the process, may irreparably damage the environment.

Compromise is the essence of situation (4). Small-scale, locally-managed tourism enterprises that may spread benefits more widely through the community are the best example. Typical are the Casamance scheme in Senegal and ecotourism developments in Belize, where a *measure* of satisfaction of a variety of sustainable aims has been achieved, according to the participants.

The various approaches to sustainable development inevitably lead to confusion and, as Burns and Holden (1995) suggest, those involved in tourism will not automatically benefit from the application of the sustainable principles that are frequently identified as a panacea for the industry (Poon 1993). While this question of the role of tourism within sustainable development is interesting, and perhaps too infrequently addressed, the role of sustainable development within tourism is widely acknowledged but imperfectly understood (Croall 1995). Both issues are incorporated within the two readings chosen for this section. They extend and explain the ideas introduced above and, in particular, identify a number of basic criteria that can be used to define sustainable tourism and can be applied to potential or actual situations to determine the nature and level of their sustainable practices.

REFERENCES

Burns, P M and Holden, A (1995) *Tourism. A New Perspective*, Prentice Hall International (UK) Limited, Hemel Hempstead

Croall, J (1995) *Preserve or Destroy. Tourism and the Environment*, Calouste Gulbenkian Foundation, London

Poon, A (1993) *Tourism, Technology and Competitive Strategies*, CAB International, Wallingford

Alternative and Sustainable Tourism Development – The Way Forward

Peter M Burns and Andrew Holden

COMPONENTS OF SUSTAINABLE TOURISM DEVELOPMENT

Murphy (in Theobold 1994, 272) gives an extensive and detailed list of the components of sustainable development in Table 2.1. Although the components apply to all forms of development they can be adapted to tourism development. Indeed, the link between these components and the guiding principles for sustainable tourism development developed by the United Kingdom's Department of the Environment (1991, 15) are axiomatic.

These guiding principles are as follows.

- The environment has an intrinsic value which outweighs its value as a tourism asset. Its enjoyment by future generations and its long-term survival must not be prejudiced by short-term considerations.
- Tourism should be recognized as a positive activity with the potential to benefit the community and the place as well as the visitor.
- The relationship between tourism and the environment must be managed so that the environment is sustainable in the long term. Tourism must not be allowed to damage the resource, prejudice its future enjoyment or bring unacceptable impacts.
- Tourism activities and developments should respect the scale, nature and character of the place in which they are sited.
- In any location, harmony must be sought between the needs of the visitor, the place and the host community.
- In a dynamic world some change is inevitable and change can often be beneficial. Adaptation to change, however, should not be at the expense of any of these principles.
- The tourism industry, local authorities and environmental agencies all have a duty to respect the above principles and to work together to achieve their practical realisation.

Central to the implementation of these principles is that consideration be given in the development process to the model shown in Figure 2.2. The emphasis in this model is for a movement towards integration of the physical environment (place), the cultural environment (host community) and the tourist. The implication is that in future planning of tourism, greater efforts need to be made to incorporate community representation into the planning process (although great difficulties may be experienced in defining the true meaning of community because of its

Table 2.1 *Sustainable development components*

Component	Description
1. Establishing ecological limits and more equitable standards	'Requires the promotion of values that encourage consumption standards that are within the bounds of the ecological possible and to which all can reasonably aspire.
2. Redistribution of economic activity and reallocation of resources	Meeting essential needs depends in part on achieving full growth potential and sustainable development clearly requires economic growth in places where such needs are not being met.
3. Population control	Though the issue is not merely one of population size but of the distribution of resources, sustainable development can only be pursued if demographic developments are in harmony with the changing productive potential of the ecosystem.
4. Conservation of basic resources	Sustainable development must not endanger the natural systems that support life on Earth: the atmosphere, the waters, the soils, and the living beings.
5. More equitable access to resources and increased technological effort to use them more effectively	Growth has no set limits in terms of population or resource use beyond which lies ecological disaster … But ultimate limits there are, and sustainability requires that long before these are reached the world must ensure equitable access to the constrained resource and reorient technological efforts to relieve the pressure.
6. Carrying capacity and sustainable yield	Most renewable resources are part of a complex and interlinked ecosystem, and maximum sustainable yield must be defined after taking into account system-wide effects of exploitation.
7. Retention of resources	Sustainable development requires that the rate of depletion of non-renewable resources foreclose as few future options as possible.
8. Diversification of the species	Sustainable development requires the conservation of plant and animal species.
9. Minimise adverse impacts	Sustainable development requires that adverse impacts on the quality of air, water and other natural elements are minimised so as to sustain the ecosystem's overall integrity.
10. Community control	Community control over development decisions affecting local ecosystems.
11. Broad national/ international policy	The biosphere is the common home of all humankind and joint management of the biosphere is prerequisite for global political security.
12. Economic viability	Communities must pursue economic well-being while recognising that [government] policies may set limits to material growth.
13. Environmental quality	Corporate environmental policy is an extension of total quality management.
14. Environmental audit	An effective environmental audit system is at the heart of good environmental management'.

Source: Murphy (in Theobald 1994, 272).

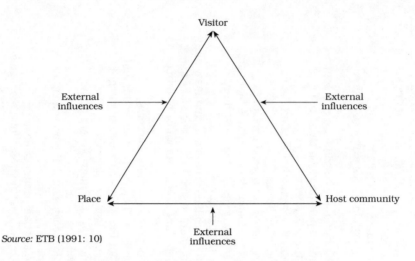

Figure 2.2 *Model for sustainable tourism*

diversity and complexity of social construction) and achieving universal agreement of such wide representations of interests may be difficult. As Haywood (1988,
105) puts it:

> *Tourism planners are now being asked to be more responsive to a broader set
> of economic and social needs. If this is to occur local governments should
> recognise that they will have to become more responsible to the local citizens
> whose lives and communities may be affected by tourism ... Local residents
> obviously become part of the tourist product attracting tourists through their
> culture and hospitality, and consequently the resident, as a community
> member, is affected by tourism in all its positive and negative manifestations.*

REFERENCES

Department of Environment (1991) *Tourism and the Environment: Maintaining the balance*,
HMSO, London

English Tourist Board (1991) *Tourism and the Environment: Maintaining the balance*, ETB,
London

Haywood, M (1988) 'Responsible and responsive tourism planning in the community',
Tourism Management, June

Murphy, P. (1994) 'Tourism and sustainable development' in Theobold, W (ed) *Global
Tourism: The next decade*, Butterworth-Heinemann Ltd, Oxford

Theobold, W (ed) (1994) *Global Tourism: The next decade*, Butterworth-Heinemann Ltd,
Oxford

The Thorny Path to Sustainable Tourism Development

Hansruedi Müller

A range of interacting issues has promoted calls for sustainable tourism development. This paper defines the subject and discusses in detail some suggestions from the well known 'Tourism with Insight' group about how to achieve sustainability. It goes on to examine why sustainable tourism is, however, very difficult to achieve in practice, noting the plethora of theoretical statements, the shortage of implementation skills, demand pressures, hedonism, and the impact of extended discussions - 'hectic continuity'. A number of ways forward are suggested, including new forms of taxation, open discussion of conflicts and environmental audits: it concludes that a search for a complex perfect formula may be counterproductive, and that simple solutions may be best.

Everybody is calling for sustainable or 'environmentally and socially compatible' tourism, but whenever these demands crop up, it becomes apparent that everybody interprets the concepts differently. So sustainable tourism runs the risk of becoming just an empty cliché. The following contribution looks into why the conserver's approach is beset with so many difficulties.

WHY THE CALL FOR SUSTAINABLE TOURISM DEVELOPMENT?

Is it perhaps because we are fast approaching the turn of the century and because we know from experience that every turn of the century has brought major structural upheavals? Is it because the year 2000 is coming up and because countless forecasts with a year–2000 deadline prompt us to think everything will be completely different in the new millennium? Or because Pisces is giving way to Aquarius? Or simply because booming post-war tourism growth is reaching a saturation point where the marginal utility of every new offer is approaching zero or even registering a negative impact? National economists call this relationship between investment efforts and the subsequent earning the 'law of decreasing growth of earnings' (cf Krippendorf and Müller 1986, 52). In any case, many of us consider that things cannot continue in the same way if they are to continue at all. All our activities have amounted to a considerable imposition on our natural environment – too much in many areas. We have neglected several aspects, for example:

- *Psychological and natural limits*, although we have all learnt in the meantime that it is extremely difficult to determine natural tolerance limits because they are constantly shifting.

Research Institute for Leisure and Tourism, University of Bern, Monbijoustrasse 29, CH 3011, Bern, Switzerland

- *The complexity of intermeshing relationships,* because tourist developments are not simple cause-and-effect relationships involving two or more factors but a complex interplay of various interacting forces.
- *Natural time lags* – effects with causes deep in the past or causes which do not take effect until years later (eg the hole in the ozone layer).
- *Assimilation period* – the time granted to nature or peoples to adapt to new situations. According to one theory, cultural development always lags behind structural development. Often, rapid changes in economic and socio-demographic structures in tourist areas take no account of this capacity for socio-cultural and natural adaptation. Paul Messerli (1989), in his final report on the research programme 'Man and Biosphere', described the assimilation period as the critical yardstick.

Negligence in this and other mattrers has put tourism in an awkward position and at least partly explains the call for 'environmentally and socially compatible' tourism.

WHAT DOES 'SUSTAINABLE TOURISM DEVELOPMENT' REALLY MEAN?

The objective of environmentally and socially compatible tourism has a lot to do with the frequently quoted and already much-abused development strategy of 'qualitative growth'. 'Qualitative growth' can be described as any increase in quality of life (ie economic health and subjective wellbeing) which can be achieved with less use of non-renewable resources and less stress on the environment and people. This demand may have its sights set high but it is very illuminating.

Thus, the objective is to influence the magic pentagon (see Figure 2.3) with the following angles:

- economic health,
- subjective wellbeing of the locals,
- unspoilt nature, protection of resources,
- healthy culture,
- optimum satisfaction of guest requirements,

by means of tourism development in such a way that no one angle predominates, ensuring that the interplay of factors becomes more and more beneficial and less and less burdensome.

The target situation is balanced tourism development. All five objectives, unspoilt nature and healthy culture, a high degree of subjective wellbeing, optimum satisfaction of guest requirements and economic health carry the same weight and are juxtaposed. Environmentally and socially compatible tourism would mean establishing harmony in this 'magic pentagon' to maximize the positive relationships between all the factors while keeping the negative repercussions (particularly on nature and culture) to a minimum.

Like the magic square in national economics (full employment, stable prices, stable balance of payments and growth), the five factors are equally important. They are objectives and prerequisites rolled into one. Compared with the present

Extract 2: *The Thorny Path to Sustainable Tourism*

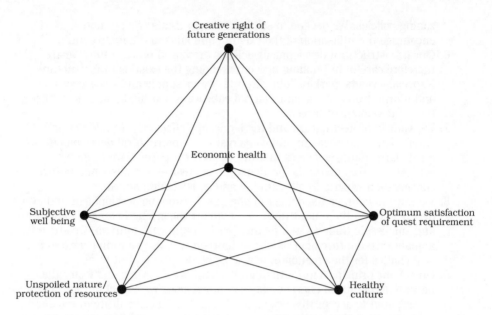

Figure 2.3 *Tourism Development's Magic Pentagon–Pyramide*

situation, this concept represents an upgrading of social and environmental interests and a comparative downgrading of purely economic ones.

There are any number of principles, theories and suggestions as to how the desired situation can be achieved. For example, the 'insights of the responsible host population' by the 'Tourism with Insight' Working Group (1992) have become internationally known:

1. Tourism should supplement our economy appropriately. We know, however, that it also represents a danger to our culture and our environment. We therefore want to supervise and control its development so that our country may be preserved as a viable economic, social and natural environment.
2. By independent decision making in tourist development we mean that the host population should decide on and participate in all matters relevant to the development of their region: tourist development by, with and for the local population. We encourage many forms of community participation in decision making, without neglecting the interests of minorities.
3. The tourist development we aim for is economically productive, socially responsible and environment-conscious. We are prepared to cease pursuing further development where it leads to an intolerable burden for our population and environment. We want to avoid the pitfalls of economic imperatives.
4. We determine the tourism development targets in our areas in a binding way, limiting them to what is desirable and not what is feasible. We adhere to this policy and are prepared to put up with the bottlenecks that may arise from doing so.
5. We want to keep control over our land. We pursue an active planning and land use policy. We limit our new construction by carefully considered

zoning policies. We decline to sell land to non-locals. We promote and encourage the utilisation of the existing buildings and infrastructure.

6. Our infrastructural development policies are based on restraint. We are therefore careful in building new or extending the existing infrastructure (especially roads, parking lots, airports, water supply and sewage system) and tourist transport facilities (aerial cableways, ski-lifts) and strictly observe the set development targets.

7. We want to protect nature and the landscape effectively. In addition to careful land management and conservative infrastructural development, we create large nature reserves in order to preserve particularly valuable ecosystems. We ensure the participation of environmentalists and nature conservation experts in all planning and construction activities.

8. We want to counter the danger of one-sided economic development and over-dependence on the tourist trade. We support the strengthening of agriculture and smallscale trade as well as their partnership with tourism. We strive for a qualitative improvement of jobs in tourism. We also continually explore all possibilities for the creation of new jobs outside the tourist trade.

9. One of our principles in tourist development is to observe and foster the natural and cultural characteristics of our region. We expect our guests to be prepared to accept this principle. We want our local culture to remain independent and alive. We protect and promote our architecture, our handi-crafts, our art, our language, our customs and our cuisine.

10. We shall provide information for all concerned: the local population, the tourist trade, politicians and tourists, and try to win their support for socially respon-sible and environmentally conscious behaviour. We shall use all tourism marketing tools and general information channels to promote our concept.

WHAT MAKES ACHIEVING SUSTAINABLE TOURISM DEVELOPMENT SO DIFFICULT?

There is nothing as practical as a good theory, but too many over-abstract theories do not get us any further either. In fact, they quickly provoke counter reactions and rejection. Researchers and critics have to realize that we are reaching a *saturation point* where there are too many 'experts' with too much advice on the one hand and too few agents with too few resources and too little time to act on the other. This may be the first difficulty.

A second possible explanation lies in continuing *pressure from demand*. The boom factors in tourism growth, in particular the still expanding leisure budget of many sectors of the population, and ever greater willingness to travel (amounting to a virtual addiction to mobility) and the increasing importance of getting away or travelling as a way of giving life a meaning, are producing a swelling torrent of travellers.

A third reason for the difficulty of achieving sustainable tourism development probably lies in the increasing *hedonistic philosophy* of many people. Although empirical research reveals a growing awareness of responsibility towards future generations or more and more environmental consciousness, the trend towards indulging in pleasure and enjoyment and living life to the full continues virtually undiminished.

Fourthly, mere talk and a few isolated changes of attitude are not enough to achieve genuine environmentally and socially compatible tourism development. This calls for a *change of paradigm* – or to quote the title of Stephan Schmidheiny's book (1992) – *a change of course*. However, we find it hard to bring about this change of paradigm, course or frame of outlook which helps us to understand the world around us or the economic fabric and to take the appropriate decisions. It is a long and difficult process. Admittedly, a radical change in human conscious-ness is emerging but there are still enough defence or delaying mechanisms in the economic and political system to prevent this change from coming about fast. One often has the impression that general uncertainty has merely resulted in a kind of 'hectic stagnation'.

Yet new approaches are becoming visible all around. More and more tour operators are reflecting on how they can implement ecological management requirements, environmental experts are being employed, 'green quality symbols' are mushrooming, ecological audits are being drawn up and existing guidelines revised. Nevertheless, this glimmer of hope on the tourism horizon should not blind us to the fact that many tourism professionals are still oblivious to the opportunity offered by this crisis.

SO JUST HOW DO WE ACHIEVE SUSTAINABLE TOURISM DEVELOPMENT?

First of all, I warmly recommend people to take their lead from the principles developed by Gerd Gerken (1988, 242):

1. Take maximum account of the value and dignity of all peoples.
2. Reduce inequality to the absolute minimum because inequality represents a waste of energy, creativity and human resources.
3. Accept planetary responsibility, ie give priority to the principles and objec-tives of the ecological environment and the biosphere.
4. Cooperate on an 'ecological generation contract' which respects the right of future generations to have a hand in shaping their world.

If we want to promote *social compatibility* in tourism, we must be prepared to:

- let locals share in the development process;
- take the wraps off cultural conflicts;
- seek dialogue, encourage discussion about future tourism development;
- prepare guests better for their holiday situation.

To advance the change of course towards *environmentally compatible* tourism, I should like to reflect on the following fundamental ideas.

Frank disclosure of the conflict between economic premises and ecological demands

There is a conflict between economic premises such as cost effectiveness, competitive ability, productivity, economic growth, job creation, etc and ecological demands such as the sparing use of raw materials, securing basic conditions for life, avoiding noise and waste, etc. Naturally, ecology means 'long-term economy', but we can only survive as a branch of industry, an economic system and the human race if we frankly expose the short-term conflict.

Advocacy of and active support for 'global control taxation'

The globalization of the problems also represents a challenge to tourism companies and tourism politicians to think globally and take appropriate action. Sustainable tourism development implies clear advocacy of 'global control taxation' (like a serious CO_2 levy or an energy tax), even if this results in temporary structural changes. The 'polluter pays' principle must be taken seriously at long last, with not only economic, but also so-called 'social' or 'external', costs being compensated for.

Environmental declaration of all aspects

I advocate an open, honest declaration of all aspects which impinge on the environment, for example the energy consumption of various means of transport (cf Müller 1993), the elimination or treatment of waste, air and water pollution (EC Blue Flag), etc. In the not-so-distant future, this environmental information should be the subject of proper ecological audits but a start could already be made in lists of hotels, travel brochures or local pamphlets.

IMPLANTING 'GREEN VIRUSES'

I would warn against waiting until all details of ecological relationships have been clarified or until a methodology for drawing up ecological audits has been established. We academics will never manage this! So visions of a desirable situation should be developed and the appropriate measures introduced. I would also recommend against beginning in the traditional way of adapting corporate objectives and developing time-consuming green strategies. It is more important to try to implant 'green viruses' which will spread awareness on their own encouraging people to act in a more environmentally compatible fashion. There are a large number of these green viruses which have to be traced, observed, nurtured or perhaps even curbed: ecological competitions, environmental information or a regular wholefood menu are often more effective faster than newly formulated guidelines or a complicated training concept.

'Think locally – act globally' must become just as important as the old adage 'Think globally – act locally'. Global challenges require big and small steps which must, however, begin with a small, very personal revolution. What is important is the right direction, and the right direction is definitely towards 'environmentally and socially compatible action'. We must take joint action, trying to make a desirable future the probable one and introducing a change of course. After all, we really have no other choice.

REFERENCES

Gerken, Gerd (1988) *Die Geburt der neuen Kultur – Vom Industrialismus zum Light-Age*, Duesseldorf/Vienna

Krippendorf, Jost and Müller, Hansruedi (1986) *Alpsegen Alptraum – Für eine Tourismus-Entwicklung im Einklang mit Mensch und Natur*, Berne

Messerli, Paul (1989) *Mensch und Natur im alpinen Lebensraum – Risiken, Chancen, Perspektiven*, Berne

Müller, Hansruedi (1991) "Öko-Management im Tourismus" in *Marketing 2000*, Österreich Werbung (Hrsg), Vienna

Müller, Hansruedi and Mezzasalma, Roman (1993) Transport-Energiebilanz: Ein erster Schritt zu einer Öko-Bilanz fur Reiseveranstalter, in *Jahrbuch der Schweiz, Tourismuswirtschaft*, C Kaspar (Hrsg) St-Gall

Schmidheiny, Stephan (1992) *Kurswechsel (Changing Course – A Global Perspective on Development and the Environment) – Globale unternehmerische Perspektiven für Entwicklung und Umwelt*, Munich.

Tourism with Insight Working Group (1992) Tourismus mit Einsicht, Munich.

Chapter 3

Changing Consumption Patterns

INTRODUCTION

'The crisis of the tourism industry is a crisis of mass tourism' (Poon 1993, 3). By implication, the tourists involved in mass tourism are usually associated with the type identified by Kilvert in the nineteenth century as 'a noisy rabble of tourists, males and females .... a kicking might tend to mind their manners' (Plomer 1986, 56). Not all mass tourists deserve such a stigma. They are taking advantage of paid holiday time, an adequate disposable income and the relatively cheap travel and accommodation that is made available by technological advances and the economies of scale that provide holidays developed along assembly-line principles (Poon 1993) to escape from often routine work in urban, industrial settings. This is clearly described in the reading from Krippendorf's seminal book *The Holiday Makers* (1987).

Mass tourism was considered 'best practice' by the tourism industry, by the tourists and by the host countries in the 1970s and early 1980s (Poon 1993), but although destination countries reaped benefits, especially in terms of foreign exchange earnings, few succeeded in avoiding at least some of the damaging effects of the industry. It has been the attitude of tourists, who continue to demand traditional types of holidays in large numbers, as well as the commercial aims of those engaged in the industry and the failure of developers and host governments to see beyond the short term, that have resulted in the continued dominance of mass tourism and created obstacles to the spread of alternative, more sustainable approaches (Croall 1995). It does appear that the era of unchecked exploitation of the environment by the tourist industry is no longer unquestioned, and there are signs that more sensitive developments are beginning to emerge (Poon 1993). But mass tourism is unlikely to disappear, since those who demand risk-free holidays at relatively low cost will continue to comprise a large share of the global tourism market, be they trend-setters from newly developing countries just starting to participate in material consumption as represented by international tourism, or the less adventurous psychocentrics from the developed world. The fashionable concern with the environment and with healthier lifestyles, together with a demand for 'something different' on the part of those who experienced traditional 'sun, sea and sand' holidays in their youth, lies behind the growth of new types of 'alternative' tourism and a search for more sustainable options. Whether these options are a myth or a reality (Niles 1991) is the subject of considerable debate, highlighted in the remaining extracts included in this section.

REFERENCES

Croall, J (1995) *Preserve or Destroy. Tourism and the Environment,* Calouste Gulbenkian Foundation, London

Krippendorf, J (1987) *The Holiday Makers. Understanding the Impact of Leisure and Travel,* Butterworth-Heinemann, Oxford

Niles, E. (1991) 'Sustainable tourism development – A myth or a reality?' *In Focus* Summer 1, pp3–4

Plomer, E (ed) (1986) *Kilvert's Diary 1870–1879,* Century Hutchinson Ltd, London

Poon, A (1993) *Tourism, Technology and Competitive Strategies,* CAB International, Wallingford

The Motives of the Mobile Leisureman – Travel Between Norm, Promise and Hope

Jost Krippendorf

THE COMPLEX WORLD OF TRAVEL MOTIVES AND EXPECTATIONS

When individual people are asked why they go on a journey, as is done in psychological tourism research in some countries every year with large-scale interview studies, it is not surprising to hear the reiteration of all the reasons that feature in advertising and which are repeated over and over again in all tourist brochures and catalogues. In this sense, the motives of the individual person are to a large extent 'ready made' or secondary. In technical terms: 'A subsequent rationalization of the unreflected, primary (social) motivation' (Hömberg 1978). Also, many of the quoted motives are nothing but empty boxes, which every individual may fill with quite different contents. Subjective wishes are thus condensed, simplified, registered and presented in the given answer formulas and statistics. Though this is probably the only way of measuring holiday-makers' motives, the reality is much more complex than appears from the results of various studies. There are always several motives that prompt a person to travel, and this is also the explanation for the overlaps in Table 3.1.

Many things remain hidden in the subconsciousness and cannot be brought to light by simple questions.

So much for the reliability of the information obtained from studies of tourists' motives and behaviour. But despite these reservations, their results are very instructive because they show the general direction of motives and provide pointers for judging the weight of each of the reasons given for travelling.

We have used the results of German studies for several reasons. The travel motives and behaviour of the German population have been systematically studied for over twenty years. In no other country can such a comprehensive body of information be found. Furthermore, an international comparative study shows that the habits of travelling holiday-makers do not differ essentially from country to country.

Little has changed in this motivation structure since the first psychological research of tourism in the early sixties. The order of priorities has remained the same. However, since the early seventies there has been a marked shift towards active holidays. The wish to sleep, rest and do nothing is mentioned much less often, while categories such as 'Be with other people, talk to people', 'have fun, have a change, enjoy oneself, play' and 'engage in hobbies' become more important. The unchanged main motive of travel has, for many years now, been 'mental hygiene', recuperation in a world which is experienced as counter-everyday life. Going a step further, these motives, and the phenomenon of travel in general, can

Extract 1: *The Motives of the Mobile Leisureman*

Table 3.1 *Main Reasons for Holiday Journeys*

Question: What were the main reasons for your 1986 (main) holiday journey?

To switch off, relax	66%
To get away from everyday life, have a change of scene	59%
To recover strength	49%
To experience nature	47%
To have time for one another	42%
To get sunshine, to escape from bad weather	39%
To be with other people, to have company	37%
To eat well	36%
To have a lot of fun and entertainment, enjoy oneself, have a good time	35%
To do as one pleases, to be free	35%
To experience a great deal, to have a lot of change (diversity)	33%
To experience something entirely different, see new things	33%
Cleaner air, clean water, to get out of the polluted environment	32%
To get exercise, to engage in light sports and games activities	30%
To experience other countries, to see the world	30%
To rest a great deal, do nothing, little exertion	29%
To be pampered, go on a spree, enjoy oneself	26%
To make new friends	23%
To do something for one's beauty, get a tan	23%
To travel a great deal, to move around	21%
To broaden one's horizons, do something for one's culture and education	20%
To pursue one's own interests	19%
To do something for one's health, prevent disease	18%
To refresh memories	18%
To see relatives and friends	16%
To have time for introspection, thought	15%
To engage actively in sport, to get fit	12%
To go on exploration trips, to take a risk, to experience something out of the ordinary	10%
To have time for one's hobbies	7%

Since the same person could name several reasons, the total percentage is over 100.

be interpreted in many ways, little of which, however, can be conclusively proved. The literature on tourism is full of different explanations and interpretations. The truth will probably not lie in one or the other of these theories, but in a mixture of various interpretations. Which does not make the thing any simpler.

TRAVEL IS RECUPERATION AND REGENERATION

This theory says: travel restores bodily and mental strength used up in everyday life, at work, school and in the family. It is a recharging of batteries; lubrication and oiling of the engine; minor maintenance on weekends, main servicing during the holidays. Taking a rest from everyday life in order that everything may run smoothly again and that productivity may remain high. The summer grazing of milked cows for future filling of the norm.

The number of sick is greater today than immediately after the Second World War. Our civilization has freed us from a large part of manual work, but in exchange we have had to buy such sedentary diseases as heart and circulation disorders. The so-called prosperity diseases have also become much more frequent: diabetes, high blood pressure, cancer of the respiratory tract as a result of cigarette smoking, alcoholism and many others. And what is especially striking: about half of the diseases are not of a primarily organic nature but the conse-quence of nervous stress, another product of the modern age. Free time and holidays in order to fill up on health seem to be more necessary than ever before.

TRAVEL IS COMPENSATION AND SOCIAL INTEGRATION

Travel compensates us for what we miss in everyday life. What people want is to find a compensation for the one-sided demands of their working life: they want to do and experience something that is different from the everyday routine, they seek diversion from the daily monotony, they long for fun and amusement. Increasing socialization, says this theory, drives people to take a holiday from society and escape into a world of leisure, which is relatively free from social and governmental constraints. After the trip they return willingly to the stable and familiar situation of everyday life. Tourism becomes a safety valve for letting off steam, a drug (as socially acceptable as aspirin) which temporarily kills the pain, but does nothing to cure the disease itself. It provides a way of channelling the disappointments over the impossibility of achieving one's aspirations into socially acceptable pursuits.

TRAVEL IS ESCAPE

This, most frequently quoted theory, says that the main motive for travelling is the wish to escape. It sees the modern industrial world as a prison from which its inmates want to break out. Working life being in fact ugly, the environment mostly unpleasant, monotonous and polluted, a compulsive and irrepressible urge to get out of it all emerges. According to this theory, tourism is assuming unmistakable characteristics of a mass flight from the reality of everyday life into an imaginary world of freedom. Because the everyday situation is unsatisfactory, people try to avoid it, at least temporarily, by travelling. What they want is to get away – though in a civilized manner – for a short while. It is the journey to the promised land. The flight to this imaginary outside world can also have the characteristics of escaping from oneself. The fear of inner emptiness and boredom, the thought that the holiday could be as lonely as solitary confinement or as boring as the assembly line, leads to an obsessive search for new experiences (Rieger in Svilar 1982, 14). The tourist industry, says one of its most vociferous critics, offers only temporary respite, but in so doing, enables one to avoid the responsibility of changing one's situation to something from which it is no longer necessary to escape (Braunschwieg quoted in Mäder 1982). Having said that, we should add that such a flight is not necessarily away from the daily routine. It could be an answer to a back-to-nature call. To fresh air as opposed to our polluted city environment. Or it could be that people are fleeing from the climate: from rain to sunshine, from the cold to the heat. This is a motive which determines the great North–South migration of tourists and which always features prominently in tourist trade publicity: 'When our roads are covered by dirty slush, when the sky weighs as heavy as lead and it seems the sun will never shine again, wouldn't you rather be...'

TRAVEL IS COMMUNICATION

Establishing contact with people, in contrast to the anonymity and alienation of everyday life, is an important aim of holiday-makers. They want to spend more time with their family and close friends as well as make new friends and acquaintances. All this is much easier during the holidays, since the atmosphere is more casual than at home. But, as we are told by psychologists, the chance to find human warmth is not limited to the small circle of the clan (Schober quoted in Wagner 1981). The submersion into the big thundering holiday herd trotting through the leisure pastures can also produce the feeling of security. This mixing with like-minded people creates an archaic feeling of pleasure absent from everyday life with its tendency towards isolation and alienation at the work place, in high-rise blocks of flats or in the standardized suburban family-house colonies. Tourism, with its masses of people, is interpreted as a chance to establish contacts and to feel at ease among the many other holiday-makers in a kind of community: togetherness enhancing new experiences, tourists among themselves. The wish to establish some kind of contact with the local population is at the bottom of the list of motives – at least judging by the results of some studies. But other studies indicate that the number of tourists who would like to get to know the host country and its people better is much greater in reality than is generally assumed (Vielhaber and Aderhold 1981). In many people, however, this apparent readiness is suppressed by uncertainty, inhibitions, lack of practice and experience. People don't quite know how to do it. So they don't. But even if this is the case, one thing is certain: the desire for contact with the native inhabitants in the country of destination is not a primary or urgent need for most tourists.

TRAVEL BROADENS THE MIND

A look at the list of motives confirms that to: 'Broaden one's horizons, do something for one's culture and education', 'experience other countries, see the world, meet local people', or 'experience something entirely different, see new things', do not belong to the dominating group. Culture? Did you say culture? Other things are in the foreground. Cultural needs can be easily satisfied with homeopathic doses, that is, with the usual sightseeing tours. And yet, there probably are tourists who would be ready to experience something more or something different. (See above.)

TRAVEL IS FREEDOM AND SELF-DETERMINATION

Freedom is, in the final analysis, the ability to make one's own decisions about a course of action. Travel liberates us from obligations. We can break loose from the 'must', from the order and regulations which oppress us in everyday life. We can finally do what we want and what we think is right. We can also do nothing. We are free, unrestrained, our own masters. For the German theologian and tourism researcher Paul Rieger, holidays are perhaps the only and last basically ungovernable and uncontrollable remnant of human freedom in our society. It is the most liberating form of leisure, because we can leave the habitual environment and, for a while at least, distance ourselves from it. Rieger believes that the various degenerations, massivity, clichés and primitivism do not change the fact that freedom is experienced during holiday travel (Rieger 1982). Travel is double free time: it frees people from work and from home. Many, of course, do not know what to do with this unfamiliar and sudden liberty, or with themselves, because they lack the practice and the confidence and therefore in their need for help, turn to what is offered by the tourist industry. This does not make them 'manipulated puppets' – far from it. It is, however, indisputable that the present pattern of tourism does not encourage the exercise of freedom and self-determination. Pattern F still dominates. To resist being pressed into it requires a great deal of initiative and independence.

TRAVEL IS SELF-REALIZATION

We have probably all experienced becoming aware of our own reality in places where everything is unfamiliar and strange. Travel, says this theory, is a chance for self-discovery. Holidays provide an opportunity to confront the Self, to test one's soul, to come to terms with oneself, to measure oneself against others and discover one's own abilities. Beautiful as these chances offered by travel may sound, holiday-makers do not seem to be really aware of them, and as a motive for going away it is certainly at the bottom of their list – though it may be hidden, lurking behind other motives.

TRAVEL IS HAPPINESS

In literature and experts' discussions on travel and holidays the most common catch phrases are: 'the most memorable days of the year', 'a sparkling two weeks spent in a festive atmosphere', 'the happiest time of the year', 'happiness in its most accessible form'. In a recent study by the Starnberg Study Group for Tourism, human happiness is described as a harmonious state, trouble and tension-free, combined with a certain degree of self-realization. The probability of experiencing this state of happiness is supposed to be much greater during the holidays than in everyday life (Hartman quoted in Rieger 1982, 15). Holiday expectations consist of images of happiness – the journey away from routine as a kind of second life, the arteries of which have been pumped full of our wishes and hopes. Travel is more than a new form of stimulant in our consumer society. Those who travel want to find a joie de vivre. Not only a vacation, 'a temporary liberation from service', but a vacation, in German 'ferien', from the Latin 'feria', meaning 'festivity' and 'celebration'. This is what holidays should in fact be: the expression of sensuality, happiness and harmony. But isn't it hard enough to find even a little happiness, not to mention the other (fulfilled) Self, on a beach squeezed between endless lines of cars and towering blocks of houses? Be that as it may, the holiday-maker's subjective freedom remains one of the great chances for personal happiness even though in reality it is often squandered.

Travel is... The list of motives could be expanded at will. The contradictions would then be even more numerous. But it is these contradictions that reveal the true nature of tourism – a scintillating and multi-faceted part of human and social reality. Indeed, every tourist is probably motivated by more than one of the reasons we have outlined above, depending on his social status and form of travel opted for. We must not forget that the traveller himself is a mixture of many characteristics that cannot be simply assigned into this category or that one.

But are we to content ourselves with this diffuse picture of travel motives, in which everything or nothing is possible and which does not help us in our investigation? A closer analysis will reveal two things that run like a thread through all the studies: first, travel is motivated by 'going *away* from' rather than 'going towards' something or somebody. To shake off the everyday situation is much more important than the interest in visiting new places and people. This is closely connected with the second point: travellers' motives and behaviour are markedly self-oriented: 'Now *I* decide what is on and it should be good for *me*.' These two observations are very important for our further considerations. They reveal already at this stage the difficulties of a harmonious tourism.

The list of motives shows quite explicitly that even if motivation is not always negative, ie based on the wish to escape, the 'going away from' element is always the dominant one. Where the journey leads is not so important, the main thing is to get away from the routine, to switch off, change the scene. To this extent travel destinations are altogether interchangeable.

What matters is that there is snow for skiing, sunshine for getting a tan, the sea for swimming, opportunities for gregariousness and entertainment. The 'toward' element, the positive motivation of experiencing something, the readiness to learn something about other people, other countries and cultures and about oneself, all play a subordinate role. By contrast, the emphasis on the Self manifests itself almost everywhere: the tourist doesn't receive orders any more, he gives them. He wants to get the best of things, have fun, be pampered. Perhaps even play a role that would be impossible in everyday life. For a short while, he wants to appear as 'King Guest' and be treated as such. He wants to have the feeling he is somebody. It is a kind of self-realization, very possibly at the expense of others. People are either not aware of it or they think it is their right. Nevertheless, whatever the motives – the weekend in the country, the cultured educational traveller, the photo-amateur on safari, the sun worshipper on the beach, the adventurer in the jungle and the skier in the mountains – egoistic motives, whether we realize it or not, are always first and foremost. Furthermore: as long as such motives predominate, as long as the visited country and its people are taken only as a holiday setting, there is no hope for a 'better' tourism.

Extract 1: J Krippendorf

REFERENCES

Braunschweig, P (1982) quoted by U Mäder, *Fluchthelfer Tourismus - Wärme in der Ferne?* rotpunktverlag, Zürich

Franke, M (1973) "Freizeit in diesem Jahrzehnt – sozialhygienisch gesehen" in *Schriftenreihe für ländliche Sozialfragen* Verlag M & H Schaper, Hannover, pp18–21

Hartmann, K D quoted by Rieger, P (1982) p15

Hömberg, S "Reisen zwischen Kritik und Analyse, Zum Stand der Tourismusforschung" in *Zeitschrift für Kulturaustausch*, No 3/1978, Michael Rehs (ed) Horst Erdmann Verlag, Tübingen, p39

Rieger, P (1982) "Die historische und psychologische Dimension – Warum reiste man fruher? Warum reisen wir heute?" in *Tourismus - das Phänomen des Reisens, Hermann Ringeling*, Maja Svilar (eds) Verlag Paul Haupt, Bern, p14

Schober, R (1981) quoted by F A Wagner, Geborgen in der donnernden Ferienherde in *Frankfurter Allgemeine Zeitung*, No 65/1981

Studienkreis für Tourismus (ed) (1987) *Urlaubsreisen 1986* Studienkreis für Tourismus e V, Starnberg, p29

Vielhaber, A and Aderhold, P *Tourismus in Entwicklungsländer* Bundesministerium für wirtschaftliche Zusammenarbeit, Bonn

Behaviour and Experiences While Travelling

Jost Krippendorf

THE MUCH MALIGNED TOURIST

The most exotic thing about tourism are tourists themselves! Our society has a distorted attitude to these strange beings called tourists. Although most of us travel – and not so infrequently – what other category of people are criticized, accused, laughed at or derided as much as tourists? They are called the new barbarians, the golden hordes, the new masters. They are compared to locust swarms appearing like a plague, laying waste and then going on. It made him quite ill to think how his fellow-countrymen carried on in Third World countries, said a German minister for development a few years back. The sigh can be heard rising all the way to heaven: 'Lord, they don't know what they are doing!'. Caricaturists the world over have made tourists their favourite subject, and booklets with cartoons about tourism can be bought in every bookshop. Whatever the tourist does, he does it wrong:

The ridiculous tourist, immediately recognizable by his camera dangling before his belly, his funny leisure clothes, pale skin, fat or half-naked body.

The naive tourist, inexperienced in travelling, speaking no languages, who can't find his way around, asks stupid questions and can easily be led up the garden path.

The organized tourist, who is dependent on the group and the guide and, like a sheep, feels well only among other tourists.

The ugly tourist, who behaves as if the whole world belongs only to him and does all the things he is forbidden to do at home.

The uncultured tourist, who spends the holidays lazing on the beach, doesn't care a damn about the country and people he is visiting and watches TV, plays cards and eats sausages and fried eggs, like at home.

The rich tourist, who can afford anything he fancies and does spend lavishly, who puts his prosperity on show and enjoys being waited upon hand and foot.

The exploiting tourist, who spends his holiday at the cost of other peoples and cultures and takes advantage of the poverty of others.

The polluting tourist, who flattens everything in the way with his car, pollutes the air with exhaust fumes, tramples over meadows and fields, leaves dirty rivers, lakes and seas and ruins landscapes.

The alternative tourist, who differs from other tourists, explores the last untouched corners of the earth, thus paving the way for mass tourism.

And, needless to say, a tourist is always the other person! Educated people, people who can speak foreign languages, and who have higher incomes and more experience in travelling, can camouflage their tourist role. They feel they are individualists and believe they are superior to other people – although basically their behaviour when travelling is the same. 'That's something for tourists', they say, and naturally exclude themselves, pleased that they have been able to see through it. For them, the word 'tourist' is an insult.

All this indicates that our thinking about tourism and tourists is still very much confused, otherwise there wouldn't be so much criticism around. But, the widespread reviling of tourists is unconsidered and unproductive. Are tourists really the infantile fools or reckless ravagers they are made out to be? Should we really blame the tourist for the fact that there is something unnatural and artificial about their role? Do they really carry the main responsibility for all the negative effects of mass mobility and worldwide tourism? Aren't they rather the culprits and the victims all in one: defenceless pawns that anyone can use and attack? Those who censure tourism are in fact not criticizing individual travellers, but the massivity of the phenomenon. The main problem of modern tourism is that of its huge number.

All holiday-makers feel like individuals even when carried along by the massive wave of other tourists, because now they themselves choose and decide their actions – including that of whether to go on holiday or not. The sum of many individual actions, however, leads to a mass cliché. Millions of people display similar behaviour. It is here the criticism begins. What is particularly disturbing about the phenomenon is that the problem of large numbers can be solved in part only by industrial methods, ie with standardization, mass production and high-capacity facilities.

The much maligned tourist is a person looking, quite legitimately, for his/her happiness, badly needing the subjective freedom supplied by travelling even if – at least in the eyes of the critics – it is perhaps not used very intelligently. The tourist is his own advocate and not an international ambassador; he is not there to aid development or protect the environment. It goes without saying, then, that he behaves in an egoistic way. Nobody has ever explained to him the consequences of his actions and drawn his attention to the responsibility that is his. The damage tourism causes to the people, economy and environment of the host area, especially in the long-term, remains hidden from the tourist. He has been left out of all discussion on the subject, even though he is one of the main protagonists. Tourists seem to enjoy some kind of special status and are almost more immune than diplomats. They are therefore carefree and ignorant rather than devious. To lay all blame at their door would be as wrong as denying their responsibility. But they should certainly be made aware of the situation!

Global Transformation

Auliana Poon

NEW TOURISM DEFINED

New tourism is a phenomenon of large-scale packaging of non-standardized leisure services at competitive prices to suit the demands of tourists as well as the economic and socioenvironmental needs of destinations. New tourism refers to key emerging characteristics of the tourism industry. As noted in Chapter 1 new tourism exists if the following conditions hold:

1. The holiday is flexible and can be purchased at prices that are competitive with mass-produced holidays.
2. Production of travel and tourism-related services are not dominated by scale economies alone. Tailor-made services will be produced while still taking advantages of scale economies where they apply.
3. Production is increasingly driven by the requirements of consumers.
4. The holiday is marketed to *individuals* with different needs, incomes, time constraints and travel interests. Mass marketing is no longer the dominant paradigm.
5. The holiday is consumed on a large scale by tourists who are more experienced travellers, more educated, more destination-oriented, more independent more flexible and more 'green'.
6. Consumers look at the environment and culture of the destinations they visit as a key part of the holiday experience.

One of the key characteristics of the new tourism is *flexibility* – flexible consumers, flexible services and the flexibility of producers to move with the market. The cornerstone of the industry's flexibility is information technology (IT). IT creates the flexibility to satisfy changing consumer needs at prices that are cost-competitive with mass-produced holidays. This practice is fundamentally different from the old paradigm where low-cost holidays were only possible within the confines of mass production, standardization and rigid packaging.

Information and communication technologies also allow producers to segment their markets and to match production more closely with the changing needs of their clients. Suppliers are now able to produce different travel, leisure and other related services (eg insurance and credit cards) along the same production line. Tourism now mimics flexible manufacturing and 'just-in-time' methods, which are now common practice in the automobile industry. What is unique about the growth of international tourism, however, is the speed at which it adopted the old mass-production manufacturing practices; the apparent short life cycle that mass production had in tourism; and the celerity with which the tourism industry is taking up the new production principle of flexibility.

As a new global best practice of flexible production takes hold, the travel and leisure sector will rapidly out-pace the manufacturing sector in adopting flexible production. Tourism will be a clear leader in the pack.

The marketing of the new tourism is also different from the old. In the old tourism, producers sold identical products to homogeneous groups of tourists. In the new tourism, there will be greater levels of market segmentation where travel and leisure services will increasingly cater to specific lifestyle characteristics of the new consumers. Marketing will be focused on the individual consumers, rather than on groups of undefined tourists.

Production will continue to be large-scale and global in nature and will take advantage of scale economies where they apply. It will, however, increasingly benefit from *scope economies* – economies associated with producing a *range* of items rather than producing a large quantity of identical units. While necessary, scale economies will no longer be sufficient to guarantee competitive success. Production will also be more flexible and closely geared to the changing needs of the consumers. *Mass customization* – the production and sale of large amounts of tailor-made services – will allow producers to supply flexible travel and tourism services to meet the demands of the new consumers. It will allow producers to supply travel and related services at prices that are competitive with mass-tourism services. Club Med is a good example for a supplier that has produced customized vacations for 'swinging singles' and marketed them to a large clientele. Cruise ships also provide an excellent example of mass customization. Armed with mega-ships and flexible itineraries, and a range of activities in which to participate at the various ports of call, cruise-holiday suppliers can offer a number of customized holidays to a large range of travellers.

EMERGENCE OF A NEW TOURISM

International tourism is undergoing rapid and radical transformation – a transformation into a new industry best practice or common sense.

As previously noted, five forces are driving the new tourism:

* consumers;
* technology;
* management techniques;
* production practices; and
* frame conditions.

These forces are summarized in Figure 3.1. It can be seen from the figure that new consumers and technologies are driving the new tourism, whilst new management techniques and production practices facilitate the development of the new services, and new frame conditions influence the speed and direction of the industry's change.

Changes in *consumer* behaviour and value provide the fundamental guiding force for the new tourism. New consumers are more informed and experienced travellers. They are products of universally accepted education. They have acquired changed values and lifestyles. They are products of changing population demographics. New tourists are flexible and more independent – they are hybrid

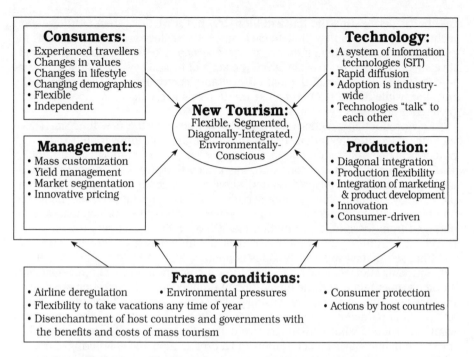

Figure 3.1 *The Driving Forces of the New Tourism*

consumers, spontaneous and unpredictable. They want to be active and in charge. They want to be different from the crowd. The increased travel experience, flexibility and independent nature of the new tourists are generating demand for more flexible holidays. Changing lifestyles and changing demographics of the new tourists are creating demand for more targeted holidays catering to their specific situations whether they be couples, families, single-parent households, empty nesters, travellers and double income and no kids (DINKS), young upwardly mobile persons (YUPPIES) or modern introverted luxury keepers (MILKIES).

Changing values are also generating demand for a more environmentally conscious and nature-oriented holiday. That it is the consumers who are driving the new tourism is reflected in a statement by Sir Colin Marshall, Deputy Chairman and Chief Executive of British Airways, as he concluded the First Annual World Travel Market Lecture in London, 1990:

> *...aside from safety and security, the shape, scope and style of the airline industry in Europe and around the world should be regulated by one force only - the choice and the preference of the air travel consumer.*

New technology provides yet another key impetus to the new tourism. It provides the wherewithal both to handle the high volumes of information that deregulation has produced (eg new fares, new airlines, new services) and the flexibility to cope with different and changing consumer requirements. Technology diffusion in tourism is so rapid and so pervasive that no segment of the industry will remain untouched. It is not merely a telephone *or* computer *or* videotext *or* teleconferencing that is permeating the tourism industry, but a whole system of information technologies that can now 'talk' to each other. Technology creates a new basis for competition in the tourism industry and has become a key determinant of competitive success. It is now possible, given the state of technology, for industry players to itemize in minute detail the many travel and leisure opportunities open to the traveller, while at the same time list the tourist's every demand, note his every preference and expectation in the quest to satisfy.

New production practices are also characteristic of the new tourism. These include: diagonal integration, production flexibility and innovation. Production practices of mass customization increasingly allow producers to satisfy the 'quirks and idiosyncrasies' of the consumers at prices that are cost-competitive with mass-produced tourism and related services. Diagonal integration makes it increasingly common sense to link services such as financial services, insurance and travel, with tremendous synergies, systems gains and scope economies to be obtained from integrated production (see Chapter 8). In a constantly changing travel environment, innovation becomes an indispensable tool for survival.

Changed management techniques is another ingredient in the making of the new tourism. Management practices of mass customization, yield management, market segmentation and the integration of production and marketing are driving the new tourism. Producers increasingly allow consumers to dictate the character and pace of production. They make a greater effort to find out what the consumers want, to produce what consumers are demanding and to sell consumers what they want to buy. Mass customization and a proliferation and splintering of brands will be the order of the day in the new tourism. Products and services will be carefully dissected and finely tuned, to meet the needs of the new consumers.

Frame conditions are the fifth and final ingredient facilitating the new tourism. Deregulation of the airline industry, limits to growth, initiatives taken by host countries, consumer protection and the increasing spread and flexibility of vacation days, are creating the conditions within which the new tourism will flourish. Deregulation has equally opened a whole new ball-game in the industry and has ushered in new airlines, mega carriers, and increased price competition. A new and more vital role for computerized reservations systems has also been ushered in. All these developments are radically changing the face of tourism.

Limits to the growth of old tourism have begun to be felt; tourism fatigue has begun to set in, and a growing global environmental consciousness limits its growth still further. Increasing levels of consumer and environmental protection will lead to improved standards in the industry and ensure that production reflects consumer choices while remaining sensitized to the needs of the eco-system. The flexibility to take vacations at any time in the year, as is now the case in Britain, will lead to a more even flow of tourism, which will reduce the high levels of seasonality – a common characteristic of the tourism industry. This could lead to a more balanced flow of visitors to resorts and attractions and lower the environmental effects of overcrowding, noise and other forms of pollution.

In what follows, the key changes in consumers, technology, management and production, and also the frame conditions that are changing tourism, shall be identified briefly.

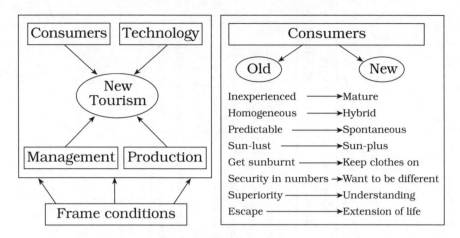

Source: Krippendorf 1987a; Poon 1987a; *Economist* 23 March 1991

Figure 3.2 *The New Consumers*

NEW CONSUMERS

New consumers are fundamentally different from the old. Some of the main differences are summarized in Figure 3.2.

Old tourists were homogeneous and predictable. They felt secure when travelling in numbers and took vacations where everything was pre-paid and pre-arranged. New tourists are spontaneous and unpredictable. They are hybrid in nature and no longer consume along linear predictable lines. The hybrid consumer may want to purchase different tourism services in different price categories for the same trip. New consumers want to be different from the crowd. They want to assert their individuality and they want to be in control.

The motivation of the new tourists is different from those of the old. For the old tourists, travel was a novelty. Travel was almost an end in itself. It mattered not where the old tourists went, once they got to a warm destination and could show others that they had been there. Quality of service was relatively unimportant and vacation was an escape from the routinization of home and work. For the new tourists, however, vacation is an extension of life. It is a journey of discovery. Vacations are taken 'just for fun', rather than to show others that one has been there. New tourists go on vacation not to see and experience the things they are used to at home and to be surrounded by it in safety; rather, they go out to see something different, something that would expand their experience. For the new tourists, quality and value for money are a premium; and expressing their individuality at the destination, their ultimate pleasure.

The attitudes of the new tourists are also very different from that of the old. Old tourists had a healthy disregard for the environment and cultures of the host countries they visited. Today, with the new tourist, there is a growing 'see and enjoy, but do not destroy' attitude. And while old tourists imposed their values on the receiving destinations with a 'West is best' attitude, among the new tourists today, there is greater understanding and appreciation for the different. The new tourists are generally better educated and informed than were the old.

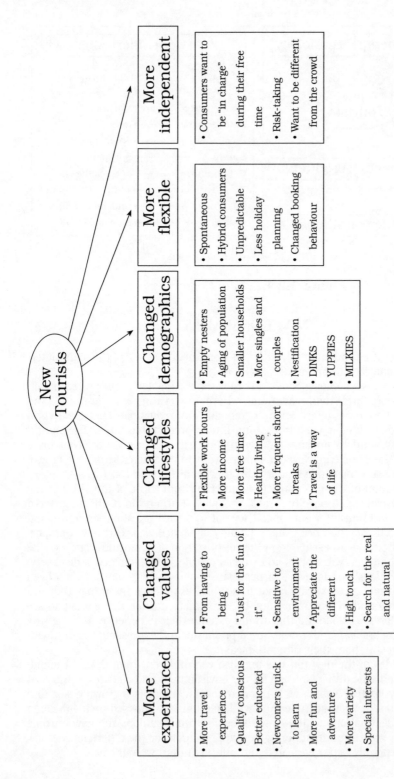

Figure 3.3 *The New Consumers*

Old tourists were content to lie in the sun and get sunburnt. They were interested in visiting attractions, had little or no special interests and ate in the hotel dining room. For the new tourists, sun is still a necessary factor in the vacation pursuit; however, sun is not sufficient to satisfy their expectation. New tourists have special interests and are more adventurous (termed 'soft, medium and hard'). They like sport and want to be active. With respect to the sun, the new tourists are more concerned about the effects of overexposure to it and its link to health.

Six key attributes are characteristic of the new tourists:

- they are more experienced;
- they have changed values;
- they have changed lifestyles;
- they are products of changed demographics;
- they are flexible; and
- they are independent-minded.

These key characteristics of the new tourists are leading to the transformation of the old tourism best practice (see Chapter 5).

REFERENCES

Economist (1991) A Survey of World Travel and Tourism, 23 March

Krippendorf, J (1987a) *The Holidaymakers: Understanding The Impact of Leisure and Travel*, Heinemann, London

Poon, A (1987a) "Information Technology and International Tourism – Implications for the Caribbean Tourism Industry", PhD Thesis, Science Policy Research Unit, Sussex University, UK

Destination Life Cycle:
The Isle of Man Case Study*

Chris Cooper and Stephen Jackson

The life cycle approach is well-developed in marketing and is increasingly being adopted to explain destination development as the Tourism Area Life Cycle (TALC). While criticized as being difficult to operationalize, the TALC does provide a useful descriptive tool for analyzing the development of destinations and the evolution of their markets. A case study of the Isle of Man exemplifies the utility of the TALC, in particular because the Island provides a long run of arrivals data and has been through all the stages of the TALC. It also demonstrates that the TALC can be viewed as being dependent upon the actions of managers and the setting of the destination. Keywords: product life cycle, tourist area life cycle, destination development, Isle of Man.

INTRODUCTION

The life cycle approach is well-developed in marketing (Day 1981, Rink and Swan 1979) where the product life cycle (PLC) is a generalization of a product's evolution as it passes through the stages of introduction, growth, maturity, and decline. In general, the growth of product sales follows an S-shaped pattern. The PLC has evoked both acclaim and disparagement. On the one hand, it is a simple concept describing the adoption of a new product by consumers. It hypothesizes that products have a limited life, profits rise and fall at different stages of the PLC, and products require different marketing strategies at each stage (Doyle 1976, Reed 1987). On the other hand, despite its logical and intuitive appeal, it is difficult to operationalize and use the PLC for, inter alia, forecasting or decision making (Brownlie 1985).

Although it could be argued that the tourism product is the sum of travel experiences from anticipation to recall (Medlik and Middleton 1973), the destination is a key element of the product and it is suggested that destinations go through a cycle of evolution similar to the PLC (Butler 1980). Here, numbers of visitors replace sales of a product. Moreover, it is possible to trace both the evolution of the market in terms of type and number of visitor and the development of the destination in terms of physical facilities, and even administrative structures. Early writers considered three stages to this tourism area life cycle: discovery, growth, and decline (Christaller 1964, Gilbert 1939), but Butler's (1980) more detailed framework is now generally accepted (Figure 3.4). This begins with 'exploration' by small numbers of visitors who are adventurous by nature and tend to

* Chris Cooper teaches and researches tourism at the University of Surrey (Department of Management Studies for Tourism and Hotel Industries, Guildford, Surrey GU2 5XH, United Kingdom) Stephen Jackson is principal lecturer in Geography, Liverpool Polytechnic. Both have a long-standing interest in the structure and development of tourist resorts and the Isle of Man as a tourism destination.

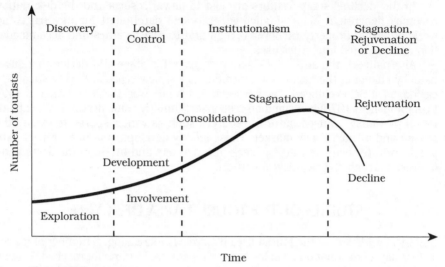

Source: Butler, 1980

Figure 3.4 *Hypothetical tourist area life cycle*

shun institutionalized travel. They are attracted by the natural beauty or cultural characteristics at the destination, but numbers are restricted by lack of access and facilities. At this stage, the attraction of the destination is that it remains unchanged by tourism and contact with local people will be high.

In the 'involvement' stage, local initiatives to provide for visitors and later advertise the destination, result in increased and regular numbers of visitors. A tourist season and market area emerge and pressures may be placed on the public sector to provide infrastructure.

The 'development' stage sees large numbers of visitors arriving. The organization of tourism begins to change as control is passed out of local hands and external companies move in to provide up-to-date facilities, which may alter the appearance of the destination. However, in this success lie the roots of failure. With increasing numbers and popularity, the destination may suffer a change in quality through problems of over-use and deterioration of facilities. Regional and national planning and control will have become necessary in part to ameliorate problems, but also to market the international tourist-generating areas, as visitors become more dependent upon travel arrangements booked through the trade.

In the 'consolidation' stage, the rate of increase of visitors has declined, though total numbers are still increasing and exceed permanent residents. The destination is now a fully fledged part of the tourism industry, with an identifiable recreational business district. Wolfe (1952) was one of the first to recognize a resort's 'divorce from the geographic environment' at this stage.

At 'stagnation', peak numbers have been reached and the destination is no longer fashionable. It relies on repeat visits from more conservative travellers, as well as business use of its extensive facilities, and major efforts are needed to maintain the number of visits. The destination may by now have environmental, social, and economic problems.

In the 'decline' stage, visitors are lost to newer resorts and the destination becomes dependent on a smaller geographical catchment for day trips and weekend visits. Property turnover is high and tourist facilities and accommodation are converted into other uses.

Alternatively, the authorities may recognize this stage and decide to 'rejuvenate' by changing the attractions. Introduction of new types of facility such as a casino, as at Scheveningen, The Netherlands (van de Weg 1982) and Atlantic City, USA (Stansfield 1978) is a common response. Similarly some destinations capitalize on previously unused natural resources such as winter sports, to extend the season and attract a new market. These facility developments often reflect joint public/private sector ventures to seek new markets and invest in the destination in order to reach a cycle/recycle pattern.

STUDIES OF THE TOURIST AREA LIFE CYCLE

Empirical evidence for the tourist area life cycle is increasing. A number of historical studies of destinations display the cycle's stages, but are approached through historical narrative rather than through explicit considerations of the life cycle stages (Clary 1984, Helleiner 1983, Moffat 1982, Snow and Wright 1976).

Others have overtly used the cycle as a framework for analysing changing destinations (Hovinen 1981, Meyer-Arendt 1985, Oglethorpe 1984, Stansfield 1978, Wilkinson 1987), but few studies actually attempt to extend the model. Exceptions here include Lundgren's (1982) examination of the spatial evolution of accommodation supply in the Laurentians and Nelson and Wall's (1986) analysis of the changing transport network on Vancouver Island. Keller (1987) develops the cycle in an examination of centre/periphery tourism.

These studies demonstrate that, as with the PLC, the shape of the curve will vary depending upon supply factors such as the rate of development, access, government policy, and competing destinations; and factors on the demand side such as the changing nature of clientele as the destination's market evolves hand in hand with supply-side developments. Each of these factors can delay or accelerate progress through the various stages (Butler 1980). Indeed development can be arrested at any stage in the cycle. Only tourist developments promising considerable financial returns will mature to experience all stages of the cycle. In turn, the length of each stage, and of the cycle itself is variable. At one extreme instant resorts such as Cancun (Mexico) or timeshare developments move almost immediately to growth. At the other extreme, well established resorts such as Scarborough (England) have taken 350 years to move from exploration to rejuvenation. Equally, there is a variety of types of cycle (Buttle 1986) – such as the scalloped pattern where a sequence of developments at the destination prompt a spurt of visitor arrivals.

UTILITY OF THE LIFE CYCLE AS A PRESCRIPTIVE TOOL

It is generally accepted that there are two basic, though interrelated, uses of the life cycle: as a guide for strategic decision making and as a forecasting tool.

The main determinant of strategy is expected market growth, while other factors include distribution of market shares, degree of competition, and profitability. Each of these vary at different stages of the cycle and a different marketing mix is appropriate (Hofer 1975, Kotler 1980, Levitt 1965, Onkvisit and Shaw 1986, Wind and Claycamp 1976). At the involvement stage, concern is with building up a strong market position and developing experience and maximizing returns on investment before competitors enter. In the development stage, emphasis changes to building market share through increased visitor numbers, pre-empting competitor's customers. As consolidation approaches, defense of share against competitors becomes important, as does maintaining margins and cash flow by cost control and avoiding price wars. However, once visitor numbers stabilize, a management should not await decline as inevitable but should seek to revitalize visits. Levitt (1965) argues that it is erroneous to assume that stage in the life cycle determines marketing strategy and the task instead is to utilize the stages of the life cycle to develop and evaluate marketing strategy. This can be done in two basic ways. First, life extension through a planned series of actions ensures that numbers of visitors and profitability are sustained for as long as possible. Second, incorporation of other inputs such as data on market share, the competitive environment, and profitability allows consolidation of market share and the search for new markets (Haywood 1986).

However, for some destinations the decision may be taken to partially withdraw from tourism and to capitalize on assets for other uses (health care, residential or business). For tourist destinations this decision is less straightforward than for product marketing, as other factors have to be taken into account. Destinations represent an investment in a community as well as the built fabric. Hence, the implications of the 'decline' stage are more severe than for a manufactured product. Seasonal unemployment, a depressed business community, and falling property prices are symptomatic of this stage. There is, therefore, a need for longer term planning at tourist destinations and a recognition of the lessons of the tourist area life cycle. In other words, visits may not increase continually with time, and if they do, this in itself has implications if the original attractions and competitiveness of the destinations are to be safeguarded. This may be achieved by constraining growth of resorts to within manageable capacity levels and developing in sympathy with the community (Murphy 1985).

Use of the life cycle approach as a forecasting tool depends upon the ability to isolate and predict the forces driving it (Onkvisit and Shaw 1986). Most forecasts assume a constraint on long-run growth, an S-shaped diffusion curve, homogeneity of customers, and give no explicit consideration of marketing decisions or the competition. Forecasts can be successful if these limiting assumptions are acceptable and long runs of visitor arrivals data are available to give stable parameter estimates (Brownlie 1985). Dewar (1983) and Nelson and Wall (1986) consider alternative data sources, such as hotel registers, in an attempt to provide data for the cycle.

Yet Butler's original conceptualization of the tourist cycle did not envisage its use as a prescriptive tool and many problems emerge when the cycle is used in this way. Accurate forecasting demands long runs of data on visitor numbers which are often lacking (Butler 1980) and the cycle, at best, can assist general trend projection rather than casual forecasts. Some argue that far from being an independent guide for strategy, the cycle is simply an outworking of management decisions and heavily dependent on external factors such as competition, development of new destinations, swings in consumer taste, government legislation, and regional policy (Dhalla and Yuspeh 1976). It may also be imprecise as a guide for strategy, because it ignores competitive settings.

A further problem here is the poor empirical validation for shape or length and danger of reacting to warning signs which may have been misinterpreted (Dhalla and Yuspeh 1976, Rink and Swan 1979). Clearly, the life cycle approach is destination specific, with each stage varying in length, shape, and pattern (Hovinen 1981). There are also difficulties involved in identifying stages and turning points (Brownlie 1985, Haywood 1986). Identification of turning points is important in the later stages of the cycle, given the increased cost of reacting as the need for change becomes more obvious. Turning points can be identified by use of leading indicators such as growth rate of visits, level of visits compared to market potential, percentage of first time visitors, numbers of competitors, levels of prices and profits, advertising, promotional and price elasticity, and emergence of new destinations meeting customer needs more effectively (Day 1981, Doyle 1976, Haywood 1986, Rink and Swan 1979). The variety of possible shapes of the curve and acceleration or delay due to external factors make it difficult to identify the stage reached by a destination. This can be done by plotting rate of change of visitor numbers, visitor expenditure, type of tourist, market share, or profitability.

Moreover, the level of aggregation is unclear (Brownlie 1985, Kotler 1980, Rink and Swan 1979). Geographical scale is important for the tourist area life cycle as each country is a mosaic of resorts and tourist areas (which in turn contain life cycles for hotels, theme parks, etc). Depending on the scale taken, each may be at a different stage in the cycle (compare, for example, resorts in eastern and southern Majorca). The unit of analysis is, therefore, crucial. At the same time, the life cycle assumes a homogeneous market, but the market can be divided into many segments and a perfectly logical stance would be for a destination to introduce segments sequentially. Equally, geographical segmentation would produce differing curves for domestic and international visitors (Brownlie 1985, Haywood 1986).

For the tourist area life cycle, decline is rooted in visitor numbers exceeding capacity levels at the destination. But carrying capacity is a notoriously difficult concept to operationalize, particularly as it is possible to 'manage' to a capacity. Also, no single capacity threshold exists for a destination. Physical, environmental, and psychological capacity may each be different. This does not take into account the spatial or temporal variations such as seasonality with the attraction of crowd-tolerant visitors in the peak season and others in the quieter off-peak (Hovinen 1981).

As a prescriptive tool, therefore, it is argued that the life cycle does not provide sufficient insight into the development of planning or policy for tourist areas. First, the cycle simply reflects policy decisions. Second, the cycle is destination specific with stages and turning points only evident with hindsight.

UTILITY OF LIFE CYCLE AS A DESCRIPTIVE TOOL

These criticisms of the life cycle approach are based on the difficulties of predicting the changing pattern of visitor numbers, product sales, and the like. However, if this pattern is taken not as an independent variable but as one dependent upon marketing and managerial action, then the life cycle can be used as an analytical framework to examine the evolution of tourist destinations within their complex economic, social, and cultural environments. On the supply-side, for example, stability of strategy during particular stages of the cycle may give way to changes in personalities, management style, and investment. Further, it may take the destination through a turning point and into the next stage of the cycle.

These developments, however, will occur hand in hand with demand for the destination in a dynamic way, with changing provision of facilities and access matched by an evolving clientele in both quantitative and qualitative terms. Different types of tourists seek different experiences. Plog (1973), for example, suggests that tourists can be characterized as allocentric (or adventurous, even seeking new destinations) or psychocentric (seeking familiar destinations and the security of the travel trade). Midcentrics have some of both of these characteristics and represent the bulk of the market. Plog envisages a destination appealing to allocentrics in the early stages of evolution, to midcentrics in the later stages of 'development' and 'consolidation', and to psychocentrics in 'stagnation' and 'decline'. Other typologies of tourists can also be used, such as Cohen's (1972) explorers in the early stages, to organized mass tourists in the latter stages. While this could be seen as simplistic and fails to take into account the mosaic of different types of tourists present at a destination, demonstration of successive waves of different numbers and types of tourists with distinctive preferences, motivations, and desires populating the resort at each stage of the life cycle is useful.

This suggests that the tourist area life cycle provides an enlightening descriptive tool for understanding how destinations and their markets evolve.

REFERENCES

Brownlie, D (1985) "Strategic Marketing Concepts and Models", *Journal of Marketing Management* 1, pp57–94

Butler, R W (1980) "The Concept of a Tourist Area Cycle of Evolution Implications for Management of Resources" *Canadian Geographer* 24, pp5–12

Buttle, F (1986) *Hotel and Food Service Marketing*, Holt, London

Christaller,W (1964) "Some Considerations of Tourism Location in Europe" *Papers of the Regional Science Association* 12, pp95–105

Clary, D (1984) "The Impact of Social Change on a Leisure Region 1960–1982. A Study of Nord Pays D'Auge" in *Leisure Tourism and Social Change*, J Long and R Hecock (eds) Centre for Leisure Research, Dunfermline, pp51–55

Cohen, E (1972) "Towards a Sociology of International Tourism" *Social Research* 39, pp164–182

Day, G S (1981) "The Product Life Cycle: Analysis and Applications Issues", *Journal of Marketing* 45, pp60–67

Dewar, K (1983) "Old Hotel Registers as a Tool in Analyzing Resort Visitation and Development" *Recreation Research Review* 10, pp5–10

Dhala, N K and S Yuspeh (1976) "Forget the Product Life Cycle Concept", *Harvard Business Review* 54, pp102–10

Doyle, P (1976) "The Realities of the Product Life Cycle", *Quarterly Review of Marketing* 1, pp1–6

Gilbert, E W (1939) "The Growth of Inland and Seaside Health Resorts in England" *Scottish Geographical Magazine* 55, pp16–35

Haywood, K M, (1986) "Can the Tourist Area Life Cycle be made Operational?", *Tourism Management* 7, pp154–167

Extract 4: *C Cooper and S Jackson*

Helleiner, F M (1983) "The Evolution and Decline of a Cottage Community in North Western Ontario", *Recreation Research Review* 10, pp34–43

Hofer, C W (1975) "Toward a Contingency Theory of Business Strategy", *Academy of Management Journal* 18, pp784–809

Hovinen, G R (1981) "A Tourist Cycle in Lancaster County, Pennsylvania", *Canadian Geographer* 25, pp283–286

Keller, C P (1987) "Stages of Peripheral Tourism Development – Canada's North West Territories", *Tourism Management* 8, pp20–32

Kotler, P, (1980) *Principles of Marketing* (3rd edition) Prentice Hall, New Jersey

Levitt, T (1965) "Exploit the Product Life Cycle", *Harvard Business Review* 43, pp81–94

Lundgren, J J (1982) "The Development of Tourist Accommodation in the Montreal Laurentians", in *Recreational Land Use: Perspectives on its Evolution in Canada*, G Wall and J Marsh (eds) Carleton University Press, Ottawa pp175–89

Medlik, S and V V Middleton (1973) "The Tourist Product and its Marketing Implications", *International Tourism Quarterly* pp28–35

Meyer-Arendt K J (1985) "The Grand Isle, Louisiana Resort Cycle", *Annals of Tourism Research* 12, pp449–65

Moffat, C A (1982) "The Development of Tourism in Nova Scotia", in *Recreational Land Use: Perspectives on its Evolution in Canada*, G Wall and J Marsh (eds) Carleton University, Ottawa, pp123–32

Murphy, P E (1985) *Tourism A Community Approach*, Methuen, London

Nelson, R and G Wall (1986) "Transport and Accommodation: Changing Interrelationships on Vancouver Island", *Annals of Tourism Research* 13, pp239–60

Oglethorpe, M (1984) "Tourism in Malta. A Crisis of Dependence", *Leisure Studies* 3, pp147–62

Onkvisit, S and J J Shaw (1986) "Competition and Product Management: Can the Product Life Cycle Help", *Business Horizons* 29, pp51–62

Plog, S C (1973) "Why Destination Areas Rise and Fall in Popularity", *Cornell Hotel and Restaurant Association Quarterly* 13, pp13–16

Reed, R (1987) "Fashion Life Cycles and Extension Theory", *European Journal of Marketing* 2, pp52–62

Rink, D R and J E Swan (1979) "Product Life Cycle Research: Literature Review", *Journal of Business Research* 78, pp219–42

Stansfield, C A (1978) "Atlantic City and the Resort Cycle Background to the Legislation of Gambling" *Annals of Tourism Research* 5, pp238–51

Snow, R E and D E Wright (1976) "Coney Island. A Case Study in Popular Culture and Technical Change", *Journal of Popular Culture* 9, pp960–75

van de Weg, H (1982) "Revitalization of Traditional Resorts" *Tourism Management* 3, pp303–07

Wilkinson, P F (1987) "Tourism in Small Island Nations: A Fragile Dependence", *Leisure Studies* 6, pp127–46

Wind, Y and H J Claycamp, (1976) "Planning Product Line Strategy: A Matrix Approach", *Journal of Marketing* 40, pp2–9

Wolfe, R I (1952) "Wasaga Beach: The Divorce from the Geographic Environment", *Canadian Geographer* 2, pp57–65

Tourism's Troubled Times
Responsible Tourism is Not the Answer

Brian Wheeller

The author argues that the fundamental problem of tourism, as a global phenomenon, is the sheer volume involved. Unless attempts to solve the ravages of tourism address this central issue of volume, then claims that there are answers to the problems of tourism are not only wrong but can be invidiously and dangerously misleading.

Rather belatedly, some sections of the media have increasingly drawn attention to the negative effects that have invariably accompanied tourism development. Recent newspaper articles and television documentaries have served as a graphic warning of the real destructive power of that potential pollutant – tourism.

At many UK tourist resorts some of the problems highlighted are all too apparent – congestion, noise, litter, environmental deterioration, etc. are depressingly familiar and examples legion.

In the wider global arena the situation is more acute. The magnitude and intensity of effects are exacerbated by the current tourist invasion in many developing countries. Environmental destruction is prevalent, cultural differences are most marked and social tensions heightened by the rapid uncontrolled flood of tourists from the alien industrialized nations into the developing world.

While notable contributions towards addressing and resolving the negative impact of tourism have been attempted, overall there has so far been little actual deployment of effective policies (Murphy 1985, Krippendorf 1987, Gunn 1988). In reality, adequate comprehensive management policies to cope with the accompanying problems of tourism development are scarce. To suggest, however, that these contributions have failed would clearly be unfair – they have at least raised the level of awareness and debate. Indeed, many would argue vehemently that firm foundations for long-term solutions have been laid. I would disagree. These 'solutions' remain essentially theoretical, are not practical answers for the future and indeed are likely to fuel the very problem they are seeking to solve.

Whether there is an overall plus or negative balance from tourism is open to conjecture, the questions involved complex. What seems indisputable, however, is that the costs and benefits do not accrue evenly. Some benefit more than others – frequently some benefit while others pay the costs.

Although many concerned parties now acknowledge some of the negative aspects of tourism, there remains the general misapprehension that these costs are only or primarily associated with mass tourism. It is not really the individual

* Brian Wheeller is at the Centre for Urban and Regional Studies, University of Birmingham, Edgbaston, Birmingham B15 2TT, UK.

tourist or small groups of tourists that are identified for criticism, nor is it travel – travel and the traveller are beyond reproach. It is in fact popular mass tourism that is seen as the villain of the peace. The volume, the huge numbers involved, are critical. We look for an answer, an alternative – ideally to plan not only to minimize the cost of tourism and maximize the benefits but simultaneously to ensure an equitable and just distribution of these costs and benefits.

RESPONSIBLE TOURISM

One way of achieving this, it is argued, is through the adoption of what has become euphemistically known as 'responsible tourism'. Although there are some variations, responsible tourism can broadly be interpreted as an umbrella term embracing this supposedly more caring, aware form of tourism. Prefixes include alternative, appropriate, sustainable, soft, green etc. In essence, the traveller is preferred to the tourist, the individual to the group, the independent specialist operators are more acceptable than large firms, indigenous homely accommodation is preferred to multinational hotel chains, etc – basically 'small' versus 'mass'. The pace of development is also vital – it must be controlled, relatively slow and capable of being absorbed into the host environment without any negative repercussions. The prevailing power base should be altered and decision-making on tourism and tourism development be in the hands of the host communities. Raising the awareness of the traveller prior to departure is also considered a vital element – education is seen by some as the key.

Responsible tourism has grown as a reaction to mass tourism, is being caught up in the groundswell of green issues and championed as a suitable way forward. I would strongly question this latter assertion – it cannot, by its very nature, be the way forward everywhere and it is, in fact, dangerously misleading. We have, on the one hand, a problem of mass tourism growing globally, out of control, at an alarming rate. And what is our answer? Small-scale, slow, steady controlled development. They just do not add up. It is true that both domestically and internationally there are many examples of small-scale 'alternative' successes. I am not suggesting that this is not a good thing, merely that they should not be cited, deliberately or inadvertently, as evidence that tourism as a whole can in a physical sense be sensitively controlled.

Although the idea of small-scale development is laudable, it does not tackle the large-scale problem of volume. If all tourist destinations could carefully calculate their appropriate tourism thresholds and then miraculously impose restrictions to keep tourist numbers below these limits and if all the tourists were indeed 'sensitive travellers' – even then the tourist problem as a whole would not be solved, as the effective demand for tourist destination at a macro level would far outstrip the supply. At best it is a micro solution to what is essentially a macro problem.

The notion of educating the tourist/traveller in destination awareness is surely idealistic. Just how is the Utopian sensitive traveller to be created? How is the exercise to be coordinated? Who pays for it? What time span is envisaged for the effect of the educative process to reach fruition, and what precisely is meant by educating? (What influence can education have in the light of such contradictory messages from, for example, *The Sun*'s 'How to be a beast in Benidorm or a terror in Torremolinos'? (*The Sun* 1988). Is the press to be controlled to eradicate such views?).

To implement effectively such a mammoth educative task in all tourist generating countries presents enormous and, I would suggest, insurmountable practical difficulties. Given the speed with which tourist impact is spreading, the reality of the situation is that if such an education programme could somehow be achieved, the time span required for its inception would inevitably witness continued irrevocable tourism damage. If we look at tourism/travel education in perspective then, however hard it is to accept, it seems the problem is now but education is for the future. There is also, of course, the salutary thought that by raising awareness (by 'better' education) we also raise demand – one of the main factors in the growth of tourist demand has undoubtedly stemmed from education itself.

In their rush to escape the mass tourist, the so-called aware, educated, 'I'm going ethnic' individual traveller is forever seeking the new, the exotic, the unspoilt – the vulnerable. Inevitably, however, they are inexorably paving the way for the package tour. The sensitive traveller is the perpetrator of the global spread, the vanguard of the package tour – where he or she goes others will, in ever increasing numbers, eventually follow. Who, in the long term, is responsible for the most damage – the mass tourist to the Mediterranean, or the sensitive traveller to the Amazon, the Himalayas or the Sahara?

It is perhaps also worth noting here the ambiguity of the term 'appropriate'. Arguments for appropriate tourism are being heard everywhere – but the vexed question of appropriate to whom or to what is left unanswered. I would suggest that for a number of interested parties, be they tour operators, international hotel chains, local indigenous beneficiaries and indeed many of the tourists themselves, we already have appropriate tourism. Vague, glib assertions as appropriate 'to the environment', 'to the host community' are not good enough. What, after all is precisely meant by the host community – the majority, those in power (democratically elected?), or the local politicians? Is, for example, the decision-making and development of the UK tourist industry in the hands of the 'host community'?

The old adage put forward by the tourist industry is that it must, by careful, sensitive and sensible management, preserve and enhance the product it is selling in order to maintain its market appeal. Tourism, it is argued, must therefore make a positive contribution to the host region. While perhaps valid in some micro-situation, this patently has not been happening on a global scale. In the context of a rapidly spreading international pleasure periphery, the philosophy of 'bugger it up and pass it down' seems to be a far more accurate description of what is actually taking place – witness the North European successive tourist invasion of Spain, Greece and Turkey and the subsequent meteoric growth of long-haul holidays. As O'Grady (1981) points out, the tourist industry inadvertently acknowledges its own destructive power when it advertises new 'unspoiled' destinations away from and, as yet unfettered by, tourist pollution.

MICRO- VERSUS MACRO-TOURISM

I understand the desire for small scale, for slow steady development, for a caring tourism. However, there are a number of fundamental economic dilemmas in converting this ideal into reality – in resolving the conundrum of size, appropriateness and economic viability of tourist activity. If, from the perspective of the host community, tourism is to create, or generate, substantial income and a significant number of jobs (full-time, all year-round?) in relation to the economic scale of the area, then surely that development has to be of a significant size?

On the micro-level of the individual firm or project, clearly there can be small-scale yet viable development. By keeping costs down, charging high prices for a specialist product etc, small firms can compensate for, and overcome, their lack of economies of scale. (We will sidestep here charges of elitism which, if proven, seem uncomfortably at odds with many of the overt liberal, caring attitudes of the green movement.) Even with high-spending customers, the fact remains that a small-scale development catering for small numbers will only have a correspondingly small effect on income and employment. The argument that together a number of small projects operating in unison could make a significant economic impact might be acceptable but then, of course, the aggregate number of tourists would also increase to significant (intolerable?) levels. This is the situation that the new forms of tourism are trying to avoid.

Sustainable tourism has burdened itself with conflicting incompatible objectives – small-scale sensitivity and limited numbers to be achieved in tandem with economic viability and significant income and employment impacts. What happens when the prerequisite size of tourism activity to ensure economic viability is too large to meet the other appropriate yardsticks of sustainability? Is tourism development run uneconomically, subsidized, abandoned or, as seems likely, are the 'appropriate' standards relaxed?

There is the school of thought that suggests sustainable does not necessarily mean small. Certainly from an economic vantage, there is credence to this. But surely there are extreme difficulties in marrying large-scale tourism developments with the concomitant beliefs of sustainable, alternative tourism. Large-scale, spatially concentrated tourism may, as it is argued, act as a 'safety-valve' syphoning off potential demand for scarce resources elsewhere and it may keep mass tourism firmly in its place – these are debatable. But surely it will not prevent the 'educated traveller' continually pursuing, and temporarily satisfying, the desire for pastures new.

There is another disturbing aspect to the question of compatible economic viability. If appropriate tourism development is seen as the answer, or partial answer, to regional regeneration then the weaker the region's economic base, the weaker its bargaining power in terms of ability responsibly to select the correct, appropriate, type of tourist development. The process can be identified clearly in developing countries under pressure to develop tourism. The weaker the economy and the greater the need for foreign exchange, then generally the weaker is that country's position in terms of imposing strict controls on the scale and form of tourism development.

Similarly, notions of community-based approaches to tourism decision making seem fine for those communities (however defined) where there is a cohesive, established network based usually on existing economic viability. These communities can perhaps be actively involved in decision making and, operating from a position of relative strength, resist unwanted, inappropriate forms of tourism. They can afford to be selective. But at a macro-level this will not stop 'unsuitable' development from taking place. It will merely transfer it spatially to another area, another community, less able – by dint of economic circumstance – to have a constructive say in its own destiny. From the initial well-intentioned starting point of wishing to maintain and respect a community's integrity, the most likely result of the 'community approach' appears to be that the strongest remain strong and intact, while putting the weaker, more vulnerable communities under increased, deflected pressure. The problem is again passed on to those less able to cope with it.

Responsible tourism is optimistically being seen as a means of sensible planning for tourism. Unfortunately responsible tourism seems to be being adopted more as a marketing tool than as a sensitive planning mechanism. There is nothing new in the confusion between the respective roles of tourism planning and tourism marketing. Many previous tourism planning policies have in fact been growth policies. Let me turn briefly to the UK both to illustrate this and to introduce another related relevant point, ie the confusion between micro- and macro-tourism planning.

Tourist boards and other official organizations point to numerous individual cases of tourist development where sensible planning and management have mitigated negative effects. By careful design, use of local materials, renovation of derelict redundant buildings, adoption of tourist flow regulatory schemes, etc they argue that tourism has actively and positively enhanced the environment and the quality of life at the tourist destination. It is a valid argument – but only up to a point. Examples of positive management of the tourist influx are the exception, not the rule. Despite suggestions to the contrary, such techniques cannot automatically be transferred from one situation and readily adopted at another. They are not universally applicable. It just does not follow that success at the localized level guarantees similar success on the wider, more complicated plane. Moving from the specific to the general is problematic, although recent rhetoric would suggest otherwise.

The process, oiled and manipulated by media interests and the tourism lobby, has become familiar. Individual examples of successful, responsible tourism are acknowledged and cited. An imperceptible shift of perspective is adopted and the transition from the specific to the general rapidly effected. The panacea to tourism problems, has, therefore, been found ('it's true, we now have successful role models') – and the 'green' light for responsible tourism development shines like a beacon while the actual realities of the situation are conveniently masked over – four easy steps in self justification.

There must be a clear distinction between planning for an individual tourism project and planning for tourism *per se*. Unfortunately this does not always appear to be the case with the all-encompassing 'planning for tourism' being misleadingly applied to these two distinct scenarios. Inconsistencies in logic and argument arise partly as a result of this confusion. Tourism on a micro-level can perhaps be sensitively planned for but at the macro-level, because of the enormity and complexity of the task, it becomes cumbersome, uncontrollable and 'unplanable'.

This might be considered to be stating the obvious. Yet it is implied by official bodies that tourism can be effectively managed and controlled. Therefore by citing examples of management techniques at the micro-level, the erroneous impression is (deliberately?) given that tourism as a mass phenomenon can similarly be successfully harnessed. It can certainly be influenced but not controlled.

GREEN POLICIES ENCOURAGE DEMAND

In this respect, the tourist boards have for years been advocating the spreading of the tourist load in both a seasonal and a spatial sense. This is seen as the panacea to the disbenefits of peak season, honey-pot tourism – avoid the jam, spread the honey. Cynically, one could view the supposed environmental and social benefits from such policies as either smoke-screens or convenient beneficial spin-offs. The unstated, underlying rationale undoubtedly remains economic. The encouragement and development of second holidays and long weekends taken in the spring and winter months are looked upon as a trend that is spreading the tourist season. These trends, however, may merely be lengthening the season – not spreading it. Tourists are encouraged to come out of season as well as, not instead of, peak times and the demands on the recipient area become all year round rather than seasonal.

Lengthening the season fails to solve many of the disbenefits associated with tourism. True, cash flow may be improved and economic returns may be greater but so too are the costs involved which are incurred by the host areas for a longer period of time. Spreading the tourist season is not a coherent, comprehensive management plan. It is a marketing strategy geared to increase cash flow by generating more tourist and more money income.

Similarly, the policy of spreading tourist demand spatially from congested to underdeveloped areas, supposedly more capable of accepting it, must be viewed with extreme caution and a healthy degree of scepticism. Both of these prerequisites are unfortunately absent from the current wave of overenthusiasm sweeping most 'green' tourism literature (Lane 1990, 44). At best it can only be regarded as an interim stop-gap policy. What happens when these areas in turn reach their own saturation thresholds? Are more new areas to be 'discovered' and promoted until eventually everywhere reaches saturation? By advertising a package of alternative attractions (usually in the same vicinity) rather than one honey-pot centre, the likely result will be an increase in overall volume of tourism – again a growth policy.

Spatially spreading tourism is a short-term means of dealing with the fundamental problem of continually encouraging tourism growth and, of course, the policy itself surreptitiously contributes to the problem. In line with responsible tourism, the policies of seasonally and spatially spreading the tourism load are deceptive and misleading. They are in fact growth policies masquerading under the guise of sensitive planning – the ultimate 'double take'. For years, the tourism industry and the affiliated pro-tourism lobby have welcomed these 'planning' policies, knowing, I believe, full well the true implications of seasonal and spatial spread – namely their marketing potential. Similarly, the irony is that responsible tourism's very ineffectiveness is likely to see its overt acceptance as global tourism strategy by an industry eager to foster a better image and keen to be seen to be green. By clothing itself in a green mantle, the industry is being provided with a shield with which it can both deflect valid criticism and improve its own image while, in reality, continuing its familiar short-term commercial march. Perhaps even more than other industries, the tourism industry can now see profit in ostensibly becoming 'green' – the perfect platitude to those of us anxious to formulate policies to rectify tourism's negative impact.

Responsible tourism is a so-called solution that keeps almost everyone happy. It appeases the guilt of the 'thinking tourist' while simultaneously providing the holiday experience they or we want. The industry is happy because the more discerning (and expensive) range of market can be catered for by 'legitimately' opening up new areas to tourism, and the overall demand for and growth of tourism, on a global basis, continues unabated. Responsible tourism is a pleasant, agreeable, but dangerously superficial, ephemeral and inadequate escape route for the educated middle classes unable, or unwilling, to appreciate or accept their/our own destructive contribution to the international tourism maelstrom.

Irresponsible tourism might be more apt terminology. The current, in-vogue 'solutions' to tourism are, I suggest, actually further fuelling the rapid spread of tourism without offering any real, lasting answers. Perhaps all the energies that have been channelled into refining this new 'good tourism' might have been better spent actually addressing the real problem of mass tourism – the massive volume and, globally, the growing absolute number of tourists. It seems to me that none of the recent suggestions are actually coming to terms with, or indeed confronting, this fact.

I am not suggesting an answer, indeed I do not think there is, as yet, an answer to tourism's global impact problems. Accepting this depressing possibility is difficult. Coming to terms with our own hypocrisy might be a start. Meanwhile, I am simply saying that we certainly have not found the answer in responsible tourism. We should not fool ourselves nor others.

REFERENCES

Gunn, C (1988) *Tourism Planning*, Taylor and Francis, London

Krippendorf, J (1987) *The Holidaymakers*, Heinemann, London

Lane, B (1990) "Spreading the tourism load", *Sunday Observer,* 4 February, p44

Murphy, P (1985) *Tourism. A Community*, Routledge, London

O'Grady, R (1981) *Third World Stop-over*, World Council of Churches, Geneva, Switzerland

The Sun (1988) "How to be a beast in Benidorm", 16 May

Ecotourism in the Third World – Problems and Prospects for Sustainability

Erlet Cater

THE INCREASING EMPHASIS ON ECOTOURISM IN THE THIRD WORLD

The development of ecotourism in the Third World appeals to destination areas, tourism enterprises and tourists alike. Its increasing popularity is highlighted by the proliferation of specialist tour operators offering experiences that range from trekking in the Himalayas to gorilla watching in Central Africa. Several destinations have hosted international ecotourism conferences, attracting a large number of delegates from a wide geographical range. The Caribbean has already fielded its fourth annual conference, with its venue in Bonaire, NA. This level of interest is the result of a number of reasons.

Comparative advantage

The less developed world has an undeniable comparative advantage in terms of the variety and extent of unspoiled natural environments. These range from tropical rainforests to savanna grasslands and secluded beaches fringed by coral reefs. Outstanding scenic attractions include spectacular waterfalls and the world's highest mountains. In addition, such countries offer the prospect of viewing unique flora and fauna in their original habitat. Ecotourism offers tourism companies and destination areas the opportunity of capitalising on this comparative advantage. Amongst the last havens of unspoiled nature, these destinations also hold considerable appeal for the ecotourist.

It is difficult to place a financial value on these natural attractions. Attempts to do so have ranged from estimates of the amount that visitors are willing to pay to visit a tropical rainforest in Costa Rica (Tobias and Mendelsohn, 1991) to attributing a financial value to wildlife in East Africa. In the latter case, about 650,000 people visit the National Parks and Protected Areas of Kenya each year, spending about US$350 million. In terms of tourist expenditures, Olindo (1991) estimates that on this basis an elephant is worth about US$14 375 a year, or US$900 000 over the course of its life. The significance of ecotourism in terms of tourism revenue to certain individual Third World nations is obvious when prime ecotourism destinations are examined. Table 3.3 shows how the increasing popularity of ecotourism is evidenced by the growth in receipts (over tenfold in the case of Belize) over the last decade. These receipts are of increasing significance to export earnings and gross domestic product (Table 3.4).

Table 3.2 Growth in tourism to selected destinations

	Tourist arrivals (thousands)		Tourism receipts (US$ millions)	
	1981	1990	1981	1900
Belize	93	222	8	91
Costa Rica	333	435	94	275
Ecuador	245	332	131	193
Dominica	16	45	2	25
Kenya	373	801	175	443
Botswana	227	844	22	65
Madagascar	12	53	5	43
Maldives	60	195	15	85

Source: World Tourism Organisation (1986; 1992)

Table 3.3 Significance of tourism receipts to selected ecotourism destinations

	Tourism receipts as a percentage of export earnings		Tourism receipts as a percentage of Gross Domestic Product	
	1981	1990	1981	1990
Belize	7.8	42.3	4.5	24.8
Costa Rica	9.7	18.9	3.6	4.8
Ecuador	5.1	7.1	1.0	1.8
Dominica	11.6	na	3.4	na
Kenya	15.3	42.9	2.5	5.9
Madagascar	1.5	12.8	0.2	1.6

Sources: World Tourism Organisation (1986; 1992), World Bank (1983; 1992), and IMF (1992).

Most Third World countries are characterized by severe balance of payments difficulties. The development of ecotourism, therefore, provides an opportunity to capitalize on bountiful natural attractions. For the ecotourist, such destinations provide a unique experience of natural environments which contrast with those of their home latitudes. The prestige element of being at the vanguard of tourist visitation is also undeniable as previously isolated areas are opened up. Just recently the Indian Government has announced a partial lifting of the restrictions on the north-eastern state of Arunchal Pradesh (*Geographical* 1993) and other 'prestige' ecotourism destinations listed recently include Patagonia and Madagascar (*Independent* 1993). Tourism operators have not been slow to recognize the potential of the fastest growing segment of the tourism industry, in its entirety now the single most important item in international trade (WTTC 1992). Not only has there been an increase in small, specialist tour operators in recent years, but the larger operators have not been slow to appeal to the ever increasing number of ecotourists. Thomas Cook's Faraway Collection, for example, suggests a visit to the primeval rainforest of Bako National Park, Sarawak.

Local involvement

Viewed as a form of alternative tourism, the emphasis in ecotourism development should be on small-scale, locally owned activities (Weaver 1991). This has three important repercussions for beleaguered Third World economies. Firstly, the facilities in terms of infrastructure and superstructure are simpler and less expensive than those demanded by conventional mass tourism, and are consequently less of a drain on the limited financial investment available. As such, ecotourism development may well prove a viable alternative in cases where funds for large-scale tourism development are not available (Sherman and Dixon 1991). Secondly, locally owned and operated businesses are not enmeshed in the need to conform to the corporate Western identity of the multinational tourism concerns, and, therefore, can have a much higher input of local products, materials and labour. This not only has greater multiplier effects throughout the local economy, but also reduces import leakages and the remittances from expatriate labour which result from large-scale, foreign-owned, operations. Thirdly, the profits made should accrue locally instead of flowing back to the parent country. In the capital-scarce situation of most Third World countries, this is a particularly attractive prospect.

Environmental sensitivity

People have become increasingly aware of the adverse socio-cultural and environmental impacts of uncontrolled mass tourism. The very incorporation of 'eco' in its title suggests that ecotourism should be an ecologically responsible form of tourism. Indeed, if it does not comply with this requirement, then the natural attractions upon which it is based will suffer degradation to the point at which tourists will cease to arrive. The scale of such ecotourism activities implies that comparatively low numbers of tourists will arrive and that supporting facilities can be kept to a minimum and will be less intrusive.

It is vital to remember that any human activity dependent on the consumptive use of ecological resources, such as ecotourism, cannot be sustained indefinitely unless an important principle underpins its organization. The resources may be regarded as the capital stock. If this is cut into, as opposed to only utilising the annual production of the biosphere (the 'interest'), then sustainability will be compromised (Rees 1990). Ecotourism, with its connotations of sound environmental management and consequent maintenance of environmental capital, should, in theory, provide a viable economic alternative to exploitation of the environment.

It is not surprising, because of these factors, that Third World destinations have turned increasingly towards ecotourism as an apparent way out of their classic impasse: the need to earn foreign exchange without, at the same time, destroying their environmental resource base and thus compromising sustainability. It is, however, necessary to determine if ecotourism development in the Third World is a truly sustainable option. This requires focusing on the different interests involved at various spatial and temporal levels.

A SUSTAINABLE ALTERNATIVE FOR THE HOST POPULATION?

Ideally, the smaller scale, dispersed nature of ecotourism development, with less sophisticated demands, should enable a much higher degree of local participation than conventional mass tourism, with the involvement of local and family-based enterprises, both directly and indirectly. This, however, may be prejudiced by several factors.

The international organisation of ecotourism

Although the emphasis may be on a smaller scale, ecotourists originate from the more developed countries (MDCs) and consequently their tour, travel and accommodation needs are largely coordinated by firms based in those countries. Whilst ecotourists may be affluent [a study by Wilson, cited by Whelan (1991) of US travellers to Ecuador found that a quarter of the group earned over US$90 000 a year in family income], much of their expenditure is not made at the destination end. Consequently, ecotourism must share many of the same characteristics as conventional tourism in terms of leakages. Britton (1982) estimates that the proportion of a total inclusive tour price that is retained locally drops to only 22–25 per cent if both the airline and hotel used are foreign-owned. Furthermore, it has been pointed out that the true wilderness tourist is a poor economic bet, because in the wilderness there is nothing to spend money on! (Butler 1991).

Foreign investment in ecotourism

This is not a surprising feature of tourism development of whatever type in the capital-scarce situation of Third World economies. As the fastest growing sector in the tourism industry, ecotourism is an attractive investment proposition and is becoming big business. Estimates of its relative significance in terms of global tourism expenditure vary considerably. The Economist Intelligence Unit (EIU) estimated the world-wide ecotourism market at US$10 billion in 1989 (EIU 1992), whereas a study by the Canadian Wildlife Service suggests that as much as US$200 billion in total was spent on ecotourism activities globally in 1990 (Ceballos Lascurain 1992).

Ecotourism is becoming the most significant tourism market segment for many Third World destinations. Overall, a World Wide Fund for Nature (WWF) study estimates that of $55 billion earned by tourism for developing countries in 1988, about $12 billion was the result of ecotourism (EIU 1992). The figures are even more striking for certain countries which are primarily ecotourism destinations (Table 3.3). In Costa Rica 40 per cent of visitors came to the country for nature-directed activities (Rovinski 1991). Ecuador, in particular the Galapagos islands, earned US$193 million in tourism receipts in 1990.

Investment in the development of ecotourism in the developing world appears to be a lucrative proposition. Foreign developers, based in the MDCs, have become increasingly involved in countries such as Belize. Of 350 delegates to the first Caribbean conference on ecotourism held in Belize in 1991, only 15–20 per cent could be said to have had no declared financial interest in the development of ecotourism (Figure 3.5). It is estimated that at least one half were either US-based or expatriates (Figure 3.6). Expatriate involvement in the Belizean tourism industry is such that 65 per cent of the members of the US Aid-initiated Belize Tourism Industry Association are expatriates (Munt 1993). The location of an English-speaking country, promoting itself as an ecotourism destination, on the doorstep of the USA is bound to prove a mecca for the American ecotourist. Over 40 per cent of tourists visiting come from the USA. Tourists to Belize from North America increased from 30 000 in 1984 to 90 000 in 1990. Inevitable pressures have been generated, to the extent that in May 1992 a scheme was exposed, amidst great controversy, to develop 3000 hectares on the prime tourism resort of Ambergris Caye by US-based developers. The proposed luxury resort included a hotel of international class, a golf course and a marina (Munt 1993).

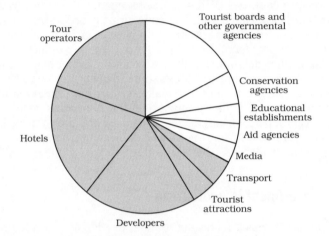

Figure 3.5 *Distribution of the 1991 Caribbean Ecotourism Conference delegates by affiliation*

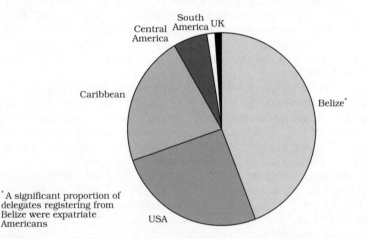

Figure 3.6 *Distribution of the 1991 Caribbean Ecotourism Conference delegates by origin*

Inflationary pressure on local economies

Largely as a result of foreign involvement, prices of land, property and sometimes even local produce are driven relentlessly upward, often beyond the reach of the local population. In Belize, the degree of foreign interest in buying land in a relatively unspoiled destination only two hours flying time from Miami, New Orleans and Houston is such that a two-bedroom villa in a coastal location on the prime resort island of Ambergris Caye commanded a price of US$135 000 in 1992. Foreign land-holdings in Belize are, in theory, restricted to 2000 m^2 in urban areas and 40 500 m^2 in rural areas. The cumulative effect, however, is such that it has been estimated that 90 per cent of all coastal development in Belize is now foreign-owned (Cater 1992). The fact that such land has been sold freehold indicates probable permanent alienation from Belizean nationals. It also implies an opportunity cost in terms of benefits that might have otherwise accrued under alternative use of that land (Sherman and Dixon 1991).

Loss of sovereignty also implies a loss of control in decision-making. Wilkinson (1989) describes how microstates have become targets for exogenous decision-making, which is often insensitive to local issues and needs.

Local participation

The degree of truly local participation is often limited not only in terms of ownership and control, but also in terms of enjoyment of the natural attraction. The cost of even a locally based day trip, for example US$100 for a day trip to Crooked Tree Sanctuary in Belize, precludes the participation of the average low income resident.

SUSTAINING VISITOR ATTRACTION

The financial significance of ecotourism to many Third World economies is evident in Table 3.4. For this contribution towards the national income to be sustained, it is vital to maintain visitor satisfaction. There are a number of factors which militate against this requirement, given the number of tourists arriving, their distribution at the destination, and their characteristics.

Rapid growth in ecotourist arrivals

An examination of the rate of growth in tourist arrivals to selected ecotourism destinations (Table 3.3) reveals how all have approximately doubled the number of visitor arrivals over the past decade. A gradualist approach towards tourism planning, to allow for adjustment, has been advocated for some time (de Kadt 1979). In contrast, the problems of managing a rapid rate of growth are considerable. More significant and lasting changes are inevitable.

Concentration at prime sites

Much attention has been drawn to the development of tourism enclaves within destinations (Jenkins 1982). Indeed, the positive aspect of this phenomenon is that the adverse effects of tourism development are usually confined to clearly defined areas. In terms of prime ecotourism sites, however, concentrated visitation may well result in an unacceptable level of degradation. At the Hol Chan Marine Reserve in Belize, snorkellers and divers are amply warned of the consequences of irresponsible behaviour, such as the careless handling of scuba equipment. The pressure of numbers is such, though, that the coral reef is showing signs of black band disease, a killer alga which attacks broken coral. Furthermore, visitors tend to be concentrated in time as well as space owing to the marked seasonality of tourism to largely tropical destinations. Vegetation cover destroyed in the dry season, the peak period, leaves fragile soils exposed to the erosive powers of tropical downpours in the wet season. The Amboseli National Park in Kenya has suffered from the excessive pressures of the 220 000 visitors it receives annually to the extent that it was withdrawn from the itineraries of some tour operators in 1992. Widespread flooding in Feburary 1993, which left 80 per cent of the game-viewing tracks under water, resulted in the temporary closure of the park.

Characteristics of ecotourists

There is an inherent risk in assuming that the ecotourist is automatically an environmentally sensitive breed. Although small, specialist, guided groups of ecotourists may attempt to conform to this identity, the net has now been cast sufficiently wide to include less responsible behaviour. Amongst those loosely defined as ecotourists will be those visiting a destination for a few days, unlikely ever to return. This can be referred to as 'this year the Galapagos, next year Antarctica' syndrome. It has been suggested that such tourists are unlikely to pay regard to the long-term repercussions of their activities, particularly as they may consider that they have a right to use the resource in light of the significant outlay they will have made for the experience (Butler 1991).

ECOTOURISM AND THE ENVIRONMENT: A SYMBIOTIC OR DESTRUCTIVE RELATIONSHIP?

Budowski (1976) suggested that the relationship between nature tourism and conservation may be mutually beneficial. However, unless the requirement of safeguarding the environment is met, ecotourism is in danger of being a self-destructive process, destroying the very resources upon which it is based. Furthermore, the present and future needs of the host population will be prejudiced and future generations of tourists will be denied the opportunity to experience environments very different to those in which they reside. As the interface between ecotourism and the environment is even closer than that of conventional tourism with its surroundings, it is probably not surprising to discover that a symbiotic relationship remains something of an ideal rather than a reality. This occurs for several reasons.

The widening locus of international tourism

The emphasis in ecotourism is on visiting unspoiled natural environments. Previously remote areas, with delicately balanced socio-cultural and physical regimes, are consequently increasingly drawn into the locus of international tourism. These vulnerable locations are thus particularly susceptible to environmental degradation and socio-cultural disruption.

The inevitability of environmental impact

It is impossible that ecotourism, based on natural attractions, will not result in some environmental impact. Even the most environmentally conscientious tourist will have some degree of impact, however small. In aggregate, such impacts become all the more significant, particularly when such activities are inevitably concentrated in time and space (Butler 1991).

The designation of protected areas

The creation of National Parks and Wildlife Reserves may well satisfy the viewing needs of tourists and, if properly managed, the requirements of conservationists. Frequently, however, the local population is excluded from traditional activities such as nomadic pastoralism, cultivation and gathering of fuel and building materials. As such, they cannot be regarded as truly sustainable constructs because they pay little regard to the needs of the host population in either the short or long term. 'It is not the rural poor who will gain most from the design of national parks, but the rich consumer in the industrialized North with leisure and wealth to be a tourist in the Third World' (Cartwright 1989).

The supreme irony is that, by ignoring the needs of the local population, the conservational objectives of protected areas may themselves be compromised. Widespread resentment exists amongst the Maasai nomadic pastoralists over their inadequately compensated displacement from traditional grazing lands through the creation of National Parks in Kenya. Wildlife in the Amboseli National Park has been killed by Maasai warriors to emphasize their dissatisfaction (Lindsay 1987). Experience elsewhere shows that once the local population has become fully integrated in tourism projects, and benefits directly from them, infringements such as indiscriminate tree-felling (Sagarmatha National Park, Nepal) and poaching of wildlife (Zimbabwe) reduce markedly.

Infrastructural and service requirements of ecotourism

Ecotourists originate largely from the MDCs. Destinations are therefore forced to cater for Western tastes and needs. In the Nepalese Himalaya, trekking lodges offer almost impossibly extensive menus, which place excessive pressures on scarce wood fuel and the cook's time as demands are juggled for dishes as diverse as pizzas and rosti. Extra porters ply the trails laden with crates of beer, trays of eggs and toilet rolls. In Belize, coastal development involves the clearance of mangrove swampland and subsequent drainage and infilling using topsoil literally shaved off the wetland savanna a few kilometres inland. This involves the destruction of two distinctive ecosystems. Ironically, the international standard Biltmore Plaza hotel, the venue of the 1991 Caribbean Ecotourism Conference, was built on land reclaimed in this way.

The cost of environmental management

The low level of development of Third World nations may preclude them from being able to afford environmental protection measures that prevent, ameliorate or restore degradation. It is also patently unfair that these countries should bear the costs of such measures, the need for which arises from the fact that ecotourism to Third World countries is essentially exploiting their environmental carrying capacity. Any efforts made by these destinations, such as the Annapurna Conservation Area Project in Nepal (Chapter 11), should receive the unqualified support of the tourism industry.

POLICY IMPLICATIONS

The foregoing discussion indicates that there are inherent dangers in regarding ecotourism in the Third World as some sort of miracle hybrid, bringing bountiful returns without any adverse impacts. It is essential to recognize some basic truths. There is no example of tourist use that is completely without impact. If protection and preservation of the environment in an untouched form is the primary goal, then there should be no tourism development at all (Butler 1991). Even a small-scale development such as that at Canaima, in southern Venezuela, owned and operated by the state domestic airline Avensa, has had a very evident impact in terms of the construction of a purpose-built airstrip and village to house employees working at the hotel complex. Indeed, unless properly managed, ecotourism may result in worse impacts than those of mass tourism to clearly defined and confined resorts. It is often undeveloped areas, all the more vulnerable to disruption and degradation, that are being drawn into the international tourism circuit. The multitude of interests scattered at the local scale may penetrate the socio-cultural and environmental fabric more deeply than conventional tourism and will probably be more difficult to control.

This should not, however, be taken against ecotourism development in the Third World. It must be remembered that sustainable development includes the human dimension; the basic needs of the local population must be satisfied. Absolute restriction may be a necessity in some instances, for example the heavily protected core area of Biosphere Reserves (Batisse 1982). Equally, whilst visitation levels must never exceed the carrying capacity of a locality, restriction is not a truly sustainable option if it results in local populations being denied the development potential that exists. In most cases the solution will be a compromise: neither strictly conservationist, nor completely meeting development needs.

For the reasons outlined in the introduction to this book, ecotourism is here to stay, it is set to grow and will undoubtedly be of increasing significance to developing nations. What is important, therefore, is to point to the particular responsibilities of the three main role players in international tourism: the tourists, the tourism enterprises and the destination areas in achieving sustainable outcomes.

Role of the tourists

Doubt has already been cast on the sustainability of the behaviour and attitudes of individual tourists (Butler 1991), intentional or otherwise. Unless these change, the cumulative effects of successive waves of ecotourists visiting a destination may progressively downgrade the distinctive characteristics which constitute its fundamental attraction and so comprommise sustainability. Sustainable ecotourism offers tourists the prospect of a guaranteed level of satisfaction whenever a destination is visited. This is a vital consideration if it is to continue to attract tourists.

Tourists should become aware of the damaging potential of their stay in Third World destinations. This will require, in many instances, considerable changes in attitudes and behaviour so that indigenous cultures and environments are respected. Often tourists visiting less developed regions must be prepared to forego accustomed standards of comfort and convenience. Properly handled, this should, in fact, prove part of the attraction of the ecotourism experience (Ruschmann 1992).

The tourists need to be properly informed about the characteristics of their destination and how to behave to reduce the impact of their stay. This is primarily the responsibility of the tourism industry. Certain tour operators, for example World Expeditions, do advise their clients along these lines. Non-governmental organizations, eg Tourism Concern in the UK and Equations in India, have made a significant contribution towards raising the level of public awareness. Destinations can reinforce this awareness by advising on ecotourism etiquette once the tourists arrive, for example via the minimum impact code printed on lodge menus in the Annapurna Conservation Area of Nepal (Chapter 11).

Thus the cornerstone to more sustainable behaviour on the part of ecotourists is a greater understanding, via the dissemination of information, on how to behave in the context they are visiting.

Role of tourism enterprises

The onus of responsibility for more sustainable ecotourism development tends to fall on ecotourism enterprises which deliver the end-product to the consumer, ie the tourists. Although profit maximization remains the prime concern of such companies, it has been suggested that historical levels of profit are not compatible with sustainable development. Resource-based companies (which, indeed, includes all tourism enterprises) should be required to demonstrate adequate maintenance of the resource base before declaring a dividend (Rees 1990). There is an increasing recognition in the trade that maintenance of the resource base is at any rate the baseline of successful operations (Chapter 4). More complete tourism accountancy procedures (Goodall 1992) would involve the concept of environmental auditing to identify why, where and how tourism products, activities and processes are damaging the environment. It is one thing to identify these factors, another to take action. Whether or not this happens will depend on how the competitive situation of the firm is changed and the organization's stance on environmental protection (Gray 1990). In some instances firms may be required to comply with the requirement for more sustainable practices initiated by the host government.

Role of destination areas

To ensure sustainable ecotourism development the governments of Third World destinations need: (a) to intervene in the market; (b) to oversee integration in planning and implementation; and (c) to encourage local involvement.

Intervention

A proactive stance is thus necessary to maximize the benefits and minimize the adverse effects of ecotourism. Allowing the free play of market forces is not conducive to sustainable outcomes. Inevitably, the carrying capacity of destinations will be exceeded as environmental costs continue to be externalized. As a result, there is a need to force tourism companies to internalize these externalities by building in appropriate cost and price signals, via legislation, together with incentives and disincentives such as appropriate taxation measures (de Kadt 1992). A problem here, however, is that often such destinations are competing with one another and are wary of frightening-off badly needed foreign investment. Indeed, the opposite approach has been for destinations to offer firms attractive tax holidays and other incentives to encourage domestic and foreign investment. Sri Lanka, for example, extended an interest-free loan programme for resort properties and reduced business turnover tax from 20 to only one per cent during the 1980s.

Countries that have attempted extra fiscal measures have sometimes been forced to step down by the threat that companies will divert their interests elsewhere; for example, a proposal that a $50 per head cruise passenger tax should be levied in the Caribbean has met with such threats from US cruise lines. It would appear, therefore, that Cohen's appraisal of the bargaining power of the unspoiled nature of developing nations remains somewhat optimistic. He suggested that, as unspoiled nature becomes rarer and competition for it stiffer, developing nations are better placed to impose the terms of its exploitation on the developed nations who seek it (Cohen 1978). Written in the aftermath of the mid-1970s oil crisis, the analogy is obvious. The collective muscle of a coordinated region-wide policy has yet to be exerted in the field of ecotourism, however.

The simplest way to raise funds for sustainable management is to introduce user fees. Although many countries already charge entry to National Parks, others, for example Dominica, have yet to do so. There is no reason why foreign visitors, who are essentially exploiting the carrying capacity of the unspoilt destination, should be effectively subsidized in this way. Sherman and Dixon (1991) suggest that even a relatively high fee of US$10 a day would be insignificant in relation to the overall cost of international travel. Two important principles need to be adopted, however. Firstly, the fees levied should be channelled back into ensuring sustainable ecotourism development, for example via environmental protection, local training, grants and incentives towards greater local involvement. Secondly, a lower charge should apply to locals. The Galapagos Islands National Park, for instance, charges international visitors higher fees than Ecuadorian citizens and does not charge local residents at all (Boo 1990).

Integration

There is no other economic activity that cuts across so many sectors, levels and interests as tourism. There is a vital need, therefore, to integrate planning for ecotourism with national development plans in general and sectoral targets in

78

particular. Ecotourism activities will concern many government ministries, for example environment, agriculture, forestry, parks, education, transportation and public works (Boo 1991). The need for horizontal integration between these ministries is evident. Vertical integration is also necessary to coordinate interests from the local, through regional, to national levels. It is also necessary to recognize the mutually dependent interests of the public and private sectors in tourism (Holder 1992). The private sector is dependent on the government because, in its broadest sense, the country is the ecotourism product. Ultimately, however, the services which the tourism enterprises need the government to provide must be paid for by them via taxation. Holder suggests that it is in the government's interests to create the conditions and business environment within which private business can make a reasonable profit. A final element of integration is required to accommodate the time dimension. Too often long-term interests are sacrificed for short-term gain. This is particularly evident in the case of the less developed countries (LDCs) where populations are forced to commit 'ecocide' in the long term to ensure short-term survival. As Blaikie (1985) suggests, environmental degradation is a result of underdevelopment, a sympton of underdevelopment and a cause of underdevelopment.

Involvement

A final general principle to ensure the sustainability of ecotourism development on the part of destination areas, but perhaps the most vital, is to increase truly local involvement. As de Kadt (1992) points out, the distributional aspects of tourism development have been all too frequently ignored. It is naive to advocate local ownership versus foreign ownership without recognizing that the interests of a local élite are often more intimately bound with those of a foreign élite than their co-residents.

The conflicts are particularly evident in the case of ecotourism development, where not only may the local population be denied any direct benefits, but may also be actively disadvantaged. They may well be physically excluded from the very resources on which they depend for their basic needs. The classic example of the Maasai pastoralists of Kenya and Tanzania has already been cited. In Belize, traditional *milpa* slash and burn cultivators are considered a threat to ecotourism (Cater 1992). It is essential, therefore, that local communities are involved directly with ecotourism development. This involvement must not only be in the form of hand-outs or doles, or even the provision of schools, hospitals and social services financed from tourism revenue, handsome show factors that these may be. If the traditional means of economic livelihood is being removed from a community, it must be replaced by an alternative.

There are sound reasons for local involvement other than a moral obligation to incorporate the people whom the projects affect. In terms of conserving the natural and socio-cultural resource base, the time perspective of the local population is longer than that of outside entrepreneurs concerned with early profits (Chambers 1988). They are also more likely to ensure that traditions and lifestyles will be respected. Their cooperation is also a vital factor in reducing infringements of conservation regulations such as poaching and indiscriminate tree-felling. There are also sound practical reasons in terms of utilising local labour. Drake (1991) points to the limited capacity of local and national governments and agencies to effectively manage the growing number of projects unless their functions are decentralized and communities involved. The Annapurna Conservation Area Project is a good example of community involvement (Chapter 11).

Such an involvement must also extend beyond economic survival, environmental conservation and socio-cultural integrity, to allow appreciation by the community of their own natural resources. They must not be excluded physically, for example by coastal development effectively isolating beaches in Barbados, or financially. It is essential to reduce inflationary pressures on land and property and avoid their permanent alienation from the indigenous population through foreign ownership. The very least that is required is that if such transfer has to occur it should be no more than leasehold. To ensure that locals can also afford to participate in the enjoyment of their own ecotourism resources, parks could charge differential, reduced rates for locals (Sherman and Dixon 1991).

This outline of the essential principles for sustainable ecotourism development in the Third World reflects a central message of collective responsibility and a holistic approach involving governments, tourists, tourism enterprises and destination areas alike. It is also vital to remember that tourism is only a process cast within a markedly inequitable structure, both internationally and intranationally. This has vital implications for sustainability. In their desperate attempts to ensure survival in the short term, the poor are forced to compromise their longer term interests. The poorest countries are the least capable of withstanding the adverse impacts on their potential for sustainability, yet these are the very nations most in need of sustainable tourism development.

REFERENCES

Batisse, M (1982) "The biosphere reserve: a tool for environmental conservation and management", *Environmental Conservation*, 9, pp101–11

Blaikie, P (1985) *The Political Economy of Soil Erosion in Developing Countries*, Longman, London

Boo, E (1990) *Ecotourism: the Potentials and Pitfalls*, Vol 1, World Wildlife Fund, Washington

Boo, E (1991) "Making ecotourism sustainable: recommendations for planning, development and management", in Whelan, T (ed) *Nature Tourism*, Island Press, Washington, pp187–99

Britton, S (1982) "International tourism and multinational corporations in the Pacific: the case of Fiji", in Taylor, M and Thrift, N J (eds) *The Geography of Multinationals*, Croom, Helm, London, pp252–74

Budowski, G (1976) "Tourism and conservation: conflict, coexistence or symbiosis", *Environmental Conservation*, 3, pp27–31

Butler, R W (1991) "Tourism, environment and sustainable development", *Environmental Conservation*, 18, pp201–9

Cartwright, J (1989) "Conserving nature, decreasing debt", *Third World Quarterly*, 11, pp114–27

Cater, E (1992) "Profits from paradise", *Geographical*, 64(3), pp16–21

Ceballos Lascurain, H (1992) "Tourists for conservation", *People and the Planet*, 1(3), pp28–30

Chambers, R (1988) "Sustainable rural livelihoods: A key strategy for people, environment and development", in Conroy, C and Litvinoff, M (eds) *The Greening of Aid: Sustainable Livelihoods in Practice*, Earthscan, London, pp1–17

Cohen, E (1978) "The impact of tourism on the physical environment", *Annals of Tourism Research*, 5, pp215–37

de Kadt, E (ed) (1979) *Tourism: Passport to Development*, Oxford University Press, New York

de Kadt, E (1992) "Making the alternative sustainable: lessons from development for tourism", in Smith, V L and Eadington, W R (eds) *Tourism Alternatives*, University of Pennsylvania Press, Philadelphia, pp47–75

Drake, S P (1991) "Local participation in ecotourism projects", in Whelan, T (ed) *Nature Tourism*, Island Press, Washington, pp132–56

Economist Intelligence Unit (1992) *The Tourism Industry and the Environment*, EIU Publications, London

Geographical (1993) "Secret state opens up", *Geographical*, 65(2) p7

Goodall, B (1992) "Environmental auditing for tourism", in Cooper, C P and Lockwood, A (eds) *Progress in Tourism, Recreation and Hospitality Management*, Vol 4, Belhaven, London, pp60–74

Gray, R H (1990) *The Greening of Accountancy: The Profession After Pearce*, Certified Accountants Publications, London

Holder, J S (1992) "The need for public–private sector cooperation in tourism", *Tourism Management*, June, pp157–62

Independent (1993) "Having a fine time: Glad you're not here", 31 January, p3

International Monetary Fund (1992) *International Financial Statistics Yearbook*, International Monetary Fund, Washington

Jenkins, C L (1982) "The effects of scale in tourism projects in developing countries", *Annals of Tourism Research*, 9, pp229–49

Lindsay, K (1987) "Integrating parks and pastoralists", in Anderson, D and Grove, R (eds) *Conservation in Africa: People, Politics and Practice*, Cambridge University Press, Cambridge, pp149–67

Munt, I (1993) "Ecotourism gone awry", *Report on the Americas*, 26(4) pp8–10

Olindo, P (1991) "The old man of nature tourism: Kenya", in Whelan, T (ed) *Nature Tourism*, Island Press, Washington, pp23–38

Rees, N E (1990) "The ecology of sustainable development", *The Ecologist*, 20(1) pp18–23

Rovinski, Y (1991) "Private reserves, parks and ecotourism in Costa Rica", in Whelan, T (ed) *Nature Tourism*, Island Press, Washington, pp39–57

Ruschmann, D (1992) "Ecological tourism in Brazil", *Tourism Management*, March, pp125–28

Sherman, P B and Dixon, V A (1991) "The economics of nature tourism: Determining if it pays", in Whelan, T (ed) *Nature Tourism*, Island Press, Washington, pp89–131

Tobias, D and Mendelsohn, R (1991) "Valuing ecotourism in a tropical rain forest reserve", *Ambio*, 20, pp91–3

Weaver, D (1991) "Alternative to mass tourism in Dominica", *Annals of Tourism Research*, 18, pp414–32

Whelan, T (1991) "Ecotourism and its role in sustainable development", in Whelan, T (ed) *Nature Tourism*, Island Press, Washington, pp3–22

Wilkinson, P F (1989) "Strategies for tourism in island microstates", *Annals of Tourism Research*, 16, pp153–77

World Bank (1983) (1992) *World Development Report*, Oxford University Press, Oxford

World Tourism Organisation (WTO) (1986) (1992) *Yearbook of Tourism Statistics*, WTO, Madrid

World Travel and Tourism Council (WTTC) (1992) *World Travel and Tourism Environment Review*, WTTC, Brussels

Chapter 4

Promoting Sustainable Development and Combating Poverty: Environmentally Sound Programmes

INTRODUCTION

It has been suggested (Ryan 1991) that it is not difficult to make the case that tourism is damaging to the environment. Indeed as early as 1961 workers (Beed and Clement quoted in Mathieson and Wall 1982, 95) postulated that, unless it was carefully managed, the rise of tourism could lead to deleterious ecological effects in Tahiti. Nevertheless, even by the early 1980s (Mathieson and Wall 1982) evidence of the environmental impacts of tourism in the literature was very sparse and scattered. Subsequent research has increased the evidence and a greater range of examples (Ryan 1991, Burns and Holden 1995) has led to a deeper understanding of the problems. A growing public awareness of, and interest in, the environment has led pressure groups like Friends of the Earth and Tourism Concern to articulate widespread concern that exerts increasing influence upon commercial and government sections of the industry. Few developments are sacrosanct. It has been argued that environmental destruction can even occur in those destinations that promote so-called 'alternative' tourism, which is alleged to be more sustainable than other forms of the industry (Burns and Holden 1995). While emphasis is frequently laid on the negative effects of tourism on the natural and man-made environment, it must be noted that benefits can also accrue. Both of these are summarized in Box 4.1.

However Box 4.2 focuses upon adverse effects of tourism, identifying the contributory factors, the underlying problem and the likely consequences. It also offers suggestions for ways to mitigate the problems and thereby increase sustainability. The readings present examples of successes and failures in attempts to reduce the environmental impacts of tourism, with the macro scale successes of Kenya contrasted with the much quoted example of Belize, that initially appeared to offer promise but has subsequently encountered difficulties. The importance of the resource base, and the dangers that tourism impacts present, are the subject of the final reading in this section.

BOX 4.1 ENVIRONMENTAL IMPACTS OF TOURISM

Benefits

1. Conservation of natural areas and wildlife
2. Environmental appreciation
3. Rehabilitation and often also transformation of old buildings and sites into new facilities
4. Introduction of planning and management

Costs

1. Energy costs of transport
2. Loss of aesthetic value
3. Noise
4. Air pollution
5. Water pollution and the generation of waste
6. Disruption of animal breeding patterns and habits
7. Deforestation
8. Impacts on vegetation through the collection of flowers and bulbs
9. Destruction of beaches, dunes, coral reefs and many National Parks and Wilderness Areas through trampling and/or the use vehicles
10. Change of landscape – permanent environmental restructuring
11. Seasonal effects on population densities and structures

Sources: Mathieson and Wall 1982, Lea 1988, Pearce 1989, Ryan 1991, Burns and Holden 1995

REFERENCES

Burns, P M and Holden, A (1995) *Tourism. A New Perspective*, Prentice Hall International (UK) Limited, Hemel Hempstead

Lea, J (1988) *Tourism and Development in the Third World*, Routledge, London

Mathieson, A and Wall, G (1982) *Tourism. Economic, Physical and Social Impacts*, Longman, Harlow

Pearce, D (1989) *Tourism Development*, 2nd ed, Longman, Harlow

Ryan, C (1991) *Recreational Tourism*, Routledge, London

BOX 4.2 THE CONNECTION BETWEEN THE DESTINATION AND ENVIRONMENTAL FACTORS

	DEMAND FOR MATERIAL IMPROVEMENTS BY GROWING POPULATIONS				CHANGING TOURIST DEMAND		INEQUITABLE LAND USE
CONTRIBUTORY FACTORS							
UNDERLYING PROBLEM	OVERUSE OF RELATIVELY SMALL AREAS OF LAND AND OCEAN THAT FREQUENTLY ARE FRAGILE						
ENVIRONMENTAL STRESS EXAMPLES	PRESSURE ON COASTS • Caribbean • Kenya • Mediterranean			PRESSURE ON MOUNTAINS Himalayas Alps		PRESSURE ON NATIONAL PARKS East Africa Himalayas	PRESSURE ON CITIES Venice
POTENTIAL ADVERSE ENVIRONMENTAL CONSEQUENCES	Beach erosion Loss of land from traditional uses Destruction of coral reefs Loss of attraction Loss of mangrove swamps Pollution of sea			Loss of vegetation Landslides/avalanches Loss of attraction	Loss of attraction	Soil erosion Loss of vegetation Landslides Adverse effect on wildlife	Congestion Pollution/litter Aesthetic degradation Changing land use
THREATS TO WELL-BEING OF HOSTS	Loss of land Loss of traditional activities Loss of familiar environment for tourism Loss of resource base for tourism			Loss of fuelwood Loss of resource base for tourism		Local population excluded from traditional activities Loss of resource base for tourism	Loss of homes Loss of familiar environment
POSSIBLE ACTION TO INCREASE SUSTAINABILITY	Increase community involvement Consider scale of tourism: establish and work within carrying capacity levels. Introduce measures to combat pollution/congestion/degradation. Ensure all new buildings harmonize with physical and cultural environment. Protect the most vulnerable areas					Increase fuel efficiency thus reduce rate of deforestation	

Must Tourism Destroy its Resource Base?

E Cater and B Goodall

THE NEED FOR SUSTAINABLE TOURISM

There is a circular and cumulative relationship between tourism development, the environment and socio-economic development. Most tourism development places additional pressures on the environmental resources upon which it is based, compromising the future prospects of the local population. The crucial issue of sustainability (defined in Chapter 2) applies to both hosts and guests as far as tourism is concerned. The destruction of tourism resources for short-term gain will deny the benefits to be gained from the mobilization of those resources in the future. Future generations of tourists will be denied the opportunity to experience environments very different from home. Host populations will be faced with environmental degradation and denied the tourism potential offered by the original attraction.

What are the prospects for sustainable tourism? Recently there has been increased emphasis on alternative forms of tourism, although none of these options constitute truly sustainable tourism. Even small group alternative tours can be damaging. In their search for 'unspoilt' locations, alternative tourists bring more and more remote communities, with delicately balanced environments and economies, into the locus of tourism. Enterprising travellers who penetrate new and as yet unspoilt areas unwittingly become the pioneers of tourism development. The principles of responsible tourism appear laudable, but are in danger of being co-opted by the tourist and the tourism industry to salve guilty consciences and promote seemingly more conscientious marketing. Green or eco-tourism may satisfy environmentalists, but unless the needs of the local population are also considered there will be no guarantee of sustainability.

Resource conservation policies may be regressive from the local population's viewpoint. The creation of National Parks to protect extensive tracts of land denies access to local populations for agriculture, the gathering of fuel, fodder and building materials. Simultaneously local populations rarely benefit from tourism. Such a conflict is evident in the National Parks of East Africa, where the pressures of a rapidly growing population and limited availability of land which can be cultivated conflict directly with wildlife tourism (Wyer and Towner 1988). The failure to integrate local involvement in the tourism industry is exemplified by the Galapagos Islands. Here, in the face of the very rapid growth of tourism, the viability of existing conservationist strategies is in question. The maximum number of visitors to be admitted has been progressively revised upwards over recent years. Local tourism is now an established and increasingly important socio-economic factor due to the increased number of tourists staying on the islands. The Ecuadorean government has yet to formulate an overall plan for sustainable tourism which effectively involves Galapagan participation.

Nepal has been a pioneer in integrating the twin goals of conservation and local development to achieve sustainable tourism. The Annapurna Conservation Area utilizes a multiple land use approach, attempting to balance the needs of the local population, tourists and the natural environment. Local villagers continue to practise traditional methods of resource utilization. They participate in decision-making via the existing village assemblies, and also benefit directly from the funds generated by tourism.

What is to be gained from balancing the needs of tourists, of the local population and of the natural environment through policies of sustainable tourism? Eco-tourism is the fastest growing tourism sector. The largest nature tour agency in Costa Rica experienced a 46% growth in 1986. Recognition of the symbiotic relationship between tourism, the environment and development should stimulate conservation of the tourism attraction. Environmental destruction will not occur if it is possible to make more money by conservation. Tourism also motivates the conservation of historical sites and buildings, for example, the Buddhist temple at Borobudur, Indonesia and the Mayan site of Tikal, Guatemala. An ultimate example of such a symbiotic relationship in the built environment is Williamsburg, Virginia, where tourists stay in conserved colonial inns and taverns which are at the same time tourist attractions.

HOW TO ACHIEVE SUSTAINABLE TOURISM

Requirements of sustainable tourism

Sustainable tourism depends on:

(a) meeting the needs of the host population in terms of improved standards of living in the short and long term
(b) satisfying the demands of increasing tourist numbers and continuing to attract them to achieve this
(c) safeguarding the environment to achieve the two foregoing aims.

To accomplish these aims attitudes and policies will have to change. This involves four viewpoints: those of tourist destinations, the tourists themselves, tourism enterprises and, lastly, global considerations.

Viewpoint of the tourist destination

Local populations must be involved in tourism development if their needs are to be met. This involves four major policy considerations: ownership, scale, timing and location. The question of ownership is particularly pertinent in LDC destinations. Net foreign exchange earnings from tourism are considerably less than the gross receipts. Substantial leakages result from the repatriation of wages and profits, and imports. Transport carriers, hotel groups and tour operators based in the MDCs have all become increasingly transnational in their operations. Third World destinations receive only a small return for the exploitation of an increasingly scarce resource, their natural environment. Such destinations have to bear certain costs, both in terms of environmental degradation and in prospects for sustainability. Furthermore, due to their low level of development, they can rarely afford preventive and restorative measures. Any extra earnings which do accrue locally benefit a small commercial elite, more concerned with early profits than environmental considerations. It is therefore insufficient to advocate local as opposed to foreign ownership without considering distributional aspects and environmental accountability.

The scale of tourism development is a complex issue. Small-scale projects, locally controlled, can have a significant impact on raising living standards (Britton and Clarke 1987), but are unlikely to meet the needs of large numbers of tourists. Some large-scale projects are inevitable, but it is important to consider the complementarity of large- and small-scale developments. As tourism development proceeds, indigenous firms and locals gain knowledge and experience. Government planners should co-ordinate investment in infrastructure with the needs of small-scale entrepreneurs and the needs of local communities, paying careful attention to the environmental component. Large-scale development is often the precursor to small-scale development. The growth in mass tourism and the building up of infrastructure in Senegal were essential prerequisites for the success of the Lower Casamance project in promoting rural development through tourism (Pearce 1989). It is a two-way process. Large-scale developments benefit from the increased local skill base.

The location of tourism development is also crucial. Development concentrated in tourism enclaves, eg Nusa Dua in Bali, may minimize adverse impacts elsewhere, but does not constitute sustainable development. The local population may be denied continuance of their traditional practices as well as being excluded from any economic benefits of such development.

There appear, therefore, to be many contradictions concerning the ownership, scale, timing and location of tourism development destinations. It is not as simple as resolving the issues of indigenous versus foreign, small versus large, gradual versus instantaneous and dispersed versus concentrated developments. It is more a question of ensuring complementarity between all these issues, so that tourism can contribute towards the development of an area while minimizing adverse environmental, social and economic effects to ensure sustainability.

The tourist's viewpoint

Are tourists aware that their actions may damage the natural environment and the culture of their destination? Do they realize their contribution to environmental damage on a global scale?

Tourists know if their holiday is unsatisfactory, although despoiled destination environments may not be the only reasons (eg flight delays, loss of baggage). Their response is to choose a different destination, hotel, or tour operation next time. Just as consumers in general have varied opinions on 'green' issues, so too with tourists. Some, eg allocentrics or explorers, are more environmentally aware of tourism's damaging potential than others, ie psychocentrics or mass tourists, who get enjoyment from holidaying in crowded situations and who seek developed ('theme park') destinations. Such facilities do not have to be located in fragile environments. Allocentrics are more of a problem, especially where demand exceeds supply. How can their tourism experiences be maintained? To spread them more widely implies more and distant destinations leading to an increase in travel consumption.

For the tourist, sustainable tourism offers the prospect of a guaranteed level of satisfaction whenever a destination is visited. But tourists' behaviour and attitudes must change – tourists must understand a destination's 'sense of place' if they are to respect its environment and culture. Tourists visiting less developed regions must forgo accustomed standards of comfort and convenience. Development using local materials and in scale with the vernacular may be more expensive. Who pays? Ultimately it is the tourist via entry charges and bed taxes. A danger is that sustainable tourism appears elitist – an up-market operation seeking longer stay tourists committed to quality crafts, organic foods, heritage, nature and quietness. It offers the richer tourist a means of preserving destinations from the masses with their noisy habits and bad tastes.

The tourism enterprise's viewpoint

Tourism enterprises are in the business for profit. If a hotel can minimize costs by discharging untreated sewage directly into the sea, because building regulations permit, it will do so. The hotel takes advantage of the sea as a common property resource (see Chapter 6) even though this imposes social costs, from pollution, on the destination as a whole. However, just as firms in retailing are responding to green consumerism, so too will tourism enterprises need to take account of environmental issues in their decision making. Indeed, some already do, for example, British Airways have an 'environmental policy' which covers all their operations.

Tourism enterprises may 'go green' operationally, ie act in an environmentally sound way. A 'green audit' of tourism enterprises would reveal the extent to which firms are conserving energy (insulation of hotels to reduce heating costs) and recycling wastes (British Airways and Consort Hotels recycle waste paper), minimizing pollution (Friendly Hotels use recycled papers products and 'ozone-friendly' toiletries and cleaning products, British Airways use lead-free petrol in their motor vehicles) and using local materials and produce (such as organic foods).

Tourism enterprises can encourage their customers to behave respectfully towards the environment. This educational role may serve as a basis for niche marketing, such as Consort Hotels' 'Go Green' weekends.

A global viewpoint

Even assuming that tourist destinations adopt sustainable tourism plans and tourism enterprises and tourists adopt more environmentally aware practices and behaviour, tourism will continue to contribute to global warming because of its heavy consumption of travel products. Can conventional tourism become more sustainable in this context? Currently tourist transport uses too much fuel. Public transport could be substituted for private transport, short-haul travel to nearer destinations for long-haul holiday journeys, high occupancy charter flights for scheduled flights and flight refuelling stops planned to minimize the need to tanker extra fuel. It is, however, questionable whether tourism can adopt measures which will reduce significantly emissions from the use of transport services and other energy sources.

Staying at home appears to be the 'greenest' way to holiday. Holographs have the potential to reproduce any environment artificially so, in the 21st century, it may be possible to holiday at home! The English Tourist Board has recently suggested the use of 'video scenics' in popular destinations such as the Lake District to dissuade tourists from visiting overcrowded locations. Alternatively, the development of holiday complexes, which provide artificial 'sun-warm water' environments (eg Center Parc villages), located at points of maximum market access, could be a way forward. What has to be faced at the global scale is that sustainable tourism could be more restrictive of holiday travel than conventional tourism.

Furthermore, global environmental change stemming from non-tourist activities will necessitate a response from the tourism industry. Global warming, for example, will alter the natural resource base and hence destinations' comparative advantages – new destinations will be developed for seaside holidays in the late 21st century.

REFERENCES

Britton, S and Clark, W C (eds) (1987) *Ambiguous Alternative: Tourism in Small Developing Countries*, University of South Pacific, Fiji

Pearce, D (1989) *Tourist Development*, Longman, London

The Old Man of Nature Tourism: Kenya

Perez Olindo

In the flatlands of Kenya's Amboseli Game Reserve, a lioness lies resting. Every few minutes, a minivan or bus drives up and the crowd of tourists inside snap their camera shutters. The animal may remain for two hours. In that time, twenty-five vehicles might stop and stare.

Kenya is the world's foremost ecotourist attraction. Some 650 thousand people visit Kenya's parks and protected areas each year, spending about $350 million. Wildlife is the magnet. One estimate holds that an elephant is worth about $14,375 a year, or $900,000 over the course of its life, in tourist expenditures.

This financial success hides a multitude of problems, however. Kenya's colonial legacy, combined with a low level of local community support for the parks, inadequate funding and enforcement powers for the ministry in charge of the parks, and poaching for ivory, has led to a dramatic decline in the elephant population, as well as the degradation of public lands. In response, the Kenyan government has launched recently a series of innovative techniques and programmes it hopes will ensure ecotourism's continued success [...].

KENYAN ECOTOURISM: HOW IT WORKS

The success of Kenya's tourism efforts, first for sports hunting, and now for ecotourism, has been based on several factors: a unique wildlife resource, an extensive system of national parks and game reserves, and an intensive promotion and investment effort. The sometimes severe problems associated with its efforts, such as environmental degradation and a dwindling wildlife resource, will be discussed in detail later.

In order to protect its unique wildlife resources, a system of wildlife conservation areas was established by the Kenya National Parks Service soon after World War II and strengthened considerably after Kenya become independent in 1963. Some 17,000 square miles, or 8 per cent of the national territory, are protected by fifty-two national parks and reserves. A further 3 per cent of the country is designated as forest reserve. These protected areas were selected based on how well they represented a cross-section of habitat and wildlife. The ranges currently under protection stretch from the highest mountains in the country (17,000 feet above sea level) to mangrove forests of the Indian Ocean and marine environments reaching a maximum depth of sixty fathoms.

Most of the protected areas are in the Great Rift Valley, which starts north of the Jordan River and extends as far south as Mozambique and is one of the world's most spectacular natural wonders. Dense wet forests inhabited by majestic crowned eagles, sweeping savannah grasslands, and sparking inland lakes: these diverse ecosystems are the heritage of the Great Rift Valley, and the Kenyan national parks system.

Several years after Kenya made the transition to ecotourism, mainly through the efforts of private individuals, the government saw that it would be in its national interest to experiment with promoting and providing incentives for ecotourism. In 1965, a special department of tourism was created as part of the Ministry of Tourism and Wildlife; its task was to develop a blueprint for the popularization of Kenya as an attractive tourist destination.

Toward that end, it set in motion a highly successful promotional effort that focused on Kenya's exotic scenery and wildlife. Writers and photographers were commissioned to prepare alluring brochures for distribution around the world. Beautiful calendars and postcards depicting Kenya's colorful wildlife were produced and sold in large quantities. Public relations representatives in key sites such as the United States, Canada, Great Britain, and Western Europe were retained to promote Kenya's image in those areas. Later, representatives were hired in Japan, Southeast Asia, Australia and New Zealand. Tourist officers were posted at Kenyan embassies and trade missions around the world and continue to be today.

The government entered into a dialogue with tour operators and travel agents in an attempt to address divisive issues such as delays of visitors at entry points and visa problems. A Kenyan Tourist Advisory Committee was formed to meet regularly on issues that appeared to be threatening the success of ecotourism efforts. Through this process, potential problems were identified and addressed. Immigration matters were discussed openly and steps taken to streamline the process. Financial issues such as tax rebates, export promotion gratuities, and duty-free imports of equipment were also tackled. No subject was deemed too big or too trivial.

Kenya also decided to provide fiscal incentives for the development of ecotourism and an ecotourism infrastructure. In order to finance its efforts, it raised funds and received technical assistance from development agencies in countries such as Great Britain, West Germany, Switzerland, and Italy, in addition to spending funds held in its own treasury. Although ultimately rejected, the idea of nationalizing the industry was considered; instead, they established the Kenya Tourist Development Corporation (KTDC) in 1966.

The new body was given a mandate to finance up-and-coming Kenyan tour operators, travel agents, and hotel owners, and to make money doing so. In the process, the KTDC embarked on a programme of buying shares in foreign-owned firms, with the aim of selling them to promising Kenyan entrepreneurs on special terms. This innovative approach to localizing the tourist industry has made it virtually impossible to distinguish between foreign and locally owned tourism firms.

The government continues to offer incentives to foreign investors, however, through the Foreign Investments Act, which guarantees them repatriation of capital and profits. The potential to attract large sums of 'bad' money (ie, that earned from gambling, drugs, prostitution, etc) is addressed through an investment vetting system that prohibits it.

Major airlines have also been wooed. Practical incentives are offered in the form of tax exemptions for capital investments and taxes only on income (to date, they do not even pay property taxes), to encourage their involvement with game lodge and hotel development, enabling airlines to earn money on two fronts, plane tickets and accommodations.

While ecotourism in Kenya has been a success, the very attraction on which it is based – wildlife – is severely threatened. Mismanagement of the protected areas, illegal hunting, and a low level of local participation and support for conservation are among the reasons why. Since independence, the Kenyan government has launched several major initiatives to tackle these problems. The jury is still out on what the future will bring, but many of the changes appear promising.

MANAGEMENT OF KENYA'S PARKS AND RESERVES

Despite the fact that nature tourism has been a big foreign exchange earner, until recently very little of that money ($7 million of $350 million) was put back into the resource that supports it – the parks system. Parks personnel and guards were underpaid and worked long hours, equipment was lacking, and poaching was rife – in short, the Department of Wildlife Conservation and Management was unable to manage the areas it was charged to protect due to a lack of funding.

In 1989, President Daniel arap Moi moved to address that problem by establishing the parastatal Kenyan Wildlife Service (KWS), which replaced the Department of Wildlife Conservation and Management. The primary role of KWS is to ensure the protection and management of wildlife both inside and outside the protected areas – and to make that wildlife accessible for viewing by tourists and so promote ecotourism. Under the new system, the income and assets associated with the national parks and game reserves are under the jurisdiction of the KWS, and thus can be ploughed back into management and conservation. In addition, the KWS can now set the prices charged for park admissions, accommodations, and so forth. (It has raised the rate 125 per cent, to Ksh 200 for foreign nationals. Kenyans continue to pay the relatively low rate of Ksh 40, as they otherwise support KWS through taxes.)

The organization is autonomous and is managed by a board of trustees, which is composed of Kenyan nationals from different sectors of the economy. The budget, however, remains subject to public and parliamentary scrutiny, in order to discourage potential abuses.

Each park and reserve is now run as a separate corporate division, responsible for its own income and expenditures. Some will be developed for high-density (minibus) tourism, other will target the high-income individual who wishes to camp in the midst of nature away from crowds, others will be set aside for as little human impact as possible, while still others will serve as multiple-use sites (research, wildlife management, education, etc). The effect of increased income for the parks can be seen already in the purchase of modern arms and new communications equipment for park guards, along with higher salaries and other benefits.

Parks personnel now receive nine months of paramilitary training and one year of education in wildlife management, and thus are better equipped to deal with the pressures, such as well-armed ivory poachers, on the areas they protect.

Few other parks management agencies, either in Africa or in the rest of the world, enjoy such autonomy and control as the newly created KWS. If managed wisely, success is guaranteed. However, if the new freedoms are abused or poorly managed, the KWS could find itself at loggerheads with other sectors of the economy.

The scars of the neglect inflicted on the parks system in earlier years through lack of financing will take substantial investment, innovation, and time to heal. KWS has been operating for less than a year and has not yet made public its long-term plans. It will have many important issues to address.

One such issue is determining the carrying capacities for Kenya's parks and reserves. The task is complicated by the fact that the carrying capacity of a given area varies from season to season or year to year depending on the amount of rainfall, and the migration habits of wildlife. In addition, the need to maintain Kenya's democratic traditions makes it difficult to deny access or development opportunities to Kenyan nationals. Nevertheless, a determination of the carrying capacities for humans, vehicles, wildlife, domestic animals, and the like must be made and enforced if the protected areas are to be viable over the long term.

Another, even more critical, issue is stopping the illegal hunting of wildlife. The solutions must address both the poaching by the local communities and the slaughter of elephants and rhinos for ivory by professional black marketeers. Fortunately, the KWS will be aided greatly in its work with the latter by the fact that in 1989, the international community of nations signed an agreement to ban ivory imports (CITES). Poaching of elephants has since scaled down dramatically – park wardens are not finding as many carcasses, and many once-thriving ivory shops have closed their doors. However, other southern African nations with thriving elephant populations (eg South Africa, Zimbabwe) continue to sell ivory, which provides incentives for poachers to kill elephants in Kenya and smuggle the ivory into these other countries, where it can be sold legally. Consequently, poaching still occurs. The next meeting on this issue will take place in 1992, at which time it is hoped that a solution for the problem will be presented, and the ban implemented in full measure; if this occurs, poaching for ivory should no longer be a problem.

KWS has also greatly strengthened enforcement. In 1988, the rangers were authorized to shoot poachers on sight, and more than seventy poachers have been killed since. Not one has been a Kenyan, however, which implies that poaching is fueled by forces outside Kenya.

LOCAL PARTICIPATION

The Kenyan government has also moved to address the problems associated with the interaction of neighbouring local communities with the protected areas.

Many of the local people are so disgruntled with decades of being ignored that today they are the enemies of the parks and national forests. Their anger has its roots in colonialism and the ban on traditional hunting, and in the fact that the wild game living in the parks are allowed to range freely over private lands, competing with domestic animals, using up essential water supplies, and sometimes contributing to soil erosion and degradation. Until recently, the private landowner saw very little monetary return from this public use of his lands.

Local landowners began to feel that their interests were being treated as less important than those of the animals, and that their good-naturedness was being abused. Some began to put up fences to keep wildlife off their property and others used innovative methods to deny water to migrating wildlife. As a result, the number of wild animals declined noticeably in the reserves, and migration patterns were disrupted.

In response, the government recently developed a number of policies aimed at increasing local participation in the development of tourism, providing financial incentives to local communities to protect the neighbouring tourism sites, and encouraging domestic tourism in order to build Kenyan support for the parks.

The Kenyan government is providing fiscal incentives to the local communities through a variety of mechanisms. First, it attempts to ensure that local goods and services, as well as local labour, are used by the tourism industry, through a series of specific requirements. Kenyans must be employed on a preferential basis, with the exception of the most senior personnel, whom the investor may appoint as desired. Hotels and lodges are required to keep imported foodstuffs to a minimum, using Kenyan products wherever possible. The visitors are charged a government hotel tax, a training levy charge, and a service charge, all of which accrue to the Kenyan government (a portion trickles down to the local populations) and are in addition to the normal corporate taxes levied by the government each year on the gross trading income.

Local participation and involvement are the keystone of a policy implemented in 1988 after being negotiated with local communities. Following lengthy discussions, it was agreed that each visitor staying in a game lodge overnight would be charged an extra USD 5 that would be allocated to the local peoples. This money is placed into a trust fund to be used by the private land owners in the area. Some tourists visit reserves that do not have game lodges nearby; in this case, a portion of the entry fee will be deposited into the trust fund.

The trust funds are managed by the people themselves under the neutral chairmanship of the district commissioner or the local game warden. In the case of wrongdoing such as misappropriation of funds, or favouritism, an appeal process has been established. If this is also unfruitful, the aggrieved person may take the case to a court of law. No such problems have yet emerged, however. The money in these trust funds is first distributed for community needs such as schools, cattle dips (where cattle are cleaned of ticks and other parasites), and hospitals. Any money that remains is distributed on a pro rata basis among the affected landowners, based on how much land is involved in the programme.

This programme is still new and as yet has been implemented only in Amboseli and Masai Mara national parks. There are no real data as yet on how well the system is functioning, though local communities now seem more positive about the parks and local poaching appears to be declining. KWS currently is conducting negotiations for similar programmes with communities surrounding other reserves.

Domestic tourism is encouraged through substantially reduced pricing, particularly during the rainy season and school holidays. Educational hostels have been built in strategic locations across the country for schoolchildren and members of the popular Kenyan wildlife clubs. Their maintenance and administration are heavily subsidized by the government. Public buses are available for organized local groups, such as schools, churches, or civic groups, to provide inexpensive transportation to these sites.

PRIVATE RESERVES

In some countries, private reserves play a large role in both preserving wildlife and distributing some of the benefits of ecotourism back to the local communities. There are at present relatively few private reserves in existence in Kenya, however. The best known number six in total. The owners of these areas are mainly wealthy foreigners. The reserves are usually part of a working ranch, located on marginal lands used primarily for cattle grazing. Portions of the ranch are devoted to the protection of wildlife, and the cattle are not allowed in those regions. Some of the more sophisticated of the reserves have built high-priced accommodations for the tourist. They all appeal to the well-heeled visitor who wants to avoid the mass tourism found on the state reserves.

In many cases, the operators of these sites claim they are losing money and that they should be supported by the government and exempted from income taxes. However, if they are truly losing money, why do they wish to continue the operation? And if it were truly nonprofitable, why are more and more people opting for this type of land use?

There are no hard data available on tourism at private reserves. There is no government oversight, either, except that wildlife is legally a national asset, so the KWS theoretically could become involved in the management of the wildlife (if hunting were to occur, for example). Currently, the government has no plans to review the issue. The KWS is, however, planning for that eventuality.

CASE STUDY: MASAI MARA/SERENGETI ECOSYSTEM

The spectacular savannah woodlands of the Mara/Serengeti are what many people envision when they think of Africa. This tropical paradise for wildlife strad-dles the borders of Kenya and Tanzania (see Figure 4.1) and is home to zebras, wildebeests, lions, antelopes, hyenas, jackals, African hunting dogs, giraffes, buffaloes, elephants, and many birds of prey. It is also home to several hundred families of Masai, a nomadic people who base their livelihoods on maintaining large herds of cattle.

Many of the 650,000 visitors to Kenya each year feel their tour is incomplete without a trip to see the Mara/Serengeti. However, the ever-increasing numbers of tourists visiting the site have led to a host of environmental problems. Previous mismanagement of the relationship of the Masai to the reserve has also led to environmental damage by Masai-owned livestock and poaching.

Until 1960, when the 750-square-mile Masai Mara County Council Game Reserve was established, the local Masai had access to all the land in the district, and were free to move southward into Tanzania in search of water and grazing when necessary. The creation of the reserve, together with the adjacent Serengeti National Park, which was established a decade earlier, greatly restricted their options without providing any alternatives. In addition, during certain months of the year, the wild game animals forage on the Masai's private lands, competing with Masai livestock and decreasing the productivity of the domestic animals.

In order to address this problem, the government and the Masai agreed on a revenue-sharing scheme (described in greater detail earlier). Each visitor staying in or around the reserve overnight (six lodges are local inside the reserve, seven outside) is charged an extra USD 10 per day, half of which goes to the county council (a local administrative authority). The other half is paid into a trust fund for the local Masai, and managed by them with the help of a locally appointed district commissioner.

As soon as the system was implemented, the shift in community attitudes was immediate and dramatic. The community began to earn a handsome income in excess of nearly USD 1 million a year, and now views wildlife as an asset rather than a liability. Poaching, which had accounted for the loss of tens of thousands of animals annually, dropped to virtually nothing.

Thus, one threat to the future of the reserve has been eliminated – perma-nently, one hopes. The impact of a virtual avalanche of tourists, however, has yet

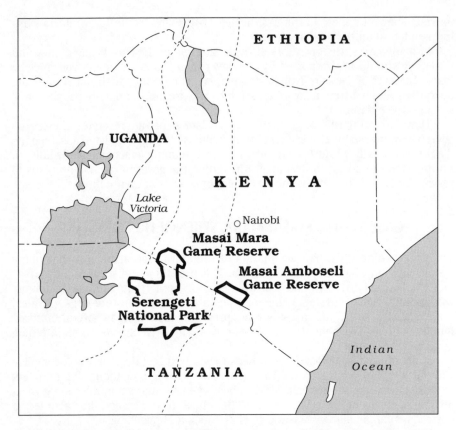

Figure 4.1 *Masai Mara and Masai Amboseli Reserves in Kenya*

to be addressed adequately.

The sensitive soils of the savannah are criss-crossed with tire tracks where tourists in search of wildlife have offered drivers large tips to go off the roads. Balloonists swoop over herds of elephants, buffalo, and other animals, causing them to scurry this way and that. (On the other hand, each individual on the balloon pays $250 for a forty five minute ride, which makes a strong economic argument in terms of short term investment criteria for continuing the practice in some form.) The feeding and mating habits of the region's wildlife have been disrupted as animals react to large numbers of viewers. Some animals, such as the cheetahs, become so disturbed that they frequently fail to feed, mate, or raise their young.

The local county council is the richest in the country, but as yet it has not invested enough funds in the development of mechanisms to better control the viewing habits of visitors to the reserves and so alleviate pressures on environmentally sensitive lands. Such an investment would suit its best interests.

Several actions are planned by the Kenyan Wildlife Service that should address the worst of these problems in the Masai Mara and other parks. A first priority is the construction of primary, secondary and tertiary roads; their use will be mandatory. Road construction is tough on the environment, but the current free-for-all is much worse. A complete ban on the development of additional tourist accommodations or expansion of existing ones is being contemplated. Casual camping will be illegal. Minimum flight levels for balloons, and fixed take-off and landing sites, will be established. Finally, tourists will be asked to be sensitive to the ecological needs of the areas they visit. Without their participation, the environment of the Mara/Serengeti ecosystem will continue to be degraded.

CONCLUSION

Tourism in Kenya has had a stormy history. However, it appears that the government, and to some degree the local communities, has decided that ecotourism is critical to the well-being of the nation and is moving to make it sustainable. The changes in governmental attitudes toward the local people, the increased financial and executive support for the protection of the parks, and the complete ban on the ivory trade have been important steps forward. The future will demonstrate if ecotourism in Kenya will indeed be sustainable, and if it can continue to provide protection for the parks and wildlife of Kenya.

Belize: Ecotourism Gone Awry

Ian Munt and Egbert Higinio

Belize has a key position in the world-wide eco-tourism wave. However, in this article IAN MUNT, who until recently worked in the planning department in Belize and now works in the geography department at South Bank University, and EGBERT HIGINIO, assistant supervisor at the School of Continuing Studies at the University of the West Indies in Belize, look at how eco-tourism in the country has become just 'like any other business': a marketing term used to capture demand from a growing social movement of 'alternative' tourists, without really changing the nature of tourism at all.

"Eco-tourism at Hachet-Cay" snapped a headline last year in the popular Belizean weekly *Amandala.* The newspaper was taking umbrage at a US resort owner who had allegedly blown up part of the coral reef to make his resort more accessible to visiting boats. The widespread media coverage and public outrage over the incident reflect Belizeans' new awareness of environmental issues in the wake of what the US-based Eco-tourism Society has coined the 'Eco-tourism Revolution'. The episode also illustrates how the original vision of ecotourism – as small-scale, locally controlled, and ecologically sensitive – is beginning to erode.

Ecotourism is the new rage in holidays. In a nutshell, westerners are now seeking out alternative tourism – what the Caribbean commentator Auliana Poon terms 'new tourism'. Tired of being chaperoned through staged cultural experiences, cocooned from the realities of everyday life, and complicit in ecologically destructive vacations, ecotourists are looking for new, lesser visited, out of the way destinations. In tune with the growth of new social movements concerned with environmental and cultural issues, these visitors are demanding vacations in pristine environments with 'uncorrupted' local culture.

On the surface, Belize would seem to have high-brow appeal to these new middle-class travellers anxious to distance themselves – both physically and socially – from the standard tourist. This former colony of British Honduras, which gained its independence in 1981, is blessed with abundant natural endowments, among them a stunning barrier reef (second only to Australia's Great Barrier Reef), large, well-reserved tracts of tropical rainforest, and idyllic tropical island cayes. Belize also boasts part of the impressive archaeological legacy of the ancient Maya civilization – now a major draw within the regional Ruta Maya. Yet, until recently, this small, officially English-speaking Caribbean nation along Central America's Atlantic coast was visited by few, and faced minimal environmental threats.

Before the 1983 election victory of the right-of-centre United Democratic Party (UDP), tourism received little government support. Sensing a change in the type of holidays that westerners were demanding, and the emergence of a new 'greener' market niche, the UDP started to promote tourism as a way to earn much-needed foreign exchange and to further economic development.

Tourism was further boosted with the return to power in 1989 of the People's United Party (PUP), and like its political rival (from which it is now indistinguishable), pro-US and free-market-orientated party. Although previously opposed to tourism, the PUP, eager to capitalize on this new trend in holidays, placed tourism second on its agenda of economic priorities.

A new international airport terminal now greets arriving visitors, and a number of luxury hotels – including the Royal Reef Ramada – have recently been built in Belize City. The government has established a range of nature, marine and archaeological reserves to ensure that tourist attractions are well-maintained. It has also encouraged local communities to tap into the tourism potential. The government's strategy is premised upon the concept of sustainability; that is, it endeavours to preserve the now highly prized local flora and fauna and to promote the sense of natural and cultural authenticity which the eco-tourist seeks. The Community Baboon Sanctuary at Bermudian Landing and the Sandy Beach Women's Co-operative run by local Garifuna women at Hopkins Village in the South are two projects which have taken the government's cue. Similar projects are sprouting up elsewhere.

These efforts are beginning to pay dividends. The number of international tourists to Belize has risen steadily from fewer than 100,000 in 1985, to a quarter of a million by 1990. Revenue from the tourism industry is estimated to account for about 26% of the Belizean GNP. Underlining the country's key position in the ecotourism wave, Belize has hosted two international conferences – the First Caribbean Eco-tourism Conference, and the First World Congress on Tourism and the Environment.

OLD TOURISM IN NEW CLOTHES?

Despite some promising results, much ecotourism in Belize merely replicates the problems characteristic of traditional mass-tourism – foreign exchange leakage, foreign ownership and environmental degradation. A case in point is the proposed multi-million dollar Belize City Tourism District project, which will no doubt involve the capital of foreign developers, or large-scale borrowing from US-dominated lending institutions like the World Bank.

New Orleans-based architects have completed a US AID-sponsored initial study for this waterfront-style regeneration project. The planners hope to build an exclusive downtown area complete with new hotels and shopping facilities, a promenade with seafront restaurants and cafes, an ethnic crafts and food market, and a marina for small yachts cruising the Caribbean. Such a development will transform the seafront district into a vacation pied-a-terre for would-be ecotourists, who presumably will feel safe and protected there from the urban problems that have become legendary in guidebooks to Belize.

Not only do ordinary Belizeans stand to gain little from this up-scale project but, to add insult to injury, local representatives were not even consulted during the planning process. Belize City's planning department first came in contact with the scheme when a three-dimensional model appeared in the window of a city supermarket. In this city of 60,000 where the government is strapped for money and poverty is increasing, the US consultants lauded the scheme for allowing the city council to 'concentrate its resources' on the upkeep of the district, including cleaning and road maintenance. Such activities, however, may have to be cut back in other neighbourhoods in order to free up the necessary funds.

Elsewhere in Belize, the lure of the tourism dollar is causing equally dismaying results and raising questions about whether the term 'ecotourism' is now being indiscriminately applied to any tourist project in an attractive natural setting. The Ambergris Caye controversy, for example, has raised serious doubts about the scale and nature of tourism development. Touted as a major contribution to re-investing in the Belizean people – a reflection of the 1989 election pledge 'Belizeans First' – the government bought back the northern two-thirds of the 20,000 acre Ambergris Caye from its US owner. Most expected the newly established Ambergris Caye Planning Authority (ACPA) to have its jurisdiction and planning powers extended over the Pinkerton Estate, as the area was formerly known. Instead, a development corporation was created by legislation unbeknownst to the Authority.

Under the guise of the corporation, appointed by and answerable to the Tourism and Environment Minister Glenn Godfrey (who is also attorney general), a $50 million 'sustainable development' has been proposed. Although its supporters claim it is 'an integrated and ecologically sound resort development' it will include the usual tourist sites: at least one international hotel, two 'all-inclusive spa hotels', three to five upscale lodges, two golf courses, town houses and villas, a thousand luxury homes, polo fields and stables.

Half of the 20,000 acres have been put aside – at least for now – for conservation and 2,500 acres are earmarked for Belizeans. Local people are enraged, however, by the transfer of the remaining 7,500 acres to the US developer as part of the deal, and by way the government attempted to foist this megacontract on the Caye. Just two days before the contract was set to be signed, Godfrey presented the document to the ACPA for the first time, claiming that negotiations – to which the ACPA was not a party – had proceeded over two years.

"If the proposed agreement for the development of North Ambergris Caye is so good, why not let the people know?" demanded Fidel Ancona, a furious member of the ACPA. "When the government acquired the Pinkerton Estate, we were told in no uncertain terms that we were getting back control of the land and meaningful participation. To me, 75 per cent to foreigners and 25 per cent to Belizeans is not fulfilling this promise."

Although the ACPA managed to temporarily stave off the signing of the contract, the incident illustrates that with large-scale development projects, local control is compromised, if not absent entirely.

POWERFUL EXPATRIATES

Much of the tourism industry is already in the hands of the country's small, but powerful expatriate community, estimated to number 1,500. Erlet Cater, a delegate at the ecotourism conference in 1991, found that 25 per cent of the registered delegates were US citizens. More significantly, among the 43 per cent who registered as Belizeans were many expatriate North Americans.

This expatriate community has become a resolute and well-represented lobby. Expatriate riverside eco-lodge owners in the western Cayo District, for example, have demanded strict zoning laws against further tourist development. The USAID initiated Belize Tourism Industry Association, an umbrella group representing private interests, faced turmoil during the 1992 election of officers, when disputes erupted among members over whether seats on its committee should be restricted to Belizeans, even though 65 per cent of the membership are expatriates.

For the time being, Belize confidently reaffirms its commitment to ecotourism and basks in the warm praise it has received from the international community for pursuing this approach. 'Conservation and therefore ecotourism' Godfrey told a receptive audience at an ecology and tourism symposium in Costa Rica at the time of the Ambergris Caye controversy, "thrives best where the sunlight penetrates to the lowest levels of autonomous local and community government." He reiterated this stance in his speech at the Rio Earth Summit, assuring his audience that: "community-based ecotourism" forms the government's main marketing and development thrust.

But it is far from clear that Belize has successfully resisted the 'seductions of mass tourism' as Godfrey claims. The dream is fading of a Belizean-controlled industry in tune with the local environment and cultural traditions. Instead, Belizean control is being sold off to the highest bidder. As an advertisement for Ambergris Caye's Club Caribbean in the US publication *Belize Currents* claims: 'own your own piece of paradise ..... Values are starting to soar'.

As foreign control of both small and large tourism enterprises increases, and as large tourism-development proposals surface that will inevitably wreak irreparable damage on the environment, tourism in Belize appears to be spinning out of control. Belize and Belizeans, as Amandala's editor concludes from the Hatchet Cay debacle, 'are beginning to be trampled in the rush by those who regard our laws and traditions as inconvenient at best, and our sovereignty as theirs.'

Chapter 5

Promoting Sustainable Development and Combating Poverty: Socio-Culturally Sensitive Programmes

INTRODUCTION

Many early studies concerned with the social and cultural impacts of tourism highlighted the costs rather than seeking a more balanced approach (Pearce 1989). Ryan (1991) has questioned whether this gradually encroaching damage to lifestyles and to values, as well as to the whole culture of the destination area, is inevitable. There is little doubt that socio-cultural factors are an important attraction for tourists, since 'myths and fantasies' (Shaw and Williams 1994, 167–8) shape a great deal of tourism advertising and publicity and thereby influence consumption patterns. Early tourists and modern explorers (Shaw and Williams 1994, Ousby 1990) have sought authenticity through the discovery of a 'Golden Age' in ancient or distinctive cultures. At the other end of the scale the tourist can be willing to accept modern and unauthentic environments created by the tourism industry for a mass market with limited financial resources and time (Urry 1990). Obviously the type of contact, characterized by the varying nature of tourism and tourists, will be one of the factors which influence the form and extent of the impact evident in the destination area. Other important influences include: the types and strengths of the beliefs and cultural systems of the hosts; the psychological effects of exceeding the carrying capacity at the destination; the transitory nature of the relationship between hosts and guests that is often exacerbated by barriers of language and/or race; the seasonality of tourism; and the implications for behaviour that stem from the fact that while the tourists are on holiday the local people are at work, which makes encounters between them even more unequal (Lea 1988, Pearce 1989, Ryan 1991).

A summary of the costs and benefits of the social and cultural impacts of tourism is given in Box 5.1 and an overview is provided in the reading from Shaw and Williams. In Box 5.2 some of the underlying problems are examined more closely, together with the consequences and possible action to reduce threats and thereby increase sustainability. A selection of illustrations of some of the ideas presented in this figure are to be found in the readings for this section. These include the often-quoted damaging effects of sex tourism in South-East Asia and an assessment of both the benefits and costs to culture as a result of tourism development in the Caribbean islands.

BOX 5.1 SOCIAL AND CULTURAL IMPACTS OF TOURISM

CULTURAL IMPACTS

COSTS

1. Disappearance, degradation or commoditization leading to a loss of authenticity of:
   • art and music
   • handicrafts
   • dance
   • ceremonies
   • architecture
   • dress
   • food

BENEFITS

1. Renaissance and/or retention of:
   • art
   • handicrafts
   • dance
   • ceremonies

2. Restoration of monuments

SOCIAL IMPACTS

COSTS

1. Local resentment resulting from the 'demonstration effect'

2. Moral problems:
   • crime
   • prostitution
   • gambling
   • decline of traditional beliefs and religion
3. Health problems, eg Aids
4. Strains on local hospitality become intolerable
5. Employment in tourism can be dehumanizing
6. Adverse effects on family and community life
7. Neo-colonialism
8. Unbalanced population structures

BENEFITS

1. Tourists gain through relaxation and recreation, a change of environment and social contact with others

2. Locals gain through:
   • impetus to modernization
   • women given a level of independence
   • people break out of traditional, restrictive roles

Sources: Mathieson and Wall (1982), Pearce (1989), Ryan (1991)

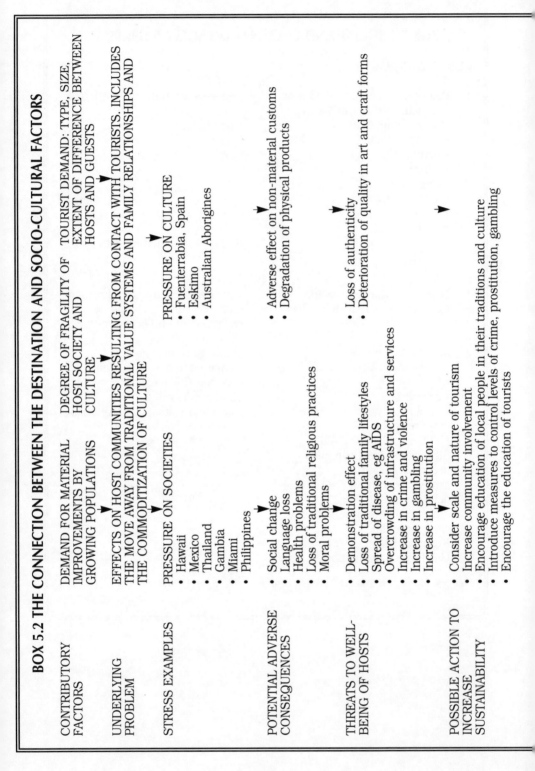

BOX 5.2 THE CONNECTION BETWEEN THE DESTINATION AND SOCIO-CULTURAL FACTORS

CONTRIBUTORY FACTORS	DEMAND FOR MATERIAL IMPROVEMENTS BY GROWING POPULATIONS	DEGREE OF FRAGILITY OF HOST SOCIETY AND CULTURE	TOURIST DEMAND: TYPE, SIZE, EXTENT OF DIFFERENCE BETWEEN HOSTS AND GUESTS
UNDERLYING PROBLEM	EFFECTS ON HOST COMMUNITIES RESULTING FROM CONTACT WITH TOURISTS. INCLUDES THE MOVE AWAY FROM TRADITIONAL VALUE SYSTEMS AND FAMILY RELATIONSHIPS AND THE COMMODITIZATION OF CULTURE		
STRESS EXAMPLES	PRESSURE ON SOCIETIES • Hawaii • Mexico • Thailand • Gambia • Miami • Philippines	PRESSURE ON CULTURE • Fuenterrabia, Spain • Eskimo • Australian Aborigines	
POTENTIAL ADVERSE CONSEQUENCES	• Social change • Language loss • Health problems • Loss of traditional religious practices • Moral problems	• Adverse effect on non-material customs • Degradation of physical products	
THREATS TO WELL-BEING OF HOSTS	• Demonstration effect • Loss of traditional family lifestyles • Spread of disease, eg AIDS • Overcrowding of infrastructure and services • Increase in crime and violence • Increase in gambling • Increase in prostitution	• Loss of authenticity • Deterioration of quality in art and craft forms	
POSSIBLE ACTION TO INCREASE SUSTAINABILITY	• Consider scale and nature of tourism • Increase community involvement • Encourage education of local people in their traditions and culture • Introduce measures to control levels of crime, prostitution, gambling • Encourage the education of tourists		

REFERENCES

Lea, J (1988) *Tourism and Development in the Third World*, Routledge, London

Mathieson, A and Wall, G (1982) *Tourism. Economic, Physical and Social Impacts*, Longman, Harlow

Ousby, I (1990) *The Englishman's England*, Cambridge University Press, Cambridge

Pearce, D (1989) *Tourist Development* 2nd ed, Longman, Harlow

Ryan, C (1991) *Recreational Tourism*, Routledge, London

Shaw, G and Williams, A M (1994) *Critical Issues in Tourism. A Geographical Perspective*, Blackwell, Oxford

Urry, J (1990) *The Tourist Gaze. Leisure and Travel in Contemporary Societies*, Sage Publications, London

Individual Consumption of Tourism

Gareth Shaw and Allan M Williams

THE SOCIOCULTURAL IMPACT OF TOURISTS

The changes brought about by host–guest encounters are transmitted through both social and cultural impacts, the dimensions of which are indicated in Figure 5.1. In reality, as Mathieson and Wall (1982) explain, it is extremely difficult to disentangle such sociocultural impacts, although for the sake of clarity we can examine some of the specific areas of change.

One of the simplest but most widely used frameworks for describing the effects of tourists on a host society is Doxey's (1976) so-called index of irritation. This represents the changing attitudes of the host population to tourism in terms of a linear sequence of increasing irritation as the number of tourists grow (Figure 5.2). In this perspective host societies in tourist destinations pass through stages of euphoria, apathy, irritation, antagonism and loss in the face of tourism development. The progression through this sequence is determined both by the compatability of each group – which is related to culture, economic status, race and nationality – as well as by the sheer numbers of tourists (Turner and Ash 1975). Indeed, one of the most important factors in the growth of hostility to tourism relates to the physical presence of large numbers of tourists. This numerical impact is clearly relative to the size and spatial distribution of the host population, as is evidenced by some of the smaller island economies: the ratio of tourists to host population ranges from 15.4 per 100 in Samoa to almost 33 per 100 in the Maldives (Crandall 1987).

A further underlying factor is the so-called 'demonstration effect', which is the adoption by local residents, especially young people, of tourist behaviour and consumption patterns (Rivers 1973). Such a process can have some benefits if

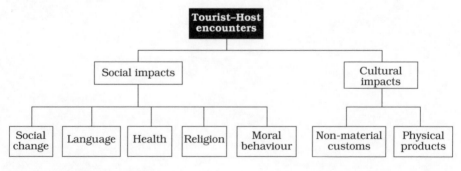

Source: modified from Lea (1988)

Figure 5.1 *The dimensions of tourist–host encounters*

Levels of host irritation

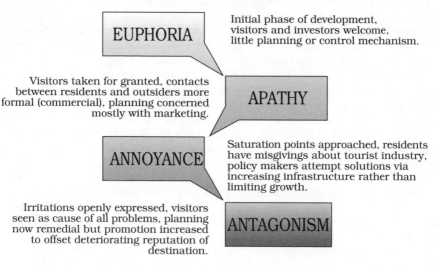

EUPHORIA

Initial phase of development, visitors and investors welcome, little planning or control mechanism.

Visitors taken for granted, contacts between residents and outsiders more formal (commercial), planning concerned mostly with marketing.

APATHY

ANNOYANCE

Saturation points approached, residents have misgivings about tourist industry, policy makers attempt solutions via increasing infrastructure rather than limiting growth.

Irritations openly expressed, visitors seen as cause of all problems, planning now remedial but promotion increased to offset deteriorating reputation of destination.

ANTAGONISM

Figure 5.2 *Doxey's index of irritation*

local people are encouraged to get a better education in order to improve their living standards. However, most evidence points to the social disbenefits as locals adopt the marks of affluence paraded by tourists, and live beyond their means. As part of this adoption process, the host population often starts to demand more luxury items which tend to be imported goods, thereby generating an economic drain on the local economy (Clevedon 1979).

The adoption of foreign values also leads to what Jafari (1973) has described as a premature departure to modernization, producing rapid and disruptive changes in the host society. Under these circumstances social tension develops as the hosts become subdivided between those adopting new values (usually young people and those deeply involved in the local tourism economy), as opposed to those retaining a traditional way of life. Such social dualism has been recorded by Smith (1977) in her study of Eskimo communities, and by Greenwood (1976) in rural Spain; while Lundberg's (1974) studies of Hawaii and Cowan's (1977) work on the Cook Islands detected societal disruptions in the form of increases in divorce rates and split families. These changes in family life are often brought about through increases in rural–urban (resort) migration, as individuals search for employment, and an increasing number of women enter the paid workforce.

The societal changes brought about by tourists are not always easy to isolate from other 'modernizing' influences, but they appear to impact on a range of social elements (Figure 5.3). It is not the intention of this chapter to review all of these, but rather to identify certain key features. Indeed, in certain areas, such as language, only limited research on the impact of tourists has been undertaken (White 1974; Mathieson and Wall 1982). In contrast, considerable and growing attention has been directed towards the moral changes attributed to tourism, particularly the rise in crime (Nicholls 1976, Pizam 1982, Chesney-Lind and Lind 1985), gambling (Pizam and Pokela 1988), prostitution (Graburn 1983, Fish 1984) and most recently the spread of AIDS through sex tourism (Cohen 1988a).

Given the difficulties in establishing tourism's role in changing the moral standards of host societies, it is not surprising that many of the early studies were empirically based and, at the same time, cautious over their findings. However, despite some methodological problems, Jud (1975) was able to present strong evidence of a positive relationship between tourism and crime in Mexico, while studies by McPheters and Stronge (1974) in Miami focused on the seasonality of crime. Within host societies in developing countries large differences between the incomes of hosts and guests, often highlighted in the demonstration effect, lead to increased frustration in the local community, which sometimes spills over as crimes against tourists (Chesney-Lind and Lind 1985). In turn, this frustration and friction is influenced by the volume of tourists, which obviously varies over the season. Thus, Rothman's (1978) study of resorts in Delaware showed massive seasonal changes in crime, which increased fivefold over a 12-month period.

Surveys amongst British tourists by the Consumer Association have revealed that the Caribbean tops the theft league, with tourists having a 1 in 14 chance of having their property stolen. Similarly high figures are recorded in the Gambia, while in Spain the risk falls to 1 in 30. As more tourists venture to an increasing number of destinations, crime does appear to be increasing, so some travel companies, such as Hogg Robinson and Tradewinds (a specialist long-haul company), even issue warnings of world trouble-spots. As the Tradewinds brochure puts it, 'beauty seldom comes without a price', although of course the price is paid by both tourists and the local community. Not all crime is directed at the tourists; indeed, many research projects have found that local people are increasingly the victims (Rothman 1978). In some circumstances the tourists themselves behave in extremely anti-social and criminal ways: as witnessed in many Spanish coastal resorts throughout the late 1980s and early 1990s, and as recorded earlier within the provincial nature parks of Canada (White et al 1978).

In their review of tourism and prostitution, Mathieson and Wall (1982, 149) suggested four main hypotheses that may be related. One was locational, in that tourism development often creates environments which attract prostitutes. The second was societal and related to the breaking of normal bonds of behaviour by tourists when away from home – circumstances conducive to the expansion of prostitution. A third hypothesis is related to economic aspects and the employment opportunities offered by prostitution to women, which may upgrade their economic status. Finally, they suggest that tourism may be a mere scapegoat for a general decline in moral standards. They go on to conclude their review with the idea that there is a lack of firm evidence concerning connections between tourism and prostitution. Recent reports have, however, exposed the development of a fully fledged 'sex tourist' industry (Lea 1988).

Sex tourism is largely focused on parts of South-East Asia, especially Thailand, the Philippines and South Korea (primary areas), together with secondary areas throughout Indonesia (Seager and Olsen 1986). The clients are normally men and the prostitutes are usually women in the particular division of labour. Tourists participating in this trade – either as individuals, small groups of friends or as employees offered a company bonus (often Japanese, as Blasing (1982) points out) – are sold holidays through sex-tour brochures. These thinly disguise the actual prostitution market by images such as 'Thailand is a world full of extremes, and the possibilities are limitless. Anything goes in this exotic country – especially when it comes to girls' (Heyzer 1986, 53).

Attempts to quantify the scale of prostitution in places such as Thailand or the Philippines are difficult, considering the nature of the activity and its supposed illegality. The numbers of masseuses and prostitutes in Bangkok are estimated to be between 100,000 and 200,000 (Phongpaichit 1980), while other studies have recorded at least 977 establishments in the same city which are associated with prostitution (Heyzer 1986). The driving force behind such developments appears to be economic, since young female prostitutes can earn at least twice as much in the so-called hospitality industry as in other forms of employment. As Heyzer (1986) explains, although tourism increases the dividends of the prostitution trade it is not totally responsible for it. Certainly in Thailand the trade in female sexuality is supported by a complex network of ideological, economic and political systems, identifying three main reasons why Thai society sanctions this high level of prostitution. These revolve around employment discrimination against females in most formal sectors of employment, the economic crises facing many rural areas from where most prostitutes are drawn, and the breakdown of many marriages, which leaves women cut off from traditional society. In Thailand, however, there are noticeable changes in the tourist industry, with a decrease since 1987 in single male tourists (usually associated with the sex tourism industry) and an increase in family tourism. This, as Cohen (1988) argues, is entirely due to the fear of contracting AIDS, and to the authorities placing greater stress on the cultural and natural attractions of the country.

Most cultures hold a fascination for tourists, who tend to be attracted by a number of overlapping cultural elements (Box 5.3). Of particular importance to tourists are those forms of culture which are based around physical objects, the purchasing of local crafts, visiting cultural sites and folk culture as reflected in daily life or special festivals (Mathieson and Wall 1982, 159). There have been numerous anthropological studies on tourism and culture (see Jafari 1989), although two main areas of interest can be identified. The first follows the ideas already discussed on societal change, and concerns the processes of acculturation, which refers to the degree of cultural borrowing between two contact cultures (Nunez 1977). An alternative conceptual approach to this theme is through the concept of 'cultural drift', as discussed by Collins (1978). Under the seasonal and

---

BOX 5.3 MAIN ELEMENTS OF CULTURE THAT ATTRACT TOURISTS

- Handicrafts
- Traditions
- History of a region   } These tend to be ranked
- Architecture   as most important by tourists
- Local food
- Art and music
- 'Ways of life'
- Religion
- Language
- Dress – traditional costumes

Source: modified from Ritchie and Zins (1978)

---

intermittent contacts that characterize host-tourist relations, cultural drift assumes that changes in the host culture are at first temporary and then exploitive. Obviously, the degree to which acculturation or cultural drift occurs is strongly related to the patterns of host-tourist encounters, as discussed in the previous section.

The second group of studies relates to the marketing and commodification of culture, as traditional ways of life become commercialized for tourist consumption (de Kadt 1979, Cohen 1988b). In some of the initial studies of the commoditization of culture by tourism, Greenwood (1977) observed, in the Spanish Basque town of Fuenterrabia, that local rituals lost all meaning when repeatedly staged for money. His more general conclusions were that local culture could be commoditized by anyone, often without the consent of local people who would, in most cases, be exploited. The destruction of local cultural products, whether rituals or craftwork, leads to what MacCannell (1973) termed 'staged authenticity'. In its most basic form it is associated with 'airport art', cheap imitation products sold to tourists as local craftwork (Graburn 1967) or fake rituals that stress exotic local customs (Boorstin 1964). Furthermore, Cohen (1988b) suggests that in some instances a contrived cultural product may, over time, become recognized as authentic both by tourists and, more importantly, by local people. This emergent authenticity has been recorded by Cornet (1975) in the case of a supposed revival of an ancient Inca festival in Cuzco. This process is also frequently to be found at the heart of many revitalized local craft industries.

There are examples of the positive impacts of tourism on local cultures mainly through the revival of craft activities, and in many circumstances these can be strongly related to the concept of emergent authenticity. Within this context Graburn's (1967) study of the emergence of Eskimo soapstone carvings provides a ready example, as does Deitch's (1977) work on the art forms of Indians in southwest America. But, of course, for each example of a more positive interplay between tourism and culture, even though such impacts derive from the process of emergent authenticity, the literature contains many more cases of negative impacts (Mathieson and Wall 1982).

Cohen (1988a) has argued that many of these studies and, indeed, Greenwood's early categorical assertion that commoditization removed all meaning from cultural products, are over-generalizations. He believes that even though events become tourist-orientated, they may still retain meanings for local people, and he argues that such impacts need to be submitted to more detailed empirical examinations, especially of a comparative nature. Such studies would make it possible to identify the conditions under which cultural meanings are preserved or emergent, as opposed to those environments under which tourism destroys culture. This debate takes us back to an assessment of tourism consumption and behaviour, which in turn calls for a reworking of tourist typologies.

REFERENCES

Blasing, A L (1982) "Prostitution tourism from Japan and other Asian countries", Paper presented to Asian Consultation of Trafficking in Women, Manila

Boorstin, O J (1964) *The Image: A Guide to Pseudo-events in America*, Harper and Row, New York

Chesney-Lind, M and Lind, I Y (1985) "Visitors as victims: crimes against tourists in Hawaii", *Annals of Tourism Research*, Vol 13, pp167–91

Clevedon, R (1979) *The Economic and Social Impact of International Tourism on Developing Countries*, EIU Special Report 60, Economist Intelligence Unit, London

Cohen, E (1988a) "Tourism and AIDS in Thailand", *Annals of Tourism Research*, Vol 15, pp467–86

Cohen, E (1988b) "Authenticity and commoditization in tourism", *Annals of Tourism Research*, Vol 15, pp371–87

Collins, L R (1978) "Review of hosts and guests. An anthropology of tourism", *Annals of Tourism Research*, Vol 5, pp278–80

Cornet, J (1975) "African art and authenticity", *African Art*, Vol 9, pp52–5

Cowan, G (1977) "Cultural impact of tourism with particular reference to the Cook Islands", in B R Finney and K A Watson (eds), *A New Kind of Sugar*, Center for South Pacific Studies, University of Santa Cruz, Santa Cruz, pp79–85

Crandall, J (1987) "The social impact of tourism on developing regions and its measurement", in J R B Ritchie and C R Goeldner (eds), *Travel, Tourism and Hospitality Research: a Handbook for Managers and Researchers*, John Wiley, New York

de Kadt, E (ed) (1979) *Tourism: Passport to Development*, Oxford University Press, Oxford

Deitch, L I (1977) "The impact of tourism upon the arts and crafts of the Indians of the Southwestern United States" in V L Smith (ed), *Hosts and Guests: an Anthropology of Tourism*, University of Pennsylvania Press, Philadelphia

Doxey, G V (1976) "When enough's enough: the natives are restless in Old Niagara", *Heritage Canada*, Vol 2, pp26–7

Fish, M (1984) "On controlling sex sales to tourists: commentary on Graburn and Cohen", *Annals of Tourism Research*, Vol 11, pp615–17

Graburn, N H H (1967) "The Eskimos and airport art", *Trans-Action*, Vol 4, pp28–33

Graburn, N H H (1983) "Tourism and prostitution", *Annals of Tourism Research*, Vol 10, pp437–43

Greenwood, D J (1976) "Tourism as an agent of change", *Annals of Tourism Research*, Vol 3, pp128–42

Greenwood, D J (1977) "Culture by the pound: an anthropological perspective on tourism as cultural commoditization", in V L Smith (ed), *Hosts and Guests*, University of Pennsylvania Press, Philadelphia

Heyzer, N (1986) *Working Women in South East Asia*, Open University Press, London

Jafari, J (1973) "Role of tourism in the socio-economic transformation of developing countries", Cornell University Press, Ithaca, New York

Jafari, J (1989) "Sociocultural dimensions of tourism: an English language literature review", in J Bustrzanowski (ed), *Tourism as a Factor of Change: A Sociocultural Study*, Economic Coordination Centre for Research and Documentation in Social Sciences, Vienna, pp17–60

Jud, G D (1975) "Tourism and crime in Mexico", *Social Science Quarterly*, Vol 56, pp324–30

Lea, J (1988) *Tourism and Development in the Third World*, Routledge, London

Lundberg, D E (1974) "Caribbean tourism: social and racial tensions", *Cornell Hotel and Restaurant Administration Quarterly*, Vol 15, pp82–7

MacCannell, D (1973) "Staged authenticity: arrangements of social space in tourist settings", *American Sociological Review*, Vol 79, pp589–603

Extract 1: G Shaw and A M Williams

McPheters, L R and Stronge, W B (1974) "Crime as an environmental externality of tourism: Florida", *Land Economics*, Vol 50, pp288–92

Mathieson, A and Wall, G (1982) *Tourism: Economic, physical and social impacts*, Longman, London

Nicholls, L L (1976) "Tourism and crime: A conference", *Annals of Tourism Research*, Vol 3, pp176–82

Nunez, T A (1977) "Touristic studies in anthropological perspectives", in V L Smith (ed) *Hosts and Guests: an Anthropology of Tourism*, University of Pennsylvania Press, Philadelphia

Phongpaichit, P (1980) "Rural women of Thailand", *ISIS International Bulletin* No 13, International Labour Office, Geneva

Pizam, A (1982) "Tourism manpower: The state of the art", *Journal of Travel Research*, Vol 21, pp5–9

Pizam, A and Pokela, J (1988) "The perceived impacts of casino gambling on a community", *Annals of Tourism Research*, Vol 12, pp147–65

Ritchie, J R and Zins, M (1978) "Culture as a determinant of the attractiveness of a tourist region", *Annals of Tourism Research*, Vol 5, pp252–67

Rivers, P (1973) "Tourist troubles", *New Society*, Vol 23, p250

Rothman, R A (1978) "Residents and transients: community reaction to seasonal visitors", *Journal of Travel Research*, Vol 16, pp8–13

Seager, J and Olsen, A (1986) *Women in the World: an International Atlas*, Pan, London

Smith, V L (ed) (1977) *Hosts and Guests: An Anthropology of Tourism*, University of Pennsylvania Press, Philadelphia

Turner, L and Ash, J (1975) *The Golden Hordes: International Tourism and the Pleasure Periphery*, Constable, London

White, P E (1974) "The social impact of tourism on host communities: a study of language change in Switzerland", Research paper No 9, School of Geography, University of Oxford

White, P, Wall, G and Priddle, G (1978) "Anti-social behaviour in Ontario Provincial Parks", *Recreational Research Review*, Vol 2, pp13–25

Sex Tourism in South-East Asia

C Michael Hall

INTRODUCTION

There are undoubtedly few issues in the study of international tourism more emotive and prone to sensationalism than that of sex tourism. Sex tourism may be defined as tourism where the main purpose of motivation is to consummate commercial sexual relations (Graburn, 1983). Sex tourism is an overt component of the touristic attractiveness of several countries of South-east Asia, with the tourism flow from tourist generating regions being partially motivated by prostitution (O'Grady 1981, Jurgensen 1987). According to Gay (1985, p34), 'Between 70 and 80 per cent of male tourists who travel from Japan, the United States, Australia, and Western Europe to Asia do so solely for the purpose of sexual entertainment'. In many countries of the region, sex tourism is 'becoming one of the most pressing social issues ... tourism prostitution in South-east Asia ... has become a multinational sex industry' (Matsui 1987, p29).

Sex tourism emerged as a legitimate area of Third World tourism studies as academic perspectives shifted 'from a generally supportive and technocratic approach to tourism's role in development to some questioning of its overall efficacy and the prevalence of its negative social impacts' (Lea 1981, p19). The study of sex tourism potentially unites many of the major research concerns of students of Third World tourism. According to Richter (1989, 2):

> the most prominent tourist-related issues tend to be associated with the exploitation of women, the advantages and disadvantages of tourism as a means of economic development, and the problems poor nations have in retaining control over their own tourism destiny.

Nevertheless, as the following discussion demonstrates, substantial methodological barriers remain in any study of this controversial area.

The study of sex tourism also has practical significance. The spread of disease, race relations issues, the connection of sex tourism to international crime, and the cultural impacts of tourism are all emerging as areas of concern for both government and industry. The appearance of new forms of sexually transmitted diseases, particularly AIDS (Acquired Immune Deficiency Syndrome), creates substantial problems for the tourism industry and for tourism generating and receiving countries, especially at those destinations where sexual attractions are a major determinant of tourism flow (Cockburn 1988a, 1988b). Similarly, negative responses to international tourists by residents because of sex tourism may discourage international visitation to particular destinations and harm international relations. [...]

Extract 2: *C M Hall*

Third World sex tourism

The relationship between tourism and prostitution has come to be regarded as particularly strong in the Third World (de Kadt 1979, O'Grady 1981). A primary attraction is the important cost differential that exists in the provision of both tourist and sexual services in the Third World and in the industrialized world. This differential, with the attraction of the exotic, provides a drawcard to sex tourists in a large number of Third World destinations and has been reported in Africa (Harrell-Bond 1978, Crush and Wellings 1983), Latin America (Roebuck and McNamara 1973), and the Caribbean (Matthews 1978, Bélisle and Hoy 1980, Ennew 1986). In the case of South-east Asia, the differential has also served to act as an inventive for the use of South-east Asian women in Japanese and European brothels. According to Matsui (1987), '100,000 women per year are arriving from the Philippines, Thailand, South Korea and Taiwan to support the Japanese sex industry'.

In Asia, despite strict Islamic laws forbidding prostitution, such countries as Bangladesh and Pakistan have major red light districts. Trafficking in women has become a serious social problem in Nepal where, because of the extreme marginality of much of the country, large numbers of women are being sent to India. Matsui (1987) states that approximately 50,000 Nepali women are being exploited in Bombay's Falkland Avenue and other brothel districts. However, while tourists and visiting businessmen do frequent these districts, the indigenous form of prostitution has long been established.

As in the case of Sri Lanka, there is perhaps some evidence that the demonstration effect of tourism may lead some men and women into prostitution (Ahmed 1986). Similarly, research by D Jones (1986) illustrates that the customers of Balinese brothels were mainly Balinese and other Indonesians. Prostitution for overseas tourists generally occurred on the beach or was provided by call-girls on a charter basis (similar to Thailand). Brothel prostitution and chartering employed very few local girls. Outdoor soliciting employed few local girls on a full-time basis, but did attract local part-timers, often of school age. Therefore, in the case of Bali, prostitution was not caused by tourism, but had changed ' its form in some senses in response to tourist demand' (Jones, D 1986, 247).

Despite Islamic laws prohibiting prostitution, tourism prostitution also exists in Malaysia, particularly Penang and Kuala Lumpur. Hong (1985) argued that sex tourism to Malaysia would grow in relation to the demands of the increasing number of Japanese tourists. However, she went on to note that the rate of STD infections was also increasing, with the tourist destination of Penang having the highest rate of infection. The growth of prostitution in Malaysia is perhaps associated with the perception among many Westerners that subservient females and free sex are more readily available in South-east Asia and the Pacific than other regions (Thitsa 1980). Indeed, advertising for many of the Asian and Pacific nations openly plays on the notion of the 'exotic orient', South Sea romanticism and the image of a 'lost paradise' which has existed since the seventeenth and eighteenth centuries (Lea 1988). For instance, Davidson (1985, 18) reported a Frankfurt advertisement that stated, 'Asian women are without desire for emancipation, but full of warm sensuality and the softness of velvet'.

In South-east Asia, prostitution clearly existed before the arrival of tourists. One of the ironies of the current Japanese involvement in sex tourism is that the Japanese used to export their own prostitutes, *Kara-Yuki San*, to their colonies.

These bonded Japanese women were sent abroad to serve as prostitutes in ports frequented by Japanese merchants and soldiers. However, in the 1920s the Japanese Government issued the Overseas Prostitution Prohibition Order and, in 1958, legal prostitution in Japan was prohibited. As a consequence, women from the former colonies 'are now imported into Japan as prostitutes' (Graburn 1983, 440). The fast-developing Japanese tourist industry has allowed the Japanese Mafia, the Yakusa, to become well established in Bangkok, Seoul, Hong Kong and Hawaii, with the result that 'almost the whole of Japan's current sex scene is Yakusa controlled, if not directly, then by minor linkage' (Lamont-Brown 1982, 335).

The post-war development of the new international division of labour has meant radical restructuring of the traditional economies of the South-east Asian region. The influx of rural women to urban centres to support village families has led to the marginalization of female participation in the labour market. In the light manufacturing industries of the electronics revolution and in the sex industries, women have been integrated into the global economy. Indeed, Ong (1985) argued that women who have lost jobs in the industrialized sector have been forced to seek work in hotels and brothels. Nevertheless, while the earning power of a prostitute may be relatively high for a short period of time and economically lucrative 'compared to other types of occupation in the industrial or services sector' (Truong 1983, 543), the costs are also extremely high. In general, health services are of a poor standard and there is a lack of protective legislation for sex workers. Therefore, the prostitute's economic gains need to be weighed 'against the psychological and social damage which their work and life style inflict upon them' (Cohen 1983, 424).

Sex tourism might be regarded as a series of linkages involving a 'legally marginalized form of commoditization (sexual services) within a national industry (entertainment), essentially dependent on, but with a dynamic function in, an international industry (travel)' (Truong 1983, 544). In South-east Asia, the institutionalization of sex tourism commenced with the prostitution associated with American military bases and Japanese colonialism and has now become transformed through the internationalization of the regional economies into a major item of systematized foreign trade. Technically, prostitution is illegal in many South-east Asian countries, but the law is poorly enforced. The prevailing sentiment appears to be, 'that what a tourist does in the hotel room, is none of the authorities' business' (Senftleben 1986, 22), particularly when it results in economic returns.

THE EVOLUTION OF SEX TOURISM IN SOUTH-EAST ASIA

The evolution of sex tourism in the region has gone through four distinct stages. The first stage is that of indigenous prostitution, in which women have been subjected to concubinage and bonded prostitution within the patriarchal nature of the majority of Asian societies.

The second stage is that of economic colonialism and militarization, where prostitution is a formalized mechanism of dominance and a means of meeting the sexual needs of occupation forces (primarily American and Japanese). In this stage, the occupied culture's general acceptance of various forms of prostitution has been used as a justification for economic or military enforced prostitution. In addition, this stage commences the economic dependency of host societies on the selling of sexual services as a means of economic development.

The third stage is marked by the substitution of international tourists for occupation forces. Following periods of occupation and the restructuring of traditional economies within the post-war international economic order, sex tourism becomes a formalized mechanism for obtaining foreign exchange and furthering national development. A common element in this stage is the authoritarian nature of governments during periods in which sex tourism has been promoted. It is possible that the denial of individual rights by authoritarian regimes may encourage the perspective that individuals are sexual commodities to be utilised for advancing the national economic good.

The fourth, and current, stage for most of the nations of the region is that of rapid economic development. In this stage, many of the primary goals of economic development have been attained or are at least within sight. However, it is as yet unknown whether increased standards of living will reduce dependency on sex tourism or whether the growth of consumerism will become a new factor in the maintenance of the sex tourism industry. In addition, the powerful forces that created the economic, political and ideological framework within which sex tourism operates may take many years to dismantle. [...]

Thailand

Prostitution and concubinage have long been accepted elements of Thai society. Nevertheless, considerable controversy has surrounded the status of women in Thailand (Truong 1983, Davidson 1985). Patriarchal Buddhist culture has allowed concubinage and polygamy to be legitimised and has cast a ready-made framework within which sex tourism can occur. 'The result was an erotic industry promoted by a government hungry for foreign exchange and built upon the solid base of a hundred years of institutionalized prostitution' (O'Malley 1988, 107). In 1957, there were 20,000 prostitutes, by 1964 there were 400,000, and by the early 1980s there were between 500,000 and a million (Phongpaichit 1982, Taylor 1984, Hong 1985). However, while the numbers are large, not all prostitutes cater to sex tourists. Nevertheless, Rogers (1989, 21) argued that tourism 'induces the demand for prostitutes, creates the available supply and hence makes a vicious cycle'.

The north-east and northern provinces of Thailand are sources of many prostitutes. Their economic marginality forces many rural households to depend on remittances provided by migrant girls (Phongpaichit, 1981, 1982). However, the northern provinces remain structurally disadvantaged within the Thai economy (O'Malley, 1988) and, given the lack of economic development in the north, the supply of workers for the sex industry in the nation's urban and industrial centres seems assured. 'The rapid and very uneven development of Thailand has closely integrated militarization, tourism, and industrialization as institutionalized systems of female exploitation' (Ong 1985).

The number of Thai women involved in sex industry activities outside of Thailand is substantial, although exact numbers are difficult to ascertain. Tourists visiting Thailand may obtain 'rented wives' (*mia chao*) who often return to tourist-generating regions, where they may suffer linguistic and social isolation while often being forced to perform sexual services. From a series of case studies of Thai women working as prostitutes in Europe, Sereewat (1983) concluded that the majority had already been working in the sex industry in Thailand, motivated mainly by the need to provide family support, and with a background of failed marriages and a lack of self esteem. However, their reasons for travelling to Europe need to be seen within the social and structural context of sex tourism and prostitution in Thailand rather than as a form of escapism.

The Thai Government places great emphasis on the promotion of tourism to Thailand and has done little to jeopardize the country's sex trade (Mingmongkol 1981, Barang 1988). For instance, Thailand's Vice Premier informed provincial governors that sexual entertainment of tourists was necessary for the creation of jobs (Gay 1985). The 1960 Prostitution Act makes prostitution illegal, but the registration of brothels and massage parlours as eating houses and the payment of protection money to government officials and the police mean that the law is rarely enforced. Nevertheless, AIDS has become a major source of concern to the Thai government. Early in 1988, government screening revealed that 194 people were HIV positive. One year later, the figure had grown to 3,138 people (*Bangkok Post* 1989a). Although the spread of AIDS in Thailand has been essentially drug-related, the sex tourism industry has been recognised as a potential channel of transmission from the drug and homosexual population to the wider heterosexual community (Cohen 1988). A study by the United Nations Fund for Population Activities found that of a sample of 1000 prostitutes, a quarter were regular drug users (Gay 1985). Indeed, despite attempts by the Thai health authorities to encourage safe sex practices, a survey published in November 1988, found that '77 per cent of addicts shared needles, only six per cent of prostitute's customers were using condoms, and 70 per cent of homosexuals still engaged in anal and oral sex, more than half of them with foreigners' (*Bangkok Post* 1989).

Sex tourism represents a major dilemma for the Thai authorities. Although it continues to be a major attraction, and hence a source of foreign currency, they are increasingly worried by Thailand's reputation as the sex capital of Asia. Nevertheless, as long as the gap between city and rural areas continues to widen and real living standards in the country remain low, Thailand's sex industry will thrive. As Richter (1989, 101) observed, 'The tragedy of Thai tourism is that one tawdry segment has been allowed to eclipse so much that is elegant, refined, and exquisite about Thailand'.

Australia and sex tourism

Australia has been a sex tourist-generating region to South-east Asia since the time of the Vietnam war and Australians have become heavily involved in the ownership of brothels and nightclubs and in the organization of sex tours, particularly to the Philippines. Probably the most conspicuous aspect of Australian sex tourism is the bar names, such as Ned Kelly and Waltzing Matilda. Although only Filipinos can hold the permit for a bar and there must be at least 60 per cent Filipino ownership, Australian criminal elements appear to have made substantial investments in the sex industry, with Angeles City being a major area of interest. Bacon (1987, 21) reported that 'Australians now have a financial interest in more than 60 per cent of the 500 bars and 7000 prostitutes around the base, although not one Australian name appears in the local register'.

In the early 1980s, Australia became one of the main destinations for Filipino mail order brides. In 1976, 1596 Filipino women were married to Australians, a figure that rose to 4470 in 1981. Promoted as 'meek, docile, submissive, home oriented and have[ing] tremendous capacities in bed', Filipino women have been sought by many Australian males through pen-pal clubs and mail order bride businesses (Philippine Women's Research Collective 1985, 19). The increase in mail order brides and Filipino marriages has led to considerable controversy over the motivations and status of Filipino women going to Australia, and the subsequent stability of their marriage (Chuah et al 1987). Opposition to marriages occurred because they were arranged and because of the stereotyped view of Asian women as subservient that developed through the debate: 'many wanted Asian wives because they were fed up with the demands Australian women make and their unfaithfulness' (Brown 1980, 10). Undoubtedly, the perception of Filipino women as subservient has substantially contributed to the demand for Filipino brides from Australian males (Shoesmith 1981). However, while the economic and cultural position of women in Filipino society is an import 'supply' factor, other considerations, such as the availability of single Australian males, contributed to the conditions that prompted the growth in arranged marriages.

A further dimension of Australia's involvement in sex tourism has been provided by the rapid growth of inbound tourism to Australia in the 1980s, particularly from Japan. Such destinations as the Gold Coast have witnessed an increase in the amount of tourist-oriented prostitution and Asian girls have often been brought into the country to cater for both Australian and Japanese tourists. As M Jones (1986, 111) contended:

> Modern tourism requires a well-regulated supply of women and the pragmatic Queensland industry knows that these services must be provided, especially if the Coast is to compete with Asia.

Jones' comments were somewhat prophetic and, in 1989, the Gold Coast Chamber of Commerce advocated the legislation and licensing of prostitution in order to attract tourists (Hall forthcoming). Prostitution tourism is an integral part of the tourist product of Australian attractions and events (Hall, 1989). As in South-east Asia, Australian governments are seeking the tourist dollar to promote economic development and overcome balance-of-payments problems. In this climate it would seem unlikely that the contributions of the sex industry to tourism will be disturbed.

CONCLUSION

Tourism-oriented prostitution has become an integral part of the economic base in several regions of South-east Asia. Sex tourism has resulted in people being regarded as commodities. The economic reliance of developing nations on tourism has led to dependence on source areas, incorporated them into the demand structures of the West and Japan, and has impeded the pursuit of autocentric development (Schürmann 1981). The 'tourist first' attitude of many governments and their advisors has transformed the processes of development to place economic 'needs' well ahead of those social concerns, for example, rural–urban migration, which feed into tourism. As Awanohara (1975, 6) commented, 'Japanese travel agents have organized these trips to Asia and not to other countries only because Asian countries allow it. They need the foreign exchange'. Fish (1984a, 1984b) has argued that a more effective mechanism of controlling sex sales to tourists would place a heavier proportion of the costs of law enforcement and sanctions on the hotels, operators and their customers. However, such an approach, built on assumptions of schedules of the elasticity of demand, fails to recognize the broader economic and socio-cultural context within which sex tourism occurs. Such short-term measures as counselling may be useful, but sex tourism demands long-term solutions (Fernand-Laurent 1985). Banning prostitution may be counterproductive and only create even greater hardship for those who engage in it. 'Legislation to protect prostitutes, and to improve their working conditions and occupational health, is preferable to legislation that would deprive them of their livelihood' (Truong 1983, 534).

The sexual relationship between prostitute and client is a mirror image of the dependency of South-east Asian nations on the developed world. The institutionalized exploitation of women within patriarchal societies of South-east Asia has been extended and systematized by the unequal power relationship that exists between genders and between host and advanced capitalist societies (Ong 1985). Demonstrations and rallies against sex tourism are likely to lead to only superficial changes in the sex industry. Profound change can occur only with the removal of the US military presence, a transformation of gender relations, and an economic development strategy that places the host first and lessens the demand for foreign exchange.

REFERENCES

Ahmed, S A (1986) 'Pereptions of the socio-economic and cultural impact of tourism in Sri Lanka', *Canadian Journal of Development Studies*, 7 (2) pp239–55

Awanohara, S (1975) 'Protesting the Sexual Imperialists', *Far Eastern Economic Review*, 87 (21st March), pp5–6

Bacon, W (1987) 'Sex in Manila for Profits in Australia', *Times on Sunday* (19th April), pp21–24

Bangkok Post (1989a) 10th February

Bangkok Post (1989b) 12th August

Barang, M (1988) 'Tourism in Thailand', *South*, December, pp72–73

Bélisle,F J, and Hoy, D R (1980) 'The Perceived Impacts of Tourism by Residents: A Case Study in Santa Marta, Columbia', *Annals of Tourism Research*, 7 (1), pp83–101

Brown, M (1980) 'Spectacular Growth in the Filipino Marriage Market', *Sydney Morning Herald*, 3rd September, p10

Center for Solidarity Tourism (1989) 'Impacts of Tourism in the Philippines', *Contours* 4 (2), p29

Chuah, F, Chuah, L D, Reid-Smith, L, Rice, A and Rowley, K (1987) 'Does Australia have a Filipina Brides Problem?', *Australian Journal of Social Issues*, 22 (4), pp573–83

Cockburn, R (1988a) 'The Geography of Tourism, Part I: The East', *The Geographical Magazine*, 60 (3), pp2–5

Cockburn, R (1988b) 'The Geography of Tourism, Part II: The West', *The Geographical Magazine*, 60 (4), pp44–7

Cohen, E (1982b) 'Thai Girls and Farang Men: The Edge of Ambiguity', *Annals of Tourism Research*, 9 (3), pp403–28

Cohen, E (1988b) 'Tourism and AIDS in Thailand', *Annals of Tourism Research*, 15 (4), pp467–86

Crush, J and Wellings, P (1983) 'The Southern Africa Pleasure Periphery, 1966–1983', *Journal of Modern African Studies*, 21 (4), pp673–98

Davidson, D (1985) 'Women in Thailand', *Canadian Women's Studies*, 16 (1), pp16–19

Ennew, J (1986) *The Sexual Exploitation of Children*, Polity Press, Cambridge

Fernand-Laurent, J (1985) *Activities for the Advancement of Women: Equality, Development and Peace*, Department of International Economic and Social Affairs, United Nations, New York

Fish, M (1984a) 'Deterring Sex Sales to International Tourists: A Case Study of Thailand, South Korea and the Philippines', *International Journal of Comparative and Applied Criminal Justice*, 8 (2), pp175–86

Fish, M (1984b) 'On Controlling Sex Sales to Tourists: Commentary on Graburn and Cohen', *Annals of Tourism Research*, 11 (4), pp615–17

Gay, J (1985) 'The Patriotic Prostitute', *The Progressive*, 49 (3), pp34–6

Graburn, N H H (1983) 'Tourism and Prostitution,' *Annals of Tourism Research*, 10 (3), pp437–42

Hall, C M (1989a) 'Impact of the America's Cup on Fremantle, Western Australia: Implications for the Hosting of Hallmark Events', in Welch, R, ed, *Geography in Action*, Department of Geography, University of Otago, Dunedin, pp74–80

Harrell-Bond, B (1978) 'A Window on an Outside World': Tourism as Development in the Gambia', American Universities Field Staff Reports, No 19, American Universities Field Staff, Hanover

Hong, E (1985) *See the Third World While it Lasts*, Consumers Association of Penang, Penang

Jones, D R W (1986) 'Prostitution and Tourism', in J S Marsh, (ed), *Canadian Studies of Parks, Recreation and Tourism in Foreign Lands*, Occasional Paper 11, Department of Geography, Trent University, Peterborough, pp241–48

Jones, M (1986) *A Shady Place for Shady People: The Real Gold Coast Story*, Allen and Unwin, Sydney

Jurgensen, O (1987) 'Tourism and Prostitution in South-east Asia', *The Manitoba Social Science Teacher*, 14 (1), pp5–12

de Kadt, E (ed) (1979) *Tourism: Passport to Development?*, Oxford University Press, New York and Oxford

Lamont-Brown, R (1982) 'The International Expansion of Japan's Criminal Brotherhood', *Police Journal*, 55 (4), pp355–9

Lea, J (1981) 'Changing Approaches towards Tourism in Africa: Planning and Research Perspectives', *Journal of Contemporary African Studies*, 1 (1), pp19–40

Matsui, Y (1987) 'The Prostitution Areas in Asia: An Experience', *Women in a Changing World*, 24 (November), pp27–32

Matthews, H G (1978) *International Tourism: A Political and Social Analysis*, Schenkman Publishing Company, Cambridge

Mingmongkol, S (1981) 'Official Blessings for the 'Brothel of Asia'', *Southeast Asia Chronicle*, 78 pp24–5

O'Grady, R (1981) *Third World Stopover*, World Council of Churches, Geneva

O'Malley, J (1988) 'Sex Tourism and Women's Status in Thailand', *Loisir et Societe*, 11 (1), pp99–114

Ong, A (1985) 'Industrialisation and Prostitution in Southeast Asia', *Southeast Asia Chronicle*, 96 pp2–6

Philippine Women's Research Collective (1985) *Filipinas for Sale: An Alternative Report on Women and Tourism*, Philippine Women's Research Collective, Quezon City

Phongpaichit, P (1981) 'Bangkok Masseuses: Holding Up the Family Sky', *Southeast Asia Chronicle*, 78 pp15–23

Phongpaichit, P (1982) *From Peasant Girls to Bangkok Masseuses*, Women, Work and Development 2, International Labour Office, Geneva

Richter, L K (1989) *The Politics of Tourism in Asia*, University of Hawaii Press, Hawaii

Roebuck, J and MacNamara, P (1973) 'Ficheras and Free-lancers: Prostitution in a Mexican Border City, *Archives of Sexual Behaviour*, 2 (3), pp231–44

Rogers, J R (1989) 'Clear Links: Tourism and Child Prostitution', *Contours*, 4 (2), pp20–2

Schürmann, H (1981) 'The effects of international tourism on the regional development of third world countries', *Applied Geography and Development*, 18, pp80–93

Sentfleben, W (1986) 'Tourism, Hot Spring Resorts and Sexual Entertainment: Observations from Northern Taiwan – A Study in Social Geography', *Philippine Geographical Journal*, 30 (Jan–June), pp21–41

Sereewat, S (1983) *Prostitution: Thai-European Connection: An Action-Oriented Study*, Commission on the Churches' Participation in Development, World Council of Churches, Geneva

Shoesmith, D (1981) 'The Fantasy Tourism Industry and Prostitution in the Philippines', *Asian Bureau Australia*, October, pp4–5

Taylor, D (1984) 'Cheap Thrills', *New Internationalist*, 142, p14

Thitsa, K (1980) *Providence and Prostitution: Image and Reality for Women in Buddhist Thailand*, Change International Reports, London

Truong, T D (1983) 'The Dynamics of Sex Tourism: The Cases of South-East Asia', *Development and Change* 14, (4), pp533–53

---

1 When undertaking the research and writing of this chapter it was originally intended to focus largely on the interaction between Australia and South-east Asia. However, because of the nature of Australia's libel laws this section has had to be severely curtailed.

Introduction to Hosts and Guests:
The Anthropology of Tourism
(2nd Edition)

V L Smith

Culture change, in the form of modernization, has made impressive inroads into the backward areas and the poverty pockets of the globe, and the process is both ongoing and accelerating. The generations born after World War II adhere far less to traditional values and mores; they seek active participation in the coming 'new order' and want to share in its benefits. Cheap radios and cassettes have brought world news and rock singers into native huts and heightened local awareness of, and demand for, roads, clean water, better medicine, electricity and entertainment. The facade of cultural homogenization appears on almost every village main street (including those of the Kuna, the Eskimo, Tana Toraja, and Bali): hamburger stands, coffeehouses, video stores, and repair shops for motorbikes, cars, and trucks. Thus the question that haunted most authors of the earlier edition of this book and other researchers in tourism a decade ago (namely 'Is tourism a major agent of culture change?') seems to have been largely resolved. The guide I met in Tana Toraja responded to that question with a straightforward) 'Tourism is not important in our lives – we see the world on television every night'; significantly, too, Kotzebue Eskimo operate their own media stations.

The tourist trade does not have to be culturally damaging. Many tourists want to forsake the 'tourist bubble' and seek opportunities to meet and become acquainted with local people. The Ecumenical Coalition on Third World Tourism (ECTWT), headquartered in Bangkok, has sought ways to curtail some of the negative effects of tourism. Prostitution, drug abuse, alcoholism, and juvenile homosexuality – though not necessarily caused by tourism *per se* – are increased due to the presence of many outsiders (as is also true of the areas surrounding army bases). In Sri Lanka ECTWT reports, for example, that children who 'beg' at airports and attractions often earn more cash in one day than their farmer–fishermen parents can earn in a month; a factor that serves as a basis for family disruption. An interesting and potentially useful device to prevent the negative cultural impacts is the use of an educational film aboard the numerous charter aircraft that bring many of the visitors to Colombo for a week's vacation. The film portrays insensitive behaviour by the tourists toward religious shrines and towards juveniles, as well as nude bathing on beaches – the latter particularly offensive to the modest Sinhalese.

Tourism can be a bridge to an appreciation of cultural relativity and international understanding. However, catering to guests is a repetitive, monotonous business, and although questions posed by each visitor may be 'new' to him, hosts can become bored as if a cassette has been turned on. If the economic goals of mass tourism are realized and the occasional visitor is replaced by a steady influx, individual guests' identities become obscured and they are labelled 'tourists' who, in turn, may be stereotyped into national character images (Pi-Sunyer, chapter 9). As guests become dehumanized objects that are tolerated for economic gain, tourists have little alternative other than to look upon their hosts only with curiosity, and, too, as objects. To overcome this impersonal attitude, some tour operators are developing 'alternative tourism' formats that feature one-to-one interaction between hosts and guests, including overnight stays in private homes. In a form of cultural mitigation, some major hotel chains have instituted training programs to teach 'service' and 'friendliness' to employees, and provide tangible rewards for the 'employee of the month' who has received the most compliments from guests.

Ethnic and cultural tourism promise the visitor the opportunity to see at least some portions of the indigenous culture. Apparently, some culture traits, such as public rituals, can be shared with outsiders without disruption, at least as long as the numbers of spectators remain small. Social stress becomes apparent, however, when tourism invades the privacy of daily lives, as among Kotzebue Eskimo, or when participants in a ritual are engulfed by grandstands full of paid audiences. Still, modernization is rapidly changing most of the tourist realm. As it does so, many problems previously associated with host-guest relationships are diminishing. Disparities between rich and poor are not as great if for no other reason than the cash flow generated by one or more decades of tourism has provided the means for employees to satisfy some of their material aspirations. Tourism is no longer an oddity, and although the people whose culture is the object of tourism may need to transfer what Nunez (chapter 14) terms 'front stage' in their lives to a private sector, a worldwide cultural homogenization is underway. As a consequence, model cultures become much more important.

THE ROLE OF MODEL CULTURES

Model cultures have been successfully developed as reconstructions of a historic past in, for example, Williamsburg, Plymouthe Plantation, old Sturbridge Village, and Mystic Seaport in the United States, as well as in the many folk museums of Europe. These turn time back a century or two, affording a scale against which visitors can measure progress, and be reminded of the hardships encountered by their forebears. Many are also 'living museums' where schoolchildren may spend a day or two and learn history firsthand. In addition to Hawaii's Polynesian Cultural Center (chapter 13), other ethnographic models include Fiji's Orchid Island, Bangkok's Rose Garden – Thailand in Miniature, and Korea's Folk Village. Smaller versions operate in cities such as Jakarta, Manila, and Cairo. Popular and profitable, these models appear to meet the ethnic expectations of the tourist. Although only a reconstruction of the life-style they had hoped to observe, these models offer a more accurate ethnographic view than is reflected in the modern native culture, and allow the visitor the freedom to wander and photograph at will.

Model cultures also offer another distinct advantage, especially at tourist sites where the physical presence of humans may cause damage. The actual Paleolithic caves of Lascaux (France) with their world-renowned polychrome paintings, are now closed to the public to prevent exfoliation of the paint; however, the surrogate display is in some ways more graphic than the original. Similarly, the Viking settlement at L'Anse aux Meadows in northern Newfoundland would have been destroyed by visitors tramping through the archaeologic pits, but the now-recon-structed village provides a fine interpretive center that documents the Viking ventures into the New World, and fully merits its number one rank on the United Nation's World Patrimony list. Even the spread of popular fantasies, in the Disneylands of Tokyo and Paris, provides forms of model cultures for 'children of all ages' for they too have internal 'theme villages' and fairy-tale motifs.

Further construction of model cultures is to be expected and should be warmly received as long as the models remain reasonably accurate: model cultures have the great advantage of structuring tourist visits to a site away from the daily lives of ordinary people. I, at least, would prefer to visit a Tana Torajan model than an inhabited village, and to photograph paid performers in traditional costumes rather than have individuals demand money for each picture taken, as is the common practice among Panama's San Blas Indians.

COME ONE OR ALL: THE EFFECTS OF NUMBERS

To a host population, tourism is often a mixed blessing: the tourist industry creates jobs and increases cash flow but the tourists themselves can become a physical as well as a social burden, especially as their numbers increase. In addition to the types of tourism suggested earlier, it appears a touristic typology can be drawn, accounting for their numbers, their goals, and their adaptations to local norms (Table 5.1).

Table 5.1 *Frequency of types of tourist and their adaptations to local norms*

Type of Tourist	Numbers of Tourists	Adaptations to Local Norms
Explorer	Very limited	Accepts fully
Elite	Rarely seen	Adapts fully
Off-beat	Uncommon but seen	Adapts well
Unusual	Occasional	Adapts somewhat
Incipient Mass	Steady flow	Seeks Western amenities
Mass	Continuous influx	Expects Western amenities
Charter	Massive arrivals	Demands Western amenities

Explorers quest for discovery and new knowledge but in a shrinking planet, their numbers are sharply restricted. By definition, they are not tourists and traditionally are almost akin to anthropologists living as active participant-observers among 'their' people. They easily accommodate to local norms in housing, food, and life-style, bolstered by an amazing array of Western technology including 'walkie-talkies', dehydrated foods, portable chemical toilets, oxygen tanks, and medicine.

Elite tourists are few in number and usually include individuals who have been 'almost everywhere' and who now, for example, choose to spend US$1500 for a week, to travel by dugout canoe, with a guide, on the Darien River in Panama. They overnight in Kuna Indian homes, sleep in hammocks, get thoroughly bitten by chiggers, eat native food, and chance the tourist 'trots'. They differ from Explorers because they are 'touring' – irrespective of whether they planned the trip in great detail in advance or not, they are using facilities that could be prearranged at home by any travel agent. However, they adapt easily with the attitude that 'if they [the natives] can live that way all their lives, we can, for a week'.

The Off-beat tourist includes those who currently visit Toraja Regency to see the funerals) 'trek' in Nepal, or go alone to Point Hope as part of an Alaskan tour. They seek either to (1) get away from the tourist crowds, or (2) heighten the excitement of their vacation by doing something beyond the norm. In general, they adapt well and 'put up with' the simple accommodations and services provided for the occasional tourist.

The Unusual tourist visits South America on an organized tour, and buys an optional one-day package tour to visit the Kuna Indians, as an alternate to a day shopping in duty-free Panama. By chartered small plane, tour members fly to a coastal airstrip where an American guide provides a motorboat to tour two or three off-shore villages; shopping for *molas* (chapter 4) is encouraged and, for a fee, tourists may photograph the women and/or the interiors of their houses. The tourist tends to be 'interested' in the 'primitive' culture but is much happier with his 'safe' box lunch and bottled soda rather than a native feast.

Incipient Mass tourism is a steady flow of people, and although the numbers are increasing, they usually travel as individuals or in small groups. The tourist industry is only one sector of the total economy, and hotels usually have a mix of guests including domestic travelers and businessmen as well as tour groups. This phase of tourist activity is exemplified by many 'popular' destinations such as Guatemala, or the summer visitors to the Arctic, the latter secure in their guided tour, heated buses, and modern hotels. These tourists seek Western amenities and, totally ignoring the fact that at great expense the hotel room in the Arctic has a private bath, many of these visitors would complain about the 'ring around the bathtub'.

Mass tourism is a continuous influx of visitors who inundate Hawaii most of the year, and other areas at least seasonally, including the European resorts (part III), and Northern Hemisphere 'winter vacation' lands such as coastal Mexico and the Caribbean. Mass tourism is built upon middle-class income and values, and the impact of sheer numbers is high. Because of the diversity of individual tastes and budgets, in Europe, for example, the tourists are everywhere – hitchhiking at the roadside, riding trains with their Eurailpasses, or huddled around a guide who is attempting to be heard above the voices of other guides in some crowded museum. With a 'you get what you pay for' attitude, they fill up hotels of every category, pensions, and hostels *but*, as a common denominator, they expect a trained, multi-lingual hotel and tourist staff to be alert and solicitous to their *wants* as well as to their needs. The 'tourist bubble' of Western amenities is very much in evidence.

Charter tourists arrive en masse, as in Waikiki, and for every 747 planeload, there is a fleet of at least ten big buses waiting to transfer them from the airport to the designated hotel, in the lobby of which is a special Tour Desk to provide itineraries and other group services. Should an individual ask even a simple, 'What time does the tour bus go?,' the immediate answer is, 'What *group* are you with?' The 'you' in the reply is spoken as to a 'living thing' and not as to a personality. Charter tourists wear name tags, are assigned to numbered buses, counted aboard, and continually reminded: 'Be sure to get on the right bus'. Given the requisite organization that makes Charter tourism a high-volume business, to avoid complaints tour operators and hotels have standardized the services to Western (or Japanese) tastes, and there are 'ice machines and soft drinks on every floor'. For Charter tourists, even destination may be of very little importance,

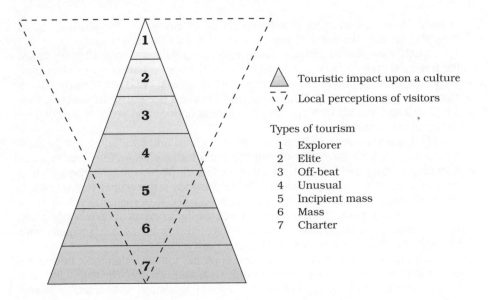

Figure 5.3 *Touristic impact upon a culture*

especially if they won the trip as part of an incentive sales program, or it coincides with tax-free convention travel.

The frequency of tourist types seems to approximate a pyramid (Figure 5.4), in which the bold triangle is a scale of increasing numbers, from top to bottom. An inverse triangle suggests the role of the host culture penetrated by the increased flow of tourists. Explorers and Elite travelers, by virtue of their limited numbers, usually make little impact upon the indigenous culture, for hotels and other services are seldom required. Their presence may be unnoticed except by the few who meet and serve them. The Off-beat and Unusual tourist commonly stays at roadhouses or hotels that locals also use, and gets about by local transportation (including the use of the school bus, for the very occasional groups who visit). The money they spend is a welcome addition, their presence is seldom disruptive, and children may delight in 'talking English' with someone other than their teacher.

However, as the number of tourists progressively increases, it appears different expectations emerge and more facilities are required to handle them. When Charter tourism appears, I suggest that nationality is no longer locally significant, for the only economic base able to generate Charter tourism is Western society, whose members are fast approaching cultural and economic homogeneity.

The stressful contacts between hosts and guests also appear to increase, proportionate to the larger numbers. I believe that the critical point in the development of a successful tourist industry occurs at or near the intersection of the two triangles, when members of Incipient Mass tourism 'seek' Western amenities, with the result that these facilities begin to be economically or even visually important, as 'tourist hotels' and privileged parking places for tour buses. The local culture is probably at the 'Y' in the road, and should decide whether to (a) consciously control or even restrict tourism, to preserve their economic and cultural integrity; or (b) to encourage tourism as a desirable economic goal and restructure their culture to absorb it. The first choice has been made by the economically powerful but socially traditional oil states adjacent to and including Saudi Arabia who refuse tourist visas. Bhutan, the tiny land-locked mountain kingdom in the eastern Himalayas, developed a second alternative (Smith 1981). Given the negative model of adjacent Nepal whose tourism was dominated through the 1970s by the drug cult and 'hippies', Bhutan opened its borders to tourism in 1974, permitting only one thousand visitors per year, each of whom paid a minimum of US$1000 for a week of group travel on a fixed itinerary. By restricting the number of visas issued annually, the Ministry of Tourism hoped to generate hard currency income and also to limit social interaction, so that little direct contact occurred between village Bhutanese and visitors. A 1986 WTO study praised the system and encouraged its perpetuation with little change. However for 1988 the government of Bhutan has closed some monasteries to foreign access because of the 'growing materialism' among monks, which was generated by visitors who thoughtlessly made token gifts of money, candy, pencils, and so forth to young trainees.

Cultural impact studies can serve tourism well and indicate which elements of a specific culture are 'public' and can be marketed as 'local color' without serious disruption. As Greenwood reassesses the Alarde in Spain (chapter 8), the festival has survived economic exploitation. Although now changed in format, its existence has made Fuentarrabia a nationally known tourist destination, and helped preserve it as a community by providing local employment in shops, pensions, and in other services. For many people, small-town living is less expensive and pleasanter among family and friends than life in major urban centres: correspondingly, one of the significant trends in tourism currently, and projected to be of greater importance in decades ahead, is the effort to disperse tourism into the countryside and small towns, to better distribute its economic benefits. In this regard, however, it is imperative that cultural assessment be undertaken to identify potential tourist use, and to develop marketing plans that will maximize the benefits of tourism without negative sociocultural impact.

If a group can survive the transition from Incipient to full-blown Mass tourism, then it may ultimately achieve what Kemper (1976) has termed 'tourist culture', or a process of full accommodation, so that large numbers of tourists are part of the 'regional scenery', as in charter tourism to Hawaii.

Tana Toraja (chapter 7), a highland area in Sulawesi, Indonesia, dramatically illustrates the potentials of tourism *and* the need for fundamental planning. When Europeans first discovered its unique funeral ceremonies (ca 1973), and government recognition that this cultural trait was a marketable commodity followed, Toraja moved from Elite to Charter tourism in only five years. Tourism became a viable economic means for widespread modernization; unfortunately, no one anticipated the demand for grave-marker souvenirs. Restrictions on public access to the sites should have been instituted immediately, for the effigies can be seen effectively from a viewing platform only a few yards distant.

However, tourism and the tourists themselves should not become scapegoats for the malaise of society as a whole. Throughout history and worldwide, the Fausts have sold their souls for a sou. In a world that many social scientists believe to be overpopulated (as does the government of the People's Republic of China), the desperately poor (or those who are simply greedy) will sell whatever they have to those who will buy – even their children, as well as their cultural patrimony. In fairness, one must consider that deep-seated economic problems which have little or nothing to do with tourism exist in many countries, including the US. The case study on Tonga (chapter 5) is instructive here. Urbanowicz points out that the islands are overpopulated, there is no additional land available, and that the importing of goods strains the economy, triggering inflation. However, if the strictures of careful scientific analysis were removed, it would be easy to conclude that food prices soared because of the fourteen thousand air visitors to Tonga in 1985. It is patently easier to blame a nameless, faceless foreigner who comes (and goes) than it is to address and solve fundamental problems.

REFERENCES

Kemper, R V (1978) 'Tourism and regional development in Taos, New Mexico', In *Tourism and economic change*, Studies in Third World Societies No 6, V Smith, (ed), pp89–103, Williamsburg, William and Mary Press, Virginia

Smith, V L (1981) 'Controlled vs uncontrolled tourism: Bhutan and Nepal' RAIN 40 (October), pp4–6.

Social Contact between Tourists and Hosts of Different Cultural Backgrounds

Y Reisinger

INTERACTION DIFFICULTIES IN CROSS-CULTURAL TOURIST–HOST CONTACT

The major interaction difficulties in the tourist–host contact due to cultural differences were found in interpersonal communication (eg polite language usage, expressing feelings and emotions, reactions to criticism, complaining, apologising); non-verbal signals (eg physical contact such as touching, spatial behaviour, facial expressions, gestures, posture, eye contact); patterns of interpersonal interaction (eg greetings, self-disclosure, self-presentation, self-restraint, managing conflict) (Bochner 1982). These differences make the interaction very difficult. The same verbal or non-verbal signals and patterns of interaction have different meanings in various cultures and are likely to be misunderstood. For instance, referring to someone by the first name to show friendliness and a lack of formality in interpersonal relations may be regarded by Australian hosts as polite but may be considered as impolite by Asian tourists. Openly disagreeing or saying 'no' may be considered by Japanese and other Asian tourists as rude; however, Australian hosts may regard it as an acceptable way of behaviour. Touching and slapping on the back may be regarded by Australian hosts as expression of friendliness but may be considered as lack of respect and dignity by Chinese tourists. Gift-giving may be regarded by Japanese tourists as an appreciation of time and effort spent with them; however, Australian hosts may consider it as bribery. Tipping may be regarded by European tourists as a reward for being well served but may be considered as an insult by Australian hosts. Expressing an interest in family matters may be regarded as polite in India and Pakistan but may be considered as rude in Australia. The 'OK' gesture in America may be confused with the Japanese gesture to refer to money (Morsbach 1973). The continuous escort of tourists by hosts everywhere may be viewed by the Chinese hosts as a courtesy. However, American tourists may consider it as an intrusion, lack of freedom in choice of activities, privacy and lack of trust (Wei et al, 1989). The Japanese hosts' willingness to take care of the affairs of their guests in advance and fulfil their needs immediately (Zimmerman 1985, Befu 1971) may be frustrating for American and Australian tourists who know best what their needs are and may regard the Japanese hosts' hospitality with discomfort. The examples of cultural differences in the tourists' and hosts' backgrounds are endless. Stringer (1981) reported that even a different custom of handling cutlery and eating habits may create interaction difficulties between tourists and hosts.

The reasons for interaction difficulties is that when tourists and hosts interact socially in their own culture they know which behaviour is proper and which is wrong. They behave in a way accepted by their respective cultures. They accept proper and reject wrong behaviour. Those who are engaged in socially unacceptable behaviour are considered as ill-mannered. Those who are engaged in socially acceptable behaviour are considered as well-mannered. But when tourists and hosts interact with someone from another culture, they do not know what behaviour is proper and what is wrong. The behaviour which is seen as proper in one culture is not always seen the same way in another culture. Since tourists and hosts are confronted with a culture different from their own, many situations are unfamiliar to them. It is difficult for them to engage in interaction with someone who has different standards of behaviour, a different way of thinking, communicating, doing things, etc. The differences in cultural values, lifestyles, traditions, etc decide how the behaviour of others is interpreted and perceived, whether it is regarded as proper or irritating or even insulting. If the behaviour of others is perceived as proper, it is likely that tourists and hosts will engage in mutual interaction. However, a common reaction to different behaviour of culturally different people is dislike, and one which leads to prejudices. The necessity to adapt to a new culture within a short period of time can cause additional frustration, leading to even more negative feelings about members of the other culture.

Brislin et al (1986) indicated that the major reasons for interactional difficulties are cultural differences in categorization, differentiation, in-group and out-group distinction, and attribution processes. According to the theory of Brislin et al (1986), conflicts arise in cross-cultural tourist–host interaction because there are major differences in the way tourists and hosts categorize the same set of behaviours. Stereotypes develop because tourists and hosts are unable to acquire and categorize appropriately much information about the other culture in a short period of time. Tourists and hosts who have not been exposed to a particular culture's standards or categorization are more likely to impose their own culture's categories on others' categories and use unfamiliar categories wrongly. Tourists and hosts also differentiate between various concepts in a distinct way. For instance, the concept of 'friendship' may have different meanings to American tourists and Chinese hosts. Americans regard friendship as superficial, without obligations. Chinese assume mutual obligations and expect reciprocation (Wei et al, 1989). This often creates false expectations and frustration due to unconfirmed expectations. Tourists and hosts also have different ways of judging others and themselves, according to their own standards.

Insensitivity to cultural differences may cause numerous problems between tourists and hosts. The major cultural problems identified by Wei et al (1989) are: ethnocentrism (belief in the superiority of own culture), communication problems (insufficient fluency in a foreign language, problems related to interpretations and lack of information), dissatisfaction with poor quality service (lack of concern for visitors, lack of tradition of hospitality, lack of interpersonal skills of the hosts), and differences in lifestyle (customs, food, etiquette, developing friendships).

The perception of service quality by tourists is particularly important for the assessment of their hosts. Interacting with service providers is the primary way in which tourists form their perceptions of service and make judgements about their hosts/service providers. Cultural differences influence the interaction processes between service providers and tourists. Service providers may be perceived differently by tourists and hosts. The tourists' and hosts' perceptions of service providers may have different implications for the assessment of service quality.

Qualities such as being friendly, prompt, helpful may have different meanings in different cultures. Being open, informal, relaxed may be admired in many Western cultures. In other cultures (eg in Asia) these qualities may be viewed as a lack of good manners, grace or efficiency and create unpleasant encounters between tourists and hosts. Therefore, there is a great scope for the development of negative perceptions of service quality by tourists when tourists and hosts have different cultural backgrounds. The ability to recognize different service expectations of tourists and the need to cater to those expectations, according to the tourists' definitions of service quality, is important. Since tourists' expectations are shaped by their culture, their culture is the basis for the service standards acceptable by tourists. It can be argued that the tourists' expectations are also shaped by other factors, eg media, intermediaries, etc. However, although the other factors exist, the influence of culture on individuals is the most important (Porter and Samovar, 1988). [...]

CONCLUSION

Cultural differences, together with asymmetry of the frequent and transitory tourist–host contact, are the most important factors which influence interaction difficulties between tourists and hosts (Pearce 1982b, Sutton 1967). Therefore, understanding of cross-cultural tourist–host contact and the influence of the cultural background of tourists and hosts is the key feature for identification of the future potential for tourist–host interaction and the effects of this interaction on the overall tourist holiday satisfaction.

RECOMMENDATIONS FOR THE DEVELOPMENT OF POSITIVE CROSS-CULTURAL TOURIST–HOST CONTACT

The following recommendations highlight the need for the improvement of tourist–host contact by better training of personnel in the tourism and hospitality industry in the area of cultural awareness and human relations.

The development of positive cross-cultural tourist–host contact depends mainly on understanding the specific nature of the tourist–host contact together with the role cultural differences play in the tourist–host interactions. The following recommendations for the development of positive cross-cultural tourist–host contact are suggested.

1. The provision is recommended of an effective educational programme and a better appreciation and understanding of foreign cultures, languages and international relations, for all those involved in international tourism, travel and hospitality at national and regional levels. The psychological study of tourists and their cultural backgrounds should be introduced. Such training would facilitate the communication between tourists and hosts and provide more relaxed conditions for tourist–host interaction, thus establishing positive tourist–host contact.
2. The range of possible culturally contrasting behaviour in tourist–host contact between different cultural groups should be analysed. Cultural

differences that lead to negative perceptions should be identified and isolated from the tourists' experiences. The development of tourist–host contact should be based on shared and internationally accepted standards of behaviour.

3. Specific attention should be given to the attributes of professional hosts who are in direct contact with tourists and provide services to tourists. The service providers' concern for tourists, welcoming attitude towards tourists, effort to understand tourists' needs, hosts' tolerance and generosity are universally expected by all international tourists. These service attributes should be emphasized in every educational and training programme.

4. The provision of well-skilled hosts is imperative. Only those employees who are suitable to the job, are interaction-oriented, and have strong interpersonal skills, should be hired.

5. The establishment of licensing or certificating requirements is needed to train all those working with international tourists. Special training for tour guides and interpreters in the tourist's language and culture is required in order to interpret, explain and respond quickly and appropriately to the cross-cultural interaction difficulties which determine the outcome of the tourist–host contact. For example, many European countries (including those in Eastern Europe), and Japan and the USA have national examinations for international tour guides in several foreign languages and examinations which test applicants' knowledge of national and foreign politics, history, geography and cultures. Aptitude, organizational skills and financial management skills tests are also common.

6. More attention should be directed towards informing tourists about host cultures through media and travel intermediaries. The tourists' respect and willingness to understand the host culture and pride in their own cultural background may result in positive tourist–host contact.

7. Raising standards of general education for local residents of tourist destinations should also be considered. For instance, short courses on international politics, world geography, history, foreign languages and cultures, and socio-cultural and economic impacts of international tourism should be offered to the general public. Free access to museums, national and international exhibitions and festivals to host communities should also be provided. Developing more links with international universities, opening new courses specializing in international relations and emphasizing the importance of coexistence with other cultural systems, supporting cross-cultural research, appointing more foreigners in academia and the public service, organizing more international student exchange programmes and youth holiday camps are also examples of improving the general education level of local hosts. This can be done via both governmental and non-governmental organizations. As a result, knowledge of different cultures and people would be improved and the ability to understand tourists with different cultural backgrounds would be enhanced. The negative experiences of tourists and hosts are caused mostly by the lack of exposure to other cultures. They can be overcome if both parties are able to appreciate and respect each other's cultural background, learn to be proud of it, and eliminate feelings of their own cultural superiority and ethnocentrism.

A number of benefits would follow for all those attending educational and training programmes:

1. greater understanding of own and others' cultures
2. the development of appreciation, respect and pride in own and others' cultures
3. an increase in self-esteem and self-worth
4. a decrease in negative attitudes, perceptions, stereo-types, prejudices and racial discrimination
5. a decrease in tension, hostility and suspicion resulting from cultural misunderstandings
6. improved communication levels and reduced culture shock
7. an increase in enjoyment from cross-cultural interaction
8. greater opportunities for developing cross-cultural friendships
9. better understanding of the everyday difficulties encountered in social relations with other cultures
10. better job performance of those who have direct contact with international tourists
11. greater satisfaction with job performance
12. the development of the positive perceptions of hosts by tourists and vice versa
13. an increase in positive economic, and socio-cultural impacts of cross-cultural interaction
14. improvement in the international tourists' cultural experiences

The responsibility for developing the educational programmes may differ depending on destinations and the importance of tourism development for the host community. The internationalization of tourism education should be considered by recognizing the important role and involvement of international tourism organizations such as World Tourism Organisation (WTO) or Pacific Asia Travel Association (PATA) that could set priorities and guidelines for the educational programmes.

8. The ratio of tourists to hosts at the destination of tourism development should be monitored.
9. Less rigid travel arrangements that would give tourists more discretionary time and opportunity to interact with native hosts, group activities that would assist in reducing cultural distance between tourists and hosts, and smaller size tour groups that would give them more independence should be offered to tourists.
10. Priority should be given to surveys of international tourists, their expectations, their satisfaction levels and the types of social interactions with hosts that would create positive experiences for tourists and hosts. Questions related to service shortcomings and suggestions for the improvement of tourist–host contact in the delivery of service should be incorporated in surveys. Service quality should be constantly monitored.

In today's competitive environment no business can survive without satisfied customers. The growth in international travel provides big markets for international tourism exports. A major obstacle that could stand in the way of potential tourist destinations fully benefiting from the increase in international travel, is lack of understanding of the importance of cultural differences. There is a need to devote efforts to understanding the tourists' cultural backgrounds and improving interaction with international tourists.

REFERENCES

Befu, H (1971) *Japan: An Anthropological Introduction*, Harper and Row, New York

Bochner, S (1982) *Cultures in Contact: Studies in Cross-Cultural Interaction*, Pergamon Press, New York

Brislin, R, Cushner, K, Craig, C, and Yong, M (1986) *Intercultural Interactions: A Practical Guide*, Sage Publications, US

Morsbach, H, (1973) 'Aspects of non-verbal communication in Japan', *Journal of Nervous and Mental Disease*, 157, pp262–77

Pearce, P (1982b) *The Social Psychology of Tourist Behaviour*, International Series in Experimental Social Psychology 3, Pergamon Press, Oxford

Porter, R and Samovar, L (1988) 'Approaching intercultural communication', in Samovar and Porter (1988)

Stringer, P (1981) 'Hosts and guests: the bed and breakfast phenomenon', *Annals of Tourism Research*, 18 (3), pp357–76

Sutton, W (1967) 'Travel and understanding notes on the social structure of touring', *International Journal of Comparative Sociology*, 8 (2), pp218–23

Wei, L, Crompton, J and Reid, L (1989) 'Cultural conflicts: experiences of US visitors to China', *Tourism Management*, 10 (4), pp322–32

Zimmerman, M (1985) *How to do Business with the Japanese*, Random House, New York

Reclaiming the Heritage Trail: Culture and Identity

Polly Patullo

'Island in the Sun' was the first number featured in the finale of Jubilation, the nightly show at the Crystal Palace Resort and Casino at Nassau's 'fabled' Cable Beach where white America is urged to 'sway to Caribbean rhythms as our Las Vegas-style revue takes on a tropical twist'. The backdrop, which had been changed for the finale, was a stretch of blue sea with a cruise ship on the horizon.

On came the male dancers in striped trousers, one on roller-skates, the prelude to the arrival of a topless female dancer, who was wheeled on to the stage lounging on a large plastic banana, waving merrily. After the gentle melody of 'Island in the Sun', the music changed to the soca number 'Dollar', and finally to 'Don't Worry, Be Happy', with the dancers in jaunty holiday hats and flowing chiffon scarves. A 'pantomime dame' waddled across the stage dressed as a large-breasted, big-bottomed black woman in a faded cotton frock, sneakers and wig.

The last number was announced by a blonde-haired singer as an expression of 'our Bahamian culture'. Musicians paraded, drumming and blowing cowbells, horns and whistles, while dancers appeared in costume in a stage recreation of the Bahamas' great post-Christmas festival, Junkanoo. Meanwhile, because it was December and Junkanoo fever at its height, a group of waiters came down the aisle, also dancing, blowing on whistles, sounding cowbells and beating drums, to great applause.

Like the Crystal Palace Resort itself, Jubilation may be in the Caribbean but it is not of the Caribbean. It was two hours of high-class American kitsch, its gesture to the Bahamas taking place in those final minutes.

The icons of the Caribbean were the songs, which were labelled 'a medley of island songs'. There was 'Island in the Sun', written by the Jamaican singer Harry Belafonte as the title song of the film of the same name in 1957. It is now an instantly recognizable anthem played to tourists all over the Anglophone Caribbean. The other two songs have different origins: the soca 'Dollar' became a commercial success for the Trinidadian singer Taxi and in the early 1990s was a dance favourite all over the region and beyond, while 'Don't Worry, Be Happy' with its calypso rhythms comes, in fact, from the 1988 film *Cocktail*, and was written by Bobby McFerrin, the black American singer, and sung with a 'Caribbean accent'.

The finale, with its holiday atmosphere and references to beaches, nudity and fun, used the banana (no joke in the region) and the cruise ship as the emblems of the Caribbean as well as the music. Of the dancers, more than half were local, including the dancer who introduced the 'our Bahamian culture' number and the Junkanoo musicians. One of the male dancers played the 'mammy', the market woman, a comforting black figure of unthreatening fun, with a feeling more of white folk memories of the American south than of the Caribbean.

Into that culturally deracinated programme came the Junkanoo waiters in their working uniforms (appropriately enough because to dress up before Junkanoo violates tradition). As if 'rushing' on the streets of Nassau, their performance was rooted in their own experience and history. They even managed to upstage the main performance.

Jubilation illustrated the two polarities of cultural expression as 'shown' to tourists in the Caribbean. The first was the formal, expensive, foreign-driven performance which is put on to please visitors, to reinforce the tourists' perceptions of the Caribbean and to give them what the Caribbean thinks they want. The second was the informal (if not spontaneous) display of local creativity by the waiters which in form represents the fusion of cultural influences (in this case from Africa and Europe) and in content remains a function of rebellion, of resistance against authority.

Jubilation (and similar representations) threaten, at many levels, to overwhelm the Caribbean with its slick otherness and metropolitan tastes. In many instances, tourism has bred cultural decline despite the efforts of those who are attempting to reclaim control. 'We are busy fighting the mentality that says that if it's not required by tourists or liked by them then it's not needed. Because if we don't stop it, we don't have anything left to give our children', says Kim Outten of the Pompey Museum, Nassau. The most recent struggle for the Caribbean has been both to nurture its indigenous art forms, to create and perform for its own peoples, amid the demands of tourism, while at the same time finding imaginative ways of 'using' tourists as patrons rather than being used by them. Indeed, there are now significant points at which the interaction between tourism and Caribbean culture has created a new dynamic.

THE INTANGIBLE HERITAGE

The genesis and expression of Caribbean culture throughout the region have been shaped by a shared experience of history: of European colonization, indigenous destruction, slavery, indentureship, the struggles for freedom, migration and independence. Those experiences have made for societies where everything and everyone which reached Caribbean shores has been creolized, that is, transformed into being part of a Caribbean identity. That force represents part of the region's creative genius and its strength.

However, most of the Caribbean (with the notable exception of post-revolutionary Cuba) has also suffered from a sense of inferiority. As William Demas, then president of the Caribbean Development Bank, said in a 1973 address to students in Jamaica: 'The deep and disturbing identity problem remains. The problem is ... one of not recognizing that we as a people have many features of uniqueness – that is to say, a basis upon which a sense of identity can be built. It is fundamentally a typical West Indian problem of lack of self-confidence.'

In the 1970s, awareness of such problems was sharpened by the recent or imminent independence of most Anglophone countries and a subsequent birth of nationhood, by the civil rights and Black Power movements in the USA and by the tensions generated by the Cold War. And as the growing tourist industry made increasing claims on the region, there was alarm about cultural dependency, the way in which the region's beliefs and values appeared to be determined by North America. This process followed the long-time cultural conditioning by Europe through colonization. The Caribbean, it was argued, was not defined by its own peoples, but by tourists and others according to their own needs and perceptions of sun-baked islands. This cultural standard-setting by metropolitan interests was linked to the Caribbean's political and economic dependence. As Demas said in an address to the University of Guyana in 1970, the 'New Caribbean Man' must 'devise ways and means of reducing the negative aspects of the metropolitan impact on the New Caribbean Society'; this society must be 'selective in its contacts with the metropolis – no less in economics, than in ideology, culture and values'.

The Caribbean was in danger of becoming in thrall to North America and Europe in a recreation of colonialism and the plantation system by other means. This imitation of the metropole (as described by the Trinidadian V S Naipaul in his novel *The Mimic Men*) was what the Bahamian-born actor Sidney Poitier experienced when he returned home one year after the Bahamas gained its independence in 1973. He wrote in his 1980 autobiography; *This Life*:

> It disturbed me deeply that there was no cultural life expressing the history of the people – absolutely none. I did see wood carvings, but they were imported from Haiti to sell to tourists in The Bahamas ... It was tourism, so enormously successful over the years, that had contaminated – diluted – debased – the shape of all things cultural in those islands, until there was no longer any real semblance of a Bahamian cultural identity. People even danced to Bahamian musicians playing other people's music – Jamaican music or American artificial calypso music; tunes from the American hit parade or the American 'soul' top ten.

Nearly a quarter of a century on from Demas' warnings and Poitier's lament, much nation-building has been done and achievements in all art forms have been recognized, not just regionally but internationally. There are the visual arts of Jamaica, Haiti, Cuba, Guyana; the great cultural festivals, now known as the festival arts, of Carnival and Junkanoo; the internationally acclaimed music of reggae, calypso, salsa, merengue and zouk; a fine body of literature (including St Lucia's Derek Walcott, the Nobel Prize winner); and a vibrant folk culture and customs that are recognized and encouraged. The expression of all this cultural activity has, since 1971, found an outlet in the regional festival, Carifesta, pioneered by Guyana's former President, Forbes Burnham, and held, at intervals, in different countries of the Caribbean. Yet, despite such achievement, the shadow of dependency remains.

Much of what is admired within the Caribbean and is seen to be 'better' remains foreign (usually North American), whether in design, technology, food or the visual arts. And while the tourists continue to flock in, the leaders of the tourist industry, whether local or foreign, have seemed generally unconcerned to protect the authenticity of Caribbean dance forms, carvings or architectural detail.

A fundamental reason for such neglect is that the Caribbean tourist industry does not depend on castles, ancient buildings, art galleries and museums. The Caribbean's cultural forms are not on display as they are in Venice or Prague, Delhi or Cairo. Such formal, urban environments are not the common currency of the Caribbean tourist industry. The heritage business has been a late arrival and only recently a tool for tourism.

Meanwhile the 'people's culture', more vulnerable and diffuse, has been at risk, sometimes appearing to be flattened into the all-purpose caricature: a smiling guitarist in a Hawaiian shirt crooning 'Jamaica Farewell', with its chorus line 'I Left My Little Girl in Kingston Town' (to be adapted to Nassau town or Castries town or whatever town is relevant). As Professor Elliott Parris, of Howard University, noted in 1983, 'If we ignore our history and the cultural legacy that it has left us, we run the risk of developing tourism as an industry which puts the dollar first and our people last. We are saying to ourselves, perhaps unconsciously: we are the field labourers on the modern plantation of the tourist industry.'

A decade later the 'modern plantation' continues. Reg Samuel is the research officer in Antigua's Ministry of Culture. His is one of the voices raised against the impact of the tourist industry on his island, blaming it for the loss and degradation of what is unique to Antigua and its history. 'Tourism has impacted on us very seriously,' he says. 'Our total lifestyle – art, food, music, dress, architecture, celebrations – has been altered. We have lost our character.' He argues that Antigua tries to please tourists by giving them what they know. 'We try to imitate Americans and their ways. We give the impression that what tourists want is what they have and not what we have. Let the tourist know what we have.'

In music, for example, Samuel points out that the steel band, which arrived in Antigua early on with returning oil workers from Trinidad, has been neglected or lost its way, while other musical forms have virtually disappeared. 'We have distinctive forms such as the iron band, which emerged in the 1940s, played with hub caps. The tourist should be hearing this particular music that's unique to Antigua.'

Instead, tourists are offered Heritage Quay, a modern duty-free complex of boutiques and souvenir shops, which promotes itself with a poster for 'a night of Antiguan culture' with 'steel band, limbo dancers, gambling, children performing, late evening shopping.' Such entertainment is common in Antigua where, according to Tim Hector, Opposition Senator and editor of *Outlet* newspaper, young people have been 'ripped from any rootedness in a folk culture'. Instead, wrote Hector (1994), 'Folk culture has become a marketable commodity, readily and monotonously packaged as Yellow Bird, limbo without meaning, except as tourist entertainment, steelbands which now draw no response from the people for whom the music is produced, and a national dish which is really Kentucky and Fries. A culture has been turned on its head.'

Antigua's disregard for its own identity is perhaps more acute than anywhere else in the Caribbean. This is partly the result of its small size, the nature of its tourist industry (largely foreign-controlled, dominated by expatriates and investors and linked to organized crime) and the debased character of its government. Antigua demonstrates the ease with which cultural patrimony becomes threatened.

Antigua is not alone. Other countries, in particular in the Anglophone Caribbean and the Dutch territories, have also failed to define themselves clearly to tourists. As a result, tourists have retained the power to create their own (often uninformed) images of the Caribbean. The whole region thus becomes a homogenized whole, its contrasts and distinctive heritages either neglected or lost.

The successful export of calypso, salsa and reggae to the USA and Europe has meant that those musical forms have become standard-bearers of Caribbean culture. The negative effect of this achievement has been to put at risk the lesser known and more fragile forms of regional music, such as Antigua's iron band and the big drums of Carriacou. On Grenada's tiny sister island Carriacou, Big Drum, three *lapeau cabrit* (goat skin) drums, is the traditional musical form. Yet when the cruise ships call, it is a steel band which goes on board to entertain: the steel band rather than the unique Big Drum has become the sound of Carriacou.

Using 'culture' as an ingredient of a tourist industry means work for performers and artists. Much of the entertainment is in hotels which put on musical evenings and floor shows and sometimes buy local paintings and carvings. Once on cruise ships or in hotels, music, dance and art tend to become part of a safe suburban environment. Like the licensed street vendors, the performers who work the hotels have to respond to the requirements of the hoteliers: they shape the tourist experience by deciding who should perform what. 'The people who run the industry are from a different culture and totally disregard our culture.' says one prominent St Lucian. 'They do not breathe down our neck, but there is a reluctance to perform anything that might raise difficulties.'

Hotel entertainment may well be the only expression of Caribbean culture offered to tourists. Along with 'saloon' reggae, steel band, and sometimes jazz, what the tourist brochures call 'native' floor shows are the most common form of hotel entertainment. These sometimes consist of a fashion show interspersed with 'exotic' dancing which may include fire-eating, limbo dancing and glass-breaking. While there is some evidence that limbo dancing is a legacy of the Middle Passage (the journey from Africa to the Caribbean), the 'native' show versions have long lost any validity, while fire-eating is usually dismissed as degrading nonsense. A lack of authenticity plagues most tourist shows all over the Third World, and the Caribbean is no exception.

In Barbados, a twice-weekly show called '1627 and All That' ('a spectacular cultural feast') takes place in the courtyard of the Museum. In a package which includes a free tour of the Museum, a 'sumptuous Barbadian buffet dinner' and a complimentary bar, the show is a private-sector initiative employing local dance groups. Alissandra Cummins, the Museum's director, has some reservations about the production. It is, she says, 'better than some shows which have no relevance at all to Barbadian culture. However, I'm not totally comfortable with what they produce.' There are elements which may come from other Caribbean cultures but are not Barbadian, she adds, and while there is 'a generous attribution to Africa', it is non-specific.

The sort of compromises imposed (or allowed) by tourism in the representation of a culture is of concern to those who seek to protect and develop it. Raymond Lawrence, Dominica's Chief Cultural Officer, has observed what has happened to other countries who have lost many of their indigenous forms through pandering to the tourist. Dominica needs to 'learn from the experience of others', he says. 'We need to strengthen Dominica's folk traditions so that authenticity can be kept when tourism hits us in a big way.' What concerns Lawrence is to continue to 'present ourselves authentically to ourselves'. He hopes that financial rewards will not tempt groups to 'dilute their presentations with dances shortened to become something without value'. *Belé*, for example, a dance in which the dancer performs to the drummer, cannot, explains Lawrence, be turned in to a 'hello' entertainment in which performers play to an audience. 'We want to keep it that way.'

Even more remote from the typical 'floor show' than the intimacy of Dominica's *belé* are, of course, Haiti's voodoo ceremonies. Before Haiti's tourist industry collapsed in the early 1980s, voodoo performances were put on for visitors. At one voodoo centre outside Port-au-Prince, for example, two-hour-long shows were put on six nights a week. Although voodoo tourism contained all the elements of a staged performance, with an entrance fee, stage and waiters serving drinks, the nature of Haitian culture blurs the edges between 'real' and 'false' and between theatre and religion. The shows were described by an anthropologist, Alan

Goldberg (1983):

> *The ceremony begins with songs for the particular spirits being called that night. The first episode of spirit possession behaviour occurs about 10.40, usually featuring the sacrifice of a pigeon which is dispatched when the possessed person bites its head off. After the first spirit is sent away another possession may occur or an intermission may mark the end of the first part of the show.*

Although performed for tourists (albeit far removed from the typical package tourists), the performers allowed the event to 'become converted into a situation of staged authenticity', according to Goldberg. The existence of a tourist audience did not in itself invalidate the experience.

STREET CULTURE

If voodoo tourism can fill that grey area between the staged and the authentic, so, in many ways, can the other great cultural set-pieces of the Caribbean, its public street festivals – Carnival, Junkanoo (Bahamas), Crop-Over (Barbados), Christmas Sports (St Kitts) and Mashramani (Guyana). These annual flowerings of music, dance, theatre, language and costume have long histories; most are rooted in the Caribbean's experience of slavery and liberation. To what extent, however, have they flourished or withered at the hands of the marketing departments of tourist boards? Or, indeed, do they and can they ignore tourism?

The best-known, biggest and most visually extravagant of all is the Trinidad Carnival, which takes place on the Monday and Tuesday before Ash Wednesday. The two days of street bacchanal date from emancipation and represent a great outpouring of black dissent and resistance through mockery, satire and display as well as commentary on contemporary life. As Gordon Lewis (1968) described it: 'From its opening moment of *jour ouvert* and the "ole mas" costume bands to its finale, forty-eight hours later, in the dusk of Mardi Carnival, the Trinidadian populace gives itself up to the 'jump up', the tempestuous abandon of Carnival'.

Richer, more naturally endowed and diversified than other economies, Trinidad has never bothered much with tourism. So Carnival in Trinidad was neither created for tourists nor has it been recreated for them like Crop-Over in Barbados, or become a distant shadow, as in St Thomas. Trinidad's Carnival has robustly retained its own identity.

Yet it has changed over the years, and it has been influenced by tourism. Even before the Second World War, Carnival organizers had an eye on the tourist market. In 1939, the Carnival Improvement Committee was established, an offshoot of what was called the new Tourist and Exhibitions Board. Its aim was to 'lift Carnival', to make it 'one of the star attractions of the tourist season'. Some calypsonians composed on this theme: Attila, for example, wrote that tourists 'get happy and gay', finding Trinidad a 'paradise on earth/that is what the tourists say' (Roehler 1990, p328).

Beneath the welcoming patter, however, there was another issue on the Carnival Improvement Committee's agenda. Its aim was to censor Carnival, to clean it up, to make it more decorous and less wild. In 1951, to the list of annual Carnival don'ts (such as don't dress in an immodest or scanty costume and don't sing any immoral or suggestive tunes) was added: 'Don't forget that visitors are in your midst. Give them the best impression of the festival' (Roehler 1990, p403). This development, according to Trinidadian writer Lawrence Scott, was 'about how organizers wanted Carnival to be presented to the outside world – it was an awareness of what others think of us'.

Middle-class tastes were also behind commercializing trends in the 1950s when company sponsorship first became a significant element of Carnival. The merchants (as in most Caribbean countries, the white and light-skinned élite) sought to take control of Carnival by putting it on Port of Spain's central open space, the Savannah, with expensive seating and big prizes, at the expense of the street calypsonians and road-marchers. The calypsonians retaliated. Sparrow's 'Carnival Boycott' pointed out that it was calypso that was the 'root' of Carnival and steelband the 'foot' (Roehler 1990, p452).

Forty years on, Carnival in the 1990s has competitions for calypso, pan and thousand-strong costume bands, all sharing in the glory, and all required set-pieces. Television rights, sponsorship from big business, recording opportunities, big prizes, expensive seats, pricey costumes and overseas marketing have contributed to a certain reduction in spontaneity. Yet Carnival remains at the centre of the nation's psyche, an expression of Trinidad's nationhood. It is a lure for Trinidadians from overseas and other Caribbean nationals more than it is for tourists.

There are other smaller, less spectacular, Lenten carnivals around the region, mainly in predominantly Catholic islands, such as Martinique and Dominica. As in Trinidad's Port of Spain, these carnivals are urban experiences and as such now have a commercial input. Yet although there are those who lament the passing of the 'good old days', regional carnivals retain their roots and many of their rituals. They are local celebrations where tourists are welcome to observe or even join in. But, as in Trinidad, tourists are peripheral. The village festivals commemorating saints' days, celebrated in Dominica, for example, are entirely local affairs as are the rural festivals of La Rose and La Marguerite in St Lucia.

In the Bahamas, the equivalent to Carnival is Junkanoo, a Christmas festival. Junkanoo (also known in Jamaica as John Canoe) reaches back to Africa, probably linked to the legendary John Konny, an eighteenth century tribal leader from the Gold Coast; and like Carnival it remains an expression of freedom, associated with acts of rebellion and challenge. Its history is also dotted with instances of threats by colonial authorities to ban the 'rush' down Nassau's business centre, Bay Street. Yet the parade of costumes, once made of sacking and sponges and now of cardboard and coloured crepe paper, and the hundreds-strong bands with goat-skin drums, cowbells and trumpets, have flourished and have become a magnificent, home-grown attraction created for and performed by groups of Bahamians for themselves. The groups represent communities with a strong sense of belonging and collective identity; in this way, tourists are almost entirely excluded from participation, their role being to observe, enjoy and spend money among the crowds of Nassau and Freeport, the two main Junkanoo locations.

Yet this spectator role of the tourist has been crucial to the survival of Junkanoo. Gail Saunders, director of the Bahamas archives, believes that without tourism Junkanoo might have died out. She dates the first impact of tourism on Junkanoo from the late 1940s when Sir Stafford Sands, the first head of the Bahamas Development Board, put some money into the festival. The white colonial elite recognized the attractions to tourists of the African Junkanoo festival and provided it with an economic framework which enabled the bands to become organized and more ambitious. In 1958, an American guide book wrote: 'costumed and masked natives dance ancient rhythms and parade ... A real experience – don't miss it.'

In the 1960s, Junkanoo was also given an extra impetus by the involvement of young middle-class Bahamian artists inspired by Black Power and the anti-colonial movement. Jackson Burnside, a Bahamian architect and artist who designs for the Saxons Superstars band, recalled) 'In Junkanoo I found how it had grown from Africa, but beyond Africa – into something that is ours, only ours. In the process, it happens to be the best show on earth' (*The Guardian* 1993). Through the nexus of community, business and tourism, Junkanoo in the Bahamas has reasserted itself. While it has changed through tourism, it is seen to have done so without compromising its integrity.

On the other side of the Caribbean, the festival of Crop-Over in Barbados is another example of how tourism realigns traditional festivals. Crop-Over evolved from the celebration of the end of the sugar-cane harvest by both planters and slaves. By the end of the nineteenth century it had developed into a procession of carts, decorated with flowers and coloured material, bearing the last of the canes into the plantation yard. After the labourers had paraded with an effigy of Mr Harding, a figure whom they sometimes burnt, there was dancing and music. However, with the decline in sugar and the arrival of more modern forms of entertainment, Crop-Over was all but dead by the 1940s, only to be revived in 1964 by the Board of Tourism.

According to the authoritative *A–Z of Barbadian Heritage* (Fraser et al, 1990), 'the present-day festival is very different from the old-time Crop-Over'. What has happened is that it has become a four-week summer festival (traditionally the low tourist season), transformed by business sponsorship and the marketing machinations of tourism officials into a sequence of organized events such as calypso, king and queen of the crop competitions and a carnival-style parade called Kadooment. The ghosts of Crop-Over past are witnessed in the parade of decorated carts. But the parade has become 'commoditized'. 'Corporate Barbados benefits enormously from Crop-Over; it is something that is mutually beneficial,' says the chief cultural officer of the National Cultural Foundation, the organizer of Crop-Over. 'We would like to see corporate Barbados advertising, using, for example, the decorated cart parade as a medium for advertising' (Dann and Potter 1994).

Other devices are used to maximize the tourist potential of indigenous local festivals, sometimes with damaging consequences. One is to move traditional celebrations from Christmas to summer. Antigua's carnival, for example, was deliberately conceived in 1957 to boost tourist arrivals during the slack season (May to July); now it has been moved to July/August (also a slow tourist period) to coincide with the anniversary of Emancipation. Without the Christmas celebrations and parades, the traditional figures, such as John Bull, the clowns and mocojumbies also disappeared.

Festivals are also invented to boost the range of tourist attractions and, by definition, tourist numbers. In the Cayman Islands, Pirates Week was coined at the end of the 1970s to take place at the end of October, again a slow tourist period. This carnival-style entertainment has become a national event, an excuse for costumes, parades and partying. In the Bahamas, Goombay (probably from a Malian word for festival) was invented by the Tourist Board as a Friday night street dance and then became limited to the summer (again an attraction for the low tourist season), an occasion for performances, food and craft.

Whatever their derivation and history, however deep or shallow their cultural roots, Caribbean festivals have remained, for the most part, a celebration that depends on the participation of local people. As much as anything, this may be a function of their location on the streets. The jump-up in Gros Islet, St Lucia, is an interesting example. Started as a local, small-business initiative, it has become a successful institution in which locals and tourists mix every Friday night on the streets of the village for music, food and drink.

Other 'cultural events' have been launched in response to tourism. When they are rooted in the community like Jamaica's Sunsplash, they tend to succeed; where they depend on tourist patronage and thus reflect tourist tastes, as with St Lucia's Jazz Festival, their success is less assured.

Sunsplash, the great annual celebration of reggae, began with a group of Jamaican businessmen who created a company called Synergy to promote reggae. Since the first Sunsplash in 1976, each year up to 100,000 people, both tourists and Jamaican, have attended the week-long event. Its achievement has been to keep the faith of its original function, to be a showcase for reggae, both homegrown and from overseas. 'The Jamaicans are proud that other countries are interested in playing reggae,' says David Roddigan, the British DJ, who has followed the fortunes of Sunsplash for many years. 'It has never compromised itself. The organisers have played it from their hearts – they are committed to the concept of Sunsplash.'

Threats to its future have come not from tourism, but from a forced change of venue and Jamaican business politics. Its first home was Montego Bay, a perfect location for tourists, for Jamaicans who would take their own holiday there and for the reggae industry. Yet in 1993, Sunsplash was forced to move from Montego Bay to Jamworld, outside Kingston. There it has not fared so well, with lower attendances and lower takings. Not being a tourist centre, Kingston does not provide a 'tap' audience, nor is it so attractive to Jamaicans themselves. In 1995 attempts were being made to move it back to the north coast, possibly to Ocho Rios.

THE HERITAGE TRAIL

Jamaica's successful promotion of reggae nationally, regionally and internationally reflects Jamaica's mature attitude towards its own rich cultural life, looking outwards but staying grounded in local experience. The example of Sunsplash has been noted and acted on elsewhere in the region. Slowly, the idea of using more than beaches to attract tourists to the region has been generating interest.

This move to widen the tourist base to include 'cultural' or 'heritage' tourism has partly been caused by increased awareness and pride in Caribbean history within the region. It has also been nudged by the global fashion for recreating history. More pragmatically, it has been prompted by concern about falling arrival rates in 'older' tourism destinations. Examples of conservation and restoration for the tourist market come from all over the region, from the Dominican Republic to Bonaire.

One interesting example of official attempts to harness heritage to tourism is the Seville Great House and Heritage Park in St Ann's Bay on the north coast of Jamaica. Seville, now owned and operated by the Jamaica National Heritage Trust, a government agency, was opened in 1994. It was an Arawak settlement before becoming the first Spanish capital of Jamaica and then, under British occupation and slavery, a sugar plantation with a great house and African village. St Ann's

Bay was also where Columbus was shipwrecked in 1493, while the town of St Ann's was the birthplace of Marcus Garvey. Speaking at its opening, the Minister of Education and Culture pointed to the value to Jamaicans (as well as to tourists) of such sites. The importance of Seville, he said, lay with its potential to provide 'an interpretation of what is basically a microcosm of Jamaica's history at one location. This is what will empower us to speak with understanding, honesty and truth about who we are as a people' (Caribbean News Agency 1994).

Jamaica's Tourism Action plan (TAP) has also been working on plans to restore and improve not just the great houses, but also towns and villages, recognizing the heritage of Jamaica's masons, carpenters and woodworkers in the creation of Jamaica-Georgian architecture. A book, *Jamaica's Heritage – An Untapped Resource*, by three English architects and conservationists, published in 1991 in co-operation with TAP, not only illustrated Jamaica's rich architectural history, but also made a proposal for a Jamaica Heritage Trail that would link the different parts of the island (the Emancipation Trail, the Gingerbread House Trail and the Plantation Trail) (Binney, Harris and Martin 1991). This would make it possible for tourists to explore Jamaica's towns and villages thematically through its architectural history. From great house to railway station and vernacular cabin, the book is enthusiastic about the potential for visitors to see the other 'remarkable' Jamaica, to enable rural Jamaica to generate its own tourist income.

In Barbados, history has been dusted down, cleaned up and put on display. But it has been more selective than the Jamaica Heritage Trail proposals. The bit of history that Barbados has chosen to market is its plantation houses, the economic epicentres of the sugar industry and slavery. Yet the reconstruction has been partial. Sunbury Plantation House, for example, is described in the 1994 tourist handout, *The Ins and Outs of Barbados*, as 'creating a vivid impression of the life of a sugar plantation in the 18th and 19th century'. Yet its blurb mentions only the house's magnificent antiques and paintings, while ignoring the slave contribution to the estate.

A similar thing has happened at the Dows Hill Interpretation Centre in Antigua. Perched on a hillside with a magnificent view of English Harbour, Nelson's old dockyard and once the base of English naval power in the West Indies, the Centre provides in light and sound a Euro-centred version of Antigua's history as narrated by a small boy. Funded and developed by the Canadian government agency, CIDA, in conjunction with the National Parks Authority, it alienates Antiguans like cultural officer Reg Samuel. 'We don't relate to it at all,' he says.

English Harbour itself has been the subject of similar criticism. Since 1955, the dockyard and its surrounding buildings have been carefully restored. Now the whole area is a marina with a ship's chandlery, marine services and yacht club. It also has a museum, restaurants, art gallery, picture framing, boutique, bakery and craft shops, all created for the tourists on a day out from their hotels. It is attractive, tasteful, expensive and very European. Most of the businesses are owned and run by whites. For Samuels 'It is an English colony run by expatriates.'

Slavery and the story of resistance to it usually remain untold in heritage tourism (museums have become the pioneers in promoting that part of Caribbean history). This is partly because most slave accommodation, built of wood or wattle and daub, has disappeared or has been destroyed. Perhaps a more fundamental reason is that, until comparatively recently, black history has been ignored. Before independence, this was because history was 'organized' by colonial officials; after independence, Caribbean tourist officials were ignorant of their own history, or unskilled in presenting it or controlled by metropolitan tour operators. One result, in contrast to Jamaica's Seville project, is that heritage tourism has become 'for tourists only' – at best being ignored by local people, at worst alienating them.

Bonaire, in the Netherlands Antilles, however, has restored an example of its slave huts. These tiny stone houses, whose entrances are only waist-high, were built by and for the slaves who worked on the nearby salt ponds. Dating from 1850, they were restored by the National Parks Foundation of the Netherlands Antilles in a rare commemoration of slavery and vernacular architecture (Caribbean Week 1993).

Alissandra Cummins of the Barbados Museum drew attention to the process in her description of the impact of Acworth's 1951 colonial survey of the historic buildings of the West Indies; this concentrated on the European-influenced estate houses and ignored the vernacular. She wrote: 'The lack of popular support for these conservation efforts was hardly surprising and historic preservation remained on the periphery of local cultural consciousness for decades' (Cummins). Jamaica, Guyana, Cuba and Haiti were the only exceptions.

The development of museums in the Caribbean in many ways paralleled that of heritage tourism with its concentration on colonial achievement. Museums were the traditional storehouses of knowledge and bearers of the cultural chalice, but their white curators had a largely Euro-centric view of the world. For tourists, a visit to the museum, if there was one, had meant exhibits of Amerindian and colonial relics mixed with natural history. As the Barbados Minister of Culture said in 1980, the Barbados Museum told the visitor about Barbadian merchants and planters but 'little or nothing about slaves, plantation labourers or peasant farmers' (Cummins).

Only in the last decade has this changed. As Ms Cummins explains: 'How Caribbean history is presented is largely the result of its institutions – the older the institution is, the greater the rigidity of interpretation, which reflects the interests largely of colonials. The new institutions have a totally different perspective.' In these there is less glass and porcelain, fewer portraits of stern white patriarchs and a new emphasis on social history and the Caribbean masses. Under Ms Cummins, the focus of the Barbados Museum has changed, showing black culture and legitimizing 'Caribbean culture, making visible what was once a hidden past'. Other Caribbean countries are making similar changes; in the Bahamas, the Pompey Museum in Nassau, the region's first museum on slavery and emancipation (named after the leader of a slave uprising against an absentee landlord in Exuma), opened in 1992, while in Tobago, the museum noticeboard contains an appeal for contributions representing Tobago's African past.

While the focus has shifted, the role of museums and historic sites ('the outside child of tourism') has yet to be, according to Ms Cummins, fully recognized or defined: 'For while each country in the region has sought to incorporate a cultural development policy in its overall national development strategy, all too often the policy option has been that of 'cultural tourism', as a justification for any activity in this section and certainly as a priority before integration within the Caribbean cultural context' (Cummins).

There is, however, enormous potential for linking tourism with museums, says Alissandra Cummins. Yet Caribbean governments have largely underestimated the interests of tourists. 'The tourist comes to the museum to get a clear picture of who Barbadians are,' she says, drawing attention to the comments in the visitors' book. 'The tourist wants a lot more in terms of slavery and the slave trade, particularly the black tourist. Tourists are also intrigued by sports. We need to get out and tell the stories about cricket and racing in Barbados.'

It is not only the Anglophone Caribbean which has experienced the difficulties surrounding some heritage tourism. In Cuba, the interests of tourism have threatened to marginalize the poor of colonial Old Havana (population 100,000). This part of the city was declared a UN World Heritage site in 1982. Since then churches, hotels and colonial mansions in the crumbling heart of the city, which dates from the sixteenth century, have been restored (part funded by UNESCO) while local housing conditions remain poor.

When the government realized that there was little for tourists to buy in Old Havana, a state agency, Habaguanex SA, was set up in 1994 to provide food and drink, entertainment and souvenirs for tourists and to earn dollars to be ploughed back into the restoration work. Yet tourism and a dollar economy sit uneasily with the peso-earning Cubans crammed into their crumbling and insanitary accommodation and struggling to eat. The potential for unrest (and so-called 'anti-social' behaviour like begging) forced a compromise, according to the magazine *Cuba Business*, which reported in June 1994 that 10 per cent of the services would be available in pesos. Where this was difficult to implement, 10 per cent of the produce would be distributed to local schools and old people's homes. Other profits from Habaguanex would go to improve housing and infrastructure for Cubans (Cuba Business 1994).

The idea that tourists could be interested in a built environment beyond a beach is not restricted to Cuba. Slowly the rest of the region has awakened to the attractions of its own architecture. Yet for decades, with a disregard for its own architectural traditions, the Caribbean tore down its old buildings to promote other people's. Both foreign chains and local developers built (and continue to do so) hotels inappropriate to place and purpose: foreigners because they did not care, locals because they associated old buildings with backwardness and assumed that foreigners required (and liked) the paraphernalia of modern, urban societies. Philistine and desperate-for-investment Caribbean governments sanctioned such developments. As a result, Caribbean resorts often look like somewhere else, usually Florida but perhaps Spain, Mexico or Italy. Hotel brochures boast that their charmless complexes have villas with 'Spanish roofs' and reception halls of 'Italian marble'.

The rush to build for tourism resulted in many pieces of vandalism. Among the worst was the destruction of the Amerindian caves in St Maarten, discovered during the construction of the Concord Hotel (now the Maho Beach Hotel). Amerindians used caves as places of worship, and petroglyphs and other images have been found there. On the discovery of the caves, the site supervisor told the government which expressed no interest, and when building began again, parts of the caves were destroyed and one was used as a septic tank. During the months that the caves were exposed, at least three limestone statues were found, one white, one red, painted with dyes, and one black. The red and white statues are thought to date from around AD1300 and to have been carved by the Tainos. Only very few such carvings have ever been found and it is not known what petroglyphs and other statues might have been in the caves now smothered by rubble and sewage.

The new trends in heritage tourism have not only turned plantation houses into museums, but have also transformed them into hotels (such as the up-market examples on Nevis), while parts of the capital of Aruba, Oranjestad, have been rebuilt in colonial style. There is also more attention paid to vernacular architecture (paralleling the developments in museums), if sometimes only in a post-modernist mode. Sandals resort in Antigua, for instance, is painted in 'Caribbean colours'; Chris Blackwell's new hotel outside Nassau has cottages, vernacular in colours and style; and even parts of downtown Philipsburg, capital of St Maarten, have been restored in 'Caribbean style'. All such appropriations draw attention to a tradition which echoes the homes of ordinary people, outside the tourist zones.

However, this trend has been criticized for encouraging an all-purpose Caribbean architectural 'heritage', which only loosely belongs in time and place. The restored tourist shopping district in Charlotte Amalie, St Thomas, for example, has architectural details which are not specific to St Thomas but rather reproduce general perceptions of gingerbread work, verandahs and hipped roofs. The result, according to the architectural historian William Chapman (1992), is the creation of 'something that is more fantasy than homage and erodes the value of remaining authentic design and fabric'.

REFERENCES

Binney, Marcus, Harris, John and Martin, Kit *Jamaica's Heritage – An Untapped Resource*, Kingston, 1991

Caribbean News Agency, 13 May 1994

Caribbean Week, 9–22 January, 1993

Chapman, William 'A Little More Gingerbread: Tourism, Design and Preservation in the Caribbean', *Places*, London, Vol 8, No 1, 1992

Cuba Business, London, June 1994

Cummins, Alissandra 'Exhibiting Culture: Museums and National Identity in the Caribbean', *Caribbean Quarterly*, vol 38, no 2, p33

Dann, Graham and Potter, Robert 'Tourism and Post-Modernity in a Caribbean Setting', *Les Cahiers du Tourisme*, Aix-en-Provence, April 1994

Demas, William (1975) 'Change and Renewal in the Caribbean', *Challenges in the New Caribbean*, No 2, p55, Caribbean Conference of Churches, Barbados

Fraser, Henry, Carrington, Sean, Forde, Addington and Gilmore, John (1990) *A–Z of Barbadian Heritage*, Jamaica

Goldberg, Alan (1983) 'Identity and Experience in Haitian Voodoo Shows', *Annals of Tourism Research*, Vol 10, pp479–95

The Guardian, 30 October 1993, London

Lewis, Gordon K (1968) *The Growth of the Modern West Indies*, New York, p30

McKay's Guide to Bermuda, the Bahamas and the Caribbean, New York, 1958, p48

Outlet, 11 March 1994, Antigua and Barbuda

Extract 5: P Patullo

Parris, Elliott (1983) 'Cultural Patrimony and the Tourist Product: Towards a Mutually Beneficial Relationship', OAS regional seminar

Poitier, cited in Philip Cash, Shirley Gordon and Gail Saunders, *Sources of Bahamian History*, London, 1991, p 337

Roehler, Gordon (1990) *Calypso and Society in Pre-Independence Trinidad*, Port of Spain, p328

Chapter 6

Promoting Sustainable Development and Combating Poverty: Empowerment and Participation

INTRODUCTION

One strand of the neo-populist paradigm, mentioned in the general Introduction, focuses on the notion of a continuum of participation. This extends from a passive acceptance and adoption of exogenous factors, such as ideas and technologies, on the part of the host countries, to an active situation in which, it is suggested, local people can solve their own problems and use opportunities to maximize and benefit from their indigenous skills. This is considered to be part of empowerment (Blaikie 1996).

These same issues are also found in post-modernism and occur within sustainable development agendas. Indeed, participation by, and the empowerment of, local people were clearly identified within Agenda 21 as among the important aims of sustainable development programmes (Agenda 21 is an action plan for sustainable development that emerged from the United Nations Conference on Environment and Development held in Rio de Janeiro in 1992).

Participation was seen to be the active involvement of people in decision making (Slocum and Thomas-Slayter 1995). It was extended to include empowerment, through which individuals, households, local groups, communities, regions and nations shape their own lives and the kind of society in which they live (Nelson and Wright 1995, Slocum and Thomas-Slayter 1995). As a process of empowerment, participation helps local people to identify problems and become involved in decision making and implementation, all of which contribute to sustainable development. The amount of control local people are able to assume within tourism developments is limited by the neo-colonial nature of this global industry. Investment and the repatriation of profits occurs, especially in the hotel and travel sectors, either to more developed areas and countries or, in some instances, to elites in other less developed countries or regions. The latter scenario can be illustrated in the Caribbean by the Sandals all-inclusive hotel chain, which is owned by one of an elite group in Jamaica; in Nepal by those hotels owned by Indians and Japanese; and in Dar es Salaam, in Tanzania, where South African capital is being used to privatize formerly state-owned hotels. A globalization process is counter-balancing, in places, a move towards local and/or national ownership. As in Tanzania, it can reflect a change in a country's ideological focus, with private capital replacing state ownership of tourism enterprises.

Participation in tourism can be related to a number of arguments. These include:

- The extent to which tourism is of benefit to host countries.
- The nature of participation within tourism. The model evolved by Pretty (1995) is a useful starting point since it identifies a spectrum, from the more common passive and incentive-driven forms of participation towards those which are more interactive. It is the passive and incentive-driven forms – which are typical of much tourism activity – which tend to be externally imposed on the host economy and society. Nevertheless, a model of this sort is not necessarily inevitable. Other approaches could include grassroots development in which local people create their own enterprises, thereby generating new skills and extending the effects of participation outside tourism. The factors that influence spatial and temporal variations include gender, age, education and ethnicity.
- Scale is an important element, and it will affect the intensity and nature of participation. Small enterprises require less capital, and so are more likely to be indigenously owned than large, capital-intensive structures, whether they are hotels, airlines, travel agents or car hire firms.

The following case studies illustrate a range of situations in which different levels of participation and empowerment are evident within tourism. They are drawn from both the developed and the developing world and focus especially on issues of gender and ethnicity.

REFERENCES

Blaikie, P (1996) 'New knowledge and rural development: A review of views and practicalities', A Paper for the 28th International Geographical Congress at the Hague, August 5–10 1996. A state-of-the-art lecture for the Third World Commission registered under No 5590

Nelson, N and Wright, S (1995) 'Participation and Power' in N Nelson and S Wright *Power and Participatory Development: Theory and Practice*, Intermediate Technology Publications Limited, London

Pretty, J (1995) 'The many interpretations of participation', *In Focus* Summer 16, 4–5

Slocum, R and Thomas-Slayter, B (1995) 'Participation, empowerment and sustainable development' in R Slocum, L Wichhart, D Rocheleau and B Thomas-Slayter *Power, Process and Participation: Tools for Change*, Intermediate Technology Publications, London

Female Employment in Tourism Development in South-West England

Sinead Hennessy

THE LABOUR FORCE IN LOOE

Given that the economy of Looe is heavily dependent on tourism there is a high incidence in the general labour force of part-time, seasonal work and female employment. While there are differences in the conditions of employment within different sectors of the economy of Looe, about two-thirds of a general sample of employees were shown to be working part-time (Hennessy et al 1986, 19). As might be expected, the proportion of part-time employment was lowest in the industrial sector and highest in self-catering accommodation. In addition, most categories of business in Looe were found to follow a seasonal pattern with some retail and industrial establishments experiencing less fluctuation in levels of employment throughout the year.

Women accounted for 39 per cent of the total labour force in Britain in 1981; however, in Looe women constituted roughly three-quarters of the workforce of a sample of businesses (Mallier and Rosser 1987, 20; Hennessy et al 1986, 19). While roughly two-thirds of a sample of all employees surveyed in Looe were found to be working part-time, it is known that nationally women, and especially married women, are more likely than men to take up part-time jobs (Mallier and Rosser 1987, 136).

The high proportion of women workers in the tourism industry in Looe may result from a number of factors. Regardless of whether labour is part-time or seasonal, the nature of occupations in the tourism industry in Looe is such that more women than men are likely to be employed. The predominance of women in tourism reflects the greater role of women in the service sector as a whole (Mallier and Rosser 1987, 44). In addition, women in Looe are likely to be restricted to locally available employment, perhaps because of the low density of urban development in the area, poor public transport and lack of access to the 'family' car (Massey 1984, 225). Moreover, levels of pay may be insufficient to cover the additional transport costs of long-distance commuting.

Given that the local economy in Looe is relatively dependent on tourism, this does not mean that there is a homogeneous form of labour and a homogeneous form of capital. While many workers hold employment which is dependent on tourism, the degree of dependence varies significantly between business establishments. For example, employment within establishments providing accommodation may be entirely dependent on tourism, while some retail and service outlets might be relatively dependent on tourism, where dependence is measured, for example, in terms of fluctuations in turnover and numbers of staff employed. The relative dependence on tourism of any specific job may be difficult to measure in that it may be calculated in terms of both the immediate income to a firm which flows from tourism and the sum of effects which follow from tourism-related expenditure within a wider economic context. While the degree to which specific forms of employment are dependent on tourism may be difficult to measure accurately, the conditions under which employees negotiate with employers may vary significantly. For example, with respect to wage negotiations, employees may work for a national or international company where wage levels and conditions of employment are established at a national level; alternatively, employees may be said to operate within a local labour market within which the conditions of employment are established on a personal and local level, as for example, where employment in a bank in Looe is compared with employment in a local guesthouse. However, it may also be evident where employment in a local hotel is compared with employment in a hotel held by a national or multinational company.

WOMEN'S TOURISM-RELATED EMPLOYMENT IN LOOE

Questionnaire surveys were administered to 125 women working in Looe at the height of the tourism season in August 1986. These women represent a random sample of women in tourism-related employment in Looe. The women surveyed in Looe were asked to relate not only the details of their employment but also details of their age, marital status, motherhood, and their roles as wage earners within the household. Thus, the study considered both the conditions of women within the economy and within the home. Moreover, the ambitions of the women were examined, together with their educational and vocational qualifications, in order to test the suitability of their employment to their ambitions.

It is interesting that the task of surveying women in tourism in itself exposes some of the conditions of their employment. For example, women were interviewed at home where they might be unrestricted in their responses to questions concerning conditions of work. Moreover employers who provide the poorest conditions of employment, or who employ workers within the 'black economy', might have been less likely to co-operate with a survey undertaken at work. While workers in the 'black economy' do not pay national insurance contributions or income tax, the employers of those workers also fail to pay the employers' national insurance contributions or to register employees with the Inland Revenue.

ECONOMIC RELATIONS AND CONDITIONS OF EMPLOYMENT

It is widely held that employment in tourism is socially classified as unskilled. Shop work, waitressing, cleaning and bar work were shown to be the most common forms of employment undertaken by women in tourism-related employment in Looe. In Looe, the women surveyed worked predominantly in retailing (30 per cent), restaurants and cafes (25 per cent) and hotels and guesthouses (15 per cent). Only 12 per cent of the women held skilled employment. However, a significant proportion of women had skills they did not use at work – even where women had more than one job. Of 125 women surveyed in Looe, ten had two jobs and one women had three jobs.

The majority of the women (58 per cent) surveyed in Looe were in part-time employment. Young women (aged 16–25) were shown to be more likely than relatively older women to work full-time. Married and divorced or separated women were more likely (than single women) to be in part-time employment which may relate to their duties as mothers. The responsibilities of working mothers with relatively young children were reflected in the low proportion of women working full-time. Of the 34 women with one child or more aged 14 years or under, only seven (20 per cent) were in full-time employment. In addition, because the proportions of full-time and part-time employment vary within individual sectors, women who are dependent on part-time work will be drawn into particular sectors of the economy. For example, women might be drawn into employment in public houses where jobs are predominantly part-time.

Seasonality is an important characteristic of tourism-related employment,. In an analysis of employment in Looe, jobs were broken down in terms of seasonal employment where the duration of employment is 1–24 weeks per year, short-term jobs (25–40 weeks per year) and annual employment (41–52 weeks per year). Given these definitions, roughly two-thirds of the women surveyed were in seasonal or short-term employment. If seasonal, short-term and annual employment is broken down in terms of individual sectors, it is shown that retail establishments provide a high proportion of annual jobs, while restaurants and cafes account for the greatest number of seasonal jobs.

The degree to which seasonal or short-term employment meets the needs of women in Looe is likely to vary with regard to marital status and whether women have children. The majority of women had a preference for annual employment, albeit on a part-time basis. Therefore, while seasonal or short-term employment draws a lower total (annual) income than year-round employment, it may also provide employment at a time which is inconvenient for women with school-going children. An examination of the interrelationships between full-time and part-time employment, and seasonal, short-term and annual employment shows that seasonal, part-time employment is the commonest form of employment for the women surveyed. However, where employment is annual, it is more likely to be full-time.

Given the relatively poor conditions of employment for women in Looe, whereby employment is largely unskilled, seasonal or part-time, the extent to which employees were found to return to employers year after year was remarkable. With respect to the main employment of 125 women surveyed, 6 per cent had worked for the same employer for 11–26 years (or seasons in the case of seasonal employees), while 15 per cent had worked for their employer for 6–10 years or seasons. Another 40 per cent of respondents had worked for their employer for 2–5 years or seasons.

In examining the conditions of employment for women attention must be given to sickness benefit, pensions and other employment benefits. National insurance contributions are payable by both employers and employees if earnings of employees are above the lower earnings limit. Payment of national insurance contributions confers eligibility for state benefits such as sick pay, unemployment benefit, maternity allowance and in some cases retirement pensions. Only 45 per cent of the women surveyed in Looe were making national insurance contributions. In the restaurants and cafes, and hotels and guesthouses sectors, approximately two thirds of the employees were not making national insurance contributions. However, roughly half the employees in the retail sector were paying national insurance, perhaps reflecting the greater number of full-time employees in this sector. While the majority of part-time employees (76 per cent) surveyed were not making national insurance contributions, almost half these were in seasonal employment. It is possible that the earnings of some of the women who were not making national insurance contributions were below the lower earnings limit, however others may have been part of the 'black economy' and did not pay national insurance or tax although eligible to do so. Some measure of the 'informal economy' in Looe may be gained from the fact that, of a sample of women who gave details of pay, 60 per cent were evading national insurance contributions. There may also be a tendency for some employers to take on a number of part-time workers whose earnings fall below the lower limit in order to avoid payment of the employer's national insurance contribution.

Only 18 per cent of the women surveyed in Looe were found to receive sick pay benefits through an employer's scheme. Moreover, only 7 per cent of these women were contributing to an employer's retirement pension scheme which would provide a pension other than a state pension.

The incidence of trade union membership among women surveyed was remarkably low. Only 4 per cent of the women surveyed were members of trade unions. It is known that on a national level women are less likely than men to join trade unions, although the proportion of women is increasing. With respect to Looe, however, where employment is part-time and within small-scale industries, employees are less likely to be unionized.

The levels of pay of the women covered by the study were conditioned both by the fact that they are women and by their geographical location as workers in Cornwall. While the average hourly earnings of women are generally lower than men, levels of pay in the south-west region, and particularly in Cornwall, are relatively low in relation to other regions of England (Trade Union Research Unit 1985, Robinson and Wallace 1984, 6). Of the women surveyed in 1986, 76 per cent earned between £1.20 and £2.00 per hour. There was a relatively wide spread of rates of pay within individual industrial sectors with the lowest rates of pay in retail establishments, restaurants and cafes.

SOCIAL CONDITIONS AND WOMEN EMPLOYED IN LOOE

The women covered by the study did not constitute a homogeneous social group but varied with respect to factors such as vocational skills, education and class. However, there is a predominance of younger women in tourism-related employment in Looe and roughly three-quarters of the women surveyed were aged 16–35 years, although roughly two-thirds were either married or divorced and 57 per cent had one or more children. Both the age profile and the number of married respondents may indicate that tourism-related employment in Looe provides supplementary incomes within the households of married women and for younger women living with parents.

Younger married women surveyed may not have completed their families, and may take up employment in Looe between periods given over to childbirth and rearing infants. Given the number of respondents with children, importance must be given to the manner in which women combine their roles as mothers and employees. In order to determine the importance of the women as wage earners, they were asked if they viewed themselves as the main 'breadwinner' within their respective households. More than one-third saw themselves as the main 'bread-winner', although the majority of those aged 16–20 did not.

EMPLOYMENT OPPORTUNITIES AND SATISFACTION

In the light of evidence that the employment held by the women in Looe is largely unskilled, consideration was given to the correlation between qualifications, skills and the nature of tourism-related employment. Attention was also given to the avail-ability of childcare and to the ambitions of women in relation to the timing and availability of employment. In short, the conditions which women require, or would prefer, were compared with the actual conditions of employment provided in Looe.

No formal educational qualifications were held by 44 per cent of the women, although 38 per cent held CSE or 'O' level qualifications. Of the total workforce in the south-west in 1985, 31 per cent had no educational qualification, and 24 per cent held CSE or 'O' level qualifications (South-West TUC 1985, 2–7). Therefore, the tourism industry in Looe might be said to absorb relatively high proportions of employees with no educational qualifications.

It is interesting that the position of the women in Looe alters if the focus is placed on skills rather than educational attainments. In order to determine whether the women in Looe were capable of taking up alternative employment, they were asked if there were any jobs requiring skills (other than those relating to their present job) which they could do. Almost one-third had vocational skills attained through vocational training which were 'higher' than the level of skills used in their present employment and were thus skilled workers in unskilled employment. However, because the economy of Looe is dominated by the tourism industry, it is unlikely that these women could obtain jobs locally which would utilise their skills. Furthermore, given the nature of the women's employment, there is little evidence that women were likely to secure further vocational training in their present employment. As already stated, only 12 per cent of the women were in skilled employment.

Access to childcare facilities is an important factor in relation to the capacity of women to take up paid employment in that it affects not only the time women are available for work, but also the levels of pay which must be achieved to pay for childcare. It is clear that the mothers of younger children covered by this study provided care for their children mainly within the family and that husbands and parents (or parents-in-law) were mainly responsible for childcare. The capacity of the husbands of working mothers to care for children reflects the general nature of employment in Looe. Moreover, employment such as cleaning, bar work and waitressing may be undertaken outside the working hours of husbands. Professional childminders played an insignificant role in the care of the children of working mothers and were used by only two of the mothers in the study. After the family, the next most frequent form of childcare was an informal arrangement with friends and neighbours. Given the low rates of pay for women in Looe, it is unlikely that wages could cover the cost of professional childcare. Thus, it may be that those women who are unable to obtain childcare through family or friends are prevented from entering the labour market.

The degree to which the flexibility of working hours in the tourism industry accommodates the needs of working women with children should not be over-estimated. That the peak in the tourism season during July and August coincides with children's school holidays is likely to present difficulties for some women.

REFERENCES

Hennessy, S, Shaw, G and Williams, A (1986) *The role of tourism in local economics: A pilot study of Looe, Cornwall*, University of Exeter, Exeter

Mallier, A T and Rosser, M J (1987) *Women and the economy: a comparative study of Britain and the USA*, Macmillan, London

Massey, D (1984) *Spatial divisions of labour: social structures and the geography of production*, Macmillan, London

Robinson, O and Wallace, J (1984) *Part-time employment and sex discrimination legislation in Great Britain*, Department of Employment, London

South-West TUC (1985) *Low pay in the South-West*, South-West TUC, Bristol

Trade Union Research Unit (1985) *Patterns of trade union development 1966–1984*, Appendix Table 3, Ruskin College, Oxford

Communal Lands, Communal Problems

Cherry Bird

Much has been written about CAMPFIRE (The Communal Areas Management Programme) in Zimbabwe since it began in 1989 and its contribution to meaningful conservation. Perhaps less emphasis has been laid on its role in sustainable development and the empowerment of rural communities. Most articles have been written by journalists who have visited one of the 12 established CAMPFIRE projects as part of a whistle-stop tour to 'meet the people' and make contact with non-governmental organisations and key people involved. This article by CHERRY BIRD gives insight from the perspective of someone who has worked at grassroots level in rural communities in Zimbabwe for the last five years.

It is all too easy for people in the West, who have enough to eat and to fulfil most of their basic needs, to think that the beautiful African wilderness must be preserved at all costs. Two things are wrong with this statement, the word 'preserved' and the phrase 'at all costs'. A better approach is to say that conservation (not preservation) can only be achieved with compromise, and consideration of the needs of all sides.

Many long-term white residents and highly educated black government employees will tell you that the environment in Zimbabwean communal areas (where the subsistence farming communities live) has been devastated by the activities of the farming communities there. This is true, and the evidence is for all to see. Areas which have been cultivated over a long period now closely resemble deserts, with very few trees and serious soil erosion problems. Even the people living there, who have actually caused the damage, will agree that it is a disaster, but they are caught in a poverty trap, powerless to do anything else. Most understand the theoretical problems and their solutions, which have been explained to them by a well organized network of government agricultural and natural resource advisors, but in most cases they are unable to follow the advice given because of their lack of resources.

Thus it is clear that if meaningful conservation is to take place, both inside and outside the national parks, there has to be an economic incentive for the people who live in the area. Something which makes it worth their while to look after the environment, and which links conservation with economic development in the communities. An additional bonus of such rural development would be to reduce the exodus of rural people to the cities, where there are no jobs, and they will merely exchange rural poverty for urban squalor. CAMPFIRE, although initiated as a tool for conservation, lays a very heavy emphasis on sustainable economic development for local people, because then conservation will be a natural consequence. Of course, the word 'sustainable' is crucial.

FUNDING

The CAMPFIRE programme in Zimbabwe has generated a great deal of interest both nationally and internationally, and has thus attracted a considerable amount of foreign aid. The Districts which have CAMPFIRE programmes vary enormously in their approach and style of management, partly due to differences in the resources available (both internal and external), and partly due to the history and problems particular to that area. Those Districts which started at the beginning of the programme tended to be ones with the most significant natural resources (ie untouched wilderness areas with large animal populations), and the lowest levels of economic development. Since interest in this innovative new scheme was then high, outside funding was plentiful and easily available, and there was no shortage of help and advice in the form of visiting trainers and researchers.

Districts which came in later generally had less spectacular resources, but benefited from the experiences and mistakes of the first generation. By then the availability of outside funding and assistance was reduced, and while this might seem to be a disadvantage, it has not always proved to be so. From my own experience of working in one of these 'second generation' Districts, and observing what was going on in other Districts, I feel very strongly that the provision of large amounts of aid for setting up complex management structures has proved to be counter-productive. In Districts where this has happened it seems that the tail began to wag the dog, and there was a loss of control and involvement by the people at grassroots level, who were supposed to be the beneficiaries of the programme. Squabbles arose amongst members of the hierarchy over status and the acquisition of vehicles and accommodation, and the families out in the fields were forgotten. Money was often wasted in the security of the knowledge that more could easily be requested, and there was no real sense of accountability.

Conversely, in my own District the only cash available was that earned from the hunting and tourism. Everyone knew exactly how much there was, and that if it was spent in one way it was not available for something else. This encouraged responsible decision making and proper budgeting.

The other important factor in making a programme successful is an effective information network within and between Districts, so that people have a real sense of involvement. If they know what is going on and they have a voice, then they will complain when something is not to their liking. In this respect, outside assistance and training is important to enable Council staff to understand and practice the techniques of participatory rural development. This often means that a larger complement of staff is needed in order to carry out an effective programme of education and consultation among the communities, but as far as possible, it is better to keep it modest and low key. The programme should be allowed to grow slowly, under its own momentum, rather than having structures imposed from the outside which force the pace of development and leave the people behind.

CASH OR PROJECTS

In my own District of Hurungwe, the programme got off the ground through a lucrative hunting contract with a local safari operator, which grossed around US$140,000 in the first year I was there (1992). Of this money, around 80 per cent went back to the communities where it was earned, while the remaining 20 per cent was used at Council level for administration costs: running workshops and meetings, paying game scouts and other staff and purchasing equipment. Since 1992 was a drought year, most of the communities opted to divide the cash between households. Two Wards bought grinding mills, with the aim of providing a cheaper service and making money for other community projects. Others bought beehives, and some money was spent on schools and clinics.

By 1994 there was a shift away from the cash option, and more of the money was spent on schools and clinics. One community opted to build a cattle dip tank, and another funded repairs for village boreholes. Within the District, both at community and Council level, there was much debate on how the money should be spent, which came down to 'cash or projects'. Most of the community leaders and Council staff recognized the benefits of well chosen projects, but a significant element of the people still called for cash in their pockets, despite the fact that the individual amounts were often very small.

There were also social issues to contend with, since the decision-making tends to be dominated by the men, who also largely control the projects, which gives a rather unbalanced community perspective. It was noticeable that the women were cautious about accepting a project, but once the decision was made, they were more likely to be the ones who did the work required, and used the service, while the men sat on the committees and did the organizing.

MAINTAINING COMMUNICATION

From the bottom upwards, the administrative structure set up started at village level, where the people elected their own representatives to sit on the Village Wildlife Committee (VWC), and also chose their own Resource Monitors, who were paid from the Ward budget to do animal surveys and report on crop raiding incidents and poaching. Representatives from the VWCs then sat on the Ward Wildlife Committee (WWC), which was chaired by the Ward Councillor. It was at this level that most of my input as District Co-ordinator occurred, as it made a convenient mid-point for general decision-making and feedback from the villages. The community bank account was also handled by the WWC. The Councillor and WWC Secretary then sat on the District Wildlife Committee (DWC), which reported directly to the District Council, and thus acted as the major policy making body. Regular meetings and workshops were held to train Committee members and consult with the people, and representatives were frequently sent into the Council offices to discuss problems and issues of immediate importance. Thus a continuous line of involvement and communication was maintained between Council and the communities.

A range of different training workshops was run, largely governed by what seemed appropriate at the time. Just to give an idea of how the programme developed, I have listed the formal workshops in chronological order:

- 1992 – General introduction to the principles of CAMPFIRE; ideas for use of CAMPFIRE revenue, wildlife management techniques, and comparisons with other Districts; problem animal control and wildlife surveys; accounting and record keeping for secretaries and treasurers.
- 1993 – Anti-poaching strategies and community by laws; analysis of tenders from safari operators to run a tourism venture; outline of achievements so

far (training for new Councillors after election); practical animal surveys; communication skills and open forum discussion of problems; focus on community problems – the participative approach to decision making on use of revenue.
• 1994 – Bee keeping; tree planting and management, and the use of indigenous species.

It is interesting to note the progression towards more sophisticated ideas and a more participative approach, which perhaps illustrates the way CAMPFIRE encourages the development of ideas and responsibility. CAMPFIRE should also establish a programme of sustainable natural resource management practice among the communities. In an ideal world this would come first, but in reality has to be striven for after the economic benefits have been seen and can be believed in. The setting up of smaller scale projects, such as tree planting, bee-keeping, fishing, properly managed stock grazing and crop rotation, is something which could and should happen in every community, and not just those where there are charismatic wildlife resources.

PHOTO-TOURISM

The safari hunting contract provided the initial impetus for the programme, and still produces the bulk of the income. However, further schemes for generating revenue are now being developed. In 1993 a contract was set up with a photo-tourism safari operator, to run walking safaris from a tented camp. From the beginning, the local people were more involved in setting this up than they had been with the hunting contract, which was done purely at Council level. Still the business belongs to the operator, so the risks and responsibility lie with him – the joint venture is purely a financial one. In 1994 a further step was taken in devolution, when one community began building their own small tourism camp. Limited funding was obtained from an outside donor, so that the local WWC had to budget and plan the project properly. They have been the decision making body at every stage, with guidance from Council and myself. Together we faced a multitude of frustrations and delays, and the camp has slowly taken shape. When it is completed it will be staffed and managed by the WWC.

The concept is very simple, three basic self-catering rondavels and a campsite beside a beautiful river, from which tourists can walk in the bush, fish in the river or visit local villages. The money-making potential is not large, since the project is very modest, aimed at the budget traveller or weekenders from the city, but it has been, and will continue to be, an enormous learning experience for the people involved, as well as being a source of pride within the community. Having worked through this project, I can see the need for a centralized training facility to serve all such ventures. As well as initial training in project planning and budgeting, it should provide a forum for sharing ideas and experiences, so that each District can learn from the activities of others. This would require outside funding to set up and run.

WILD NOT CUTE

A major issue which is still far from being solved is crop raiding by wild animals – problem animal control. It is the single issue which causes the most bitterness and anger among the people. No matter what we say about the wonders of CAMPFIRE – cash in pocket, community projects etc, the people are first and last farmers. Their livelihood and security lies in growing crops, and to see a herd of elephant trampling a field of maize which represents hours of back-breaking toil and a year's food supply for the family generates understandably strong feelings of fury and anxiety. In addition there is the personal safety factor – sometimes people are killed by elephants, and when a herd is in the area children are afraid to go to school and people's movements are constrained. Often wells are destroyed and scarce community water resources are used up by animals unable to find water out in the bush. The problem is exacerbated by the movement of people into areas which are traditional animal feeding grounds, and in some cases it would be better if the people moved out, but they have nowhere else to go.

During the growing season, staff at the Council are inundated by complaints and calls for crop raiding animals to be shot. They cannot possibly act on every complaint, or there would be no animals left. Many reports are exaggerated, due to natural anxiety and/or the desire for some free meat, so staff have first to sort out which are the serious cases which really do require action. It is a somewhat long winded process and is intended to avoid killing animals if at all possible.

At every stage advice is given to local people on what they can do for themselves, such as avoiding planting pumpkins near maize, since pumpkins attract elephants. Plans are also being discussed to set up water points away from the villages, so that animals are not attracted to the houses and gardens for water. Sometimes electric fencing can help to separate wildlife areas from cultivated areas, though this is an expensive option requiring careful maintenance, and is not always appropriate for the geographical and ecological situation. In the end, problem animal control will always be imperfect, so the rewards of CAMPFIRE, combined with the most effective management which can be devised, have to tip the balance towards acceptance of the nuisance caused by the animals.

While still far from perfect, CAMPFIRE has none-the-less gone a significant distance along the road to sustainable natural resource management which takes the needs of people, animals and the environment into account.

TAKING ON RESPONSIBILITY

The connection between the hunting, photo-tourism and small scale projects is community participation and responsibility. For too long rural people have been told what to do – whether by a white colonial government or an independent black administration, it has amounted to the same thing for them. The result has been their abdication of all responsibility for their own welfare and environment. They have been reduced to the role of beggars who hold out their hands where there is a drought, and continue abusing the land without consideration for the future. In early traditional societies this was not so. Communities took responsibilities for themselves in their own ways. CAMPFIRE is a small step towards regenerating that spirit of local independence. It is about empowerment of the people as much as conservation of the environment, and the two are inextricably linked.

Involving Maasai Women

Sylvia van der Cammen

The Maasai have long been excluded from having access to the benefits of tourism development, and women Maasai, whose access to land and water for grazing their livestock and feeding their children is restricted, are hit particularly hard. In this article Sylvia van der Cammen of Retour, a Dutch non-governmental organisation specialising in tourism development consultancy, tells of how some of the Maasai women are now beginning to participate.

The Maasai in Tanzania have always had an ambivalent relationship with tourism. The Serengeti – where they have lived in harmony with nature for centuries – was one of the best spots to see wildlife, so the Maasai were expelled and replaced by tourists. Because those tourists are also interested in seeing fierce Maasai warriors, they have become a living attraction. But the Maasai, being regarded as backward and stubborn were not involved in the tourism operations, and now, having been forced to sell their culture, many feel as though they are victims of tourism.

Pushed by droughts and decreasing sources of income, some Maasai groups from north Tanzania asked Retour to explore the opportunities tourism could offer in the process of empowerment: more jobs, higher incomes, better organizational structures, better contacts with governments based on equity and strengthening their culture. In the Loliondo area (near the Serengeti National Park), Maasai groups are losing land to private landowners. They can no longer graze their cows and live as pastoralists and have to settle in one place. As the number of cows per person is decreasing they have had to find additional income – a difficult task since they have had little education and are in a subordinate position in Tanzanian society. Over-population and droughts deteriorated their situation further, especially for Maasai women who are responsible for finding water and food for the children and the livestock.

The first Retour mission, a team of men only, soon found out that they would not be able to communicate with the women's groups. I was therefore invited to join in the second mission as a female organizational expert. Whereas in Europe the distinction between the worlds of men and women is hierarchical, in the Maasai culture, they are almost completely separated and it makes more sense to think of them as parallel worlds. Men are responsible for the social life and the decision making systems, and women are responsible for the world inside the community such as feeding the cattle and the children, cleaning the houses, fetching the water and firewood. The women have no income or possessions of their own.

The male leaders were very reluctant to allow the women to become involved in tourism. When I talked to the men I had to be accompanied by our male project leader, and in the end three aspects convinced them that women should be involved. Firstly, there was a drought and it was obvious that women suffered in particular. Secondly, when different types of tourism and tourist were presented to choose from, the leaders selected the culturally-oriented tourist. We convinced them that such people would be critical of the oppression of women and would never return if they found out this was happening. Thirdly, we argued that if women weren't involved there would be no funding by development organizations.

After the men approved we started working with the women's groups and concentrated on strengthening organizational structures, training and education, creating jobs and generating income for them. I first interviewed the ten different women groups to assess strengths, weaknesses and possibilities that were present. Through these informal discussions, in which I paid a lot of attention to sharing information and experiences, the women and I could get to know each other. In the meantime I tried to teach them to think in terms of possibilities instead of impossibilities, and although I had to talk to them through a male interpreter, it was easy to communicate non-verbally, and I felt that I gained their trust.

Because tourism is a complex process involving many persons and groups, it offers opportunities for women to meet others, and as women have special knowledge of handicrafts, walking routes (for fetching water), herbs, plants and crops, women skills are especially well-suited for developing tourism products. As soon as possible we brought a small group of tourists with us, so they could see the project could actually lead to results. Thus the ice was broken and the women were motivated to go on. The results were used in discussions with men and led to the formation of the Maasai Tourism Organisation (MTO) in which all youth and women's groups were represented and included two men and two women on the board.

Together with the local authorities, the MTO decided on an integrated approach to tourism in which the youth and women's groups developed products and activities which were complementary: two campsites, walking safaris and beadwork shops. We provided training in book-keeping, organizational management, and tourism skills and made contacts with a Dutch tour operator who visited with five groups. Jobs were created for women in making and selling beadwork and in campsite cleaning and cooking. Through intensive lobbying with the male leaders the women were allowed to keep the income from selling beadwork.

For tourism to contribute to empowerment, some aspects are particularly important. It is crucial to look at problems women face in relation to the problems the whole society faces and the traditional power structures. It is definitely worthwhile investing time in finding the right contact persons, not only inside the target groups, but also outside, such as government officials and teachers, male and female. In order to achieve long-term goals, it is also essential to achieve short-term successes, so including targets that are within reach, such as opening a bank account, organizing workshops, or carrying out a small pilot programme, are particularly important.

A final question which is always raised, especially by critical men, is whether there is a strong element of cultural imperialism when white westerners help other women of a radically different culture. Maasai women don't want to radically change their culture. But they do want to create incomes of their own and to put more pressure on men if necessary, to cope with growing needs for income, healthcare and education for their children. Empowerment is a process to enable them to achieve these goals, thus enabling the whole Maasai society to cope with the changing challenges of the future.

Chapter 7

Economic Perspectives

INTRODUCTION

The detailed economic appraisal of specific tourism structures and activities, individually or collectively, is achieved by the application of measurable indicators of economic performance (Lea 1988). Unfortunately this approach to the study of the economic impacts of tourism, essential at a micro scale, is too narrow to judge the overall value of the industry to the destination area. Hence we focus here on the political economy perspectives of tourism in which much of the theory is grounded. Indeed Van Doorn (1979) suggested that it was only possible to understand tourism evolution within the framework of the level of development reached by the country or area concerned. A great deal of attention has been given to the structure of the industry, especially in developing countries (Shaw and Williams 1994), and the role of entrepreneurs – notably through the operation of multinational companies – has been highlighted (Shaw and Williams 1994, Burns and Holden 1995).

It is also worth stressing that the particular moment in time at which any evaluation occurs can be critical. During the construction phase capital is provided by developers and state expenditure on infrastructure is considerable. Many unskilled and skilled jobs are generated that can often be filled by local people. In the operation phase, when the facilities are being used by tourists, income derives from them to local and non-local commercial interests, as well as to the state. Skilled posts are often occupied by non-local labour (Pearce 1989). These situations introduce a range of costs and benefits, listed in Box 7.1, that focus on a number of important groups.

Income

Tourism can help the national balance of payments by attracting hard currency. In many poor countries with few alternatives for development, such as Nepal, Antigua and the Maldives, it is the main export industry and contributes greatly to gross national product. However these countries often suffer from high leakages, because many goods and services essential for the operation of the industry must be imported, while profits are repatriated. Britton's model (1980) highlights these difficulties and stresses the dangers of dependency and neo-colonialism that apply not simply to developing countries where tourism has assumed importance, but also to relatively underdeveloped parts of the more advanced nations, like the Highlands of Scotland. The role of multinational companies, acting in a neo-colonial capacity, has come to be seen as a key to understanding the operation and effects of the industry. Though often denigrated (Ferguson 1990, O'Grady 1990), it has been suggested (Shaw and Williams 1994)

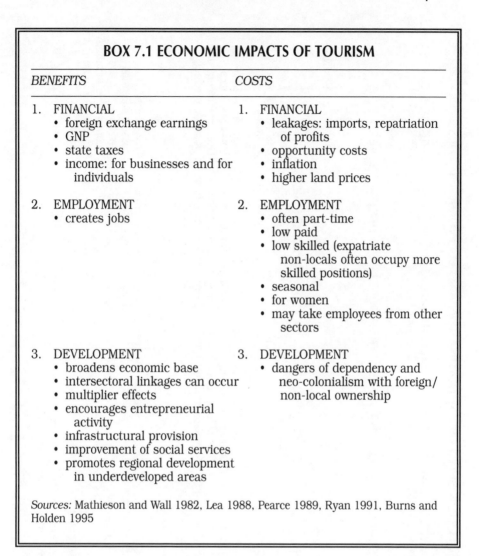

BOX 7.1 ECONOMIC IMPACTS OF TOURISM

BENEFITS	*COSTS*

1. FINANCIAL
   • foreign exchange earnings
   • GNP
   • state taxes
   • income: for businesses and for individuals
	1. FINANCIAL
	   • leakages: imports, repatriation of profits
	   • opportunity costs
	   • inflation
	   • higher land prices

2. EMPLOYMENT
   • creates jobs
	2. EMPLOYMENT
	   • often part-time
	   • low paid
	   • low skilled (expatriate non-locals often occupy more skilled positions)
	   • seasonal
	   • for women
	   • may take employees from other sectors

3. DEVELOPMENT
   • broadens economic base
   • intersectoral linkages can occur
   • multiplier effects
   • encourages entrepreneurial activity
   • infrastructural provision
   • improvement of social services
   • promotes regional development in underdeveloped areas
	3. DEVELOPMENT
	   • dangers of dependency and neo-colonialism with foreign/ non-local ownership

Sources: Mathieson and Wall 1982, Lea 1988, Pearce 1989, Ryan 1991, Burns and Holden 1995

that such a reaction is oversimplistic since organizations of this type, through their training programmes, can spread desperately needed skills more widely.

Employment

Tourism creates much-needed jobs in destination areas that, often because of their relative underdevelopment, are attractive to visitors. Nevertheless it is argued (Lea 1988, Pearce 1989, Burns and Holden 1995) that such jobs are not 'real' jobs but are usually low-skilled and low-paid, seasonal, part-time and for which women are favoured. They can draw workers away from other sectors of the economy and thereby cause a fall in output levels in those sectors. The more skilled and higher-paid positions are frequently occupied by non-local or expatriate labour, leading to further leakages from the economy, as well as social strains among less favoured

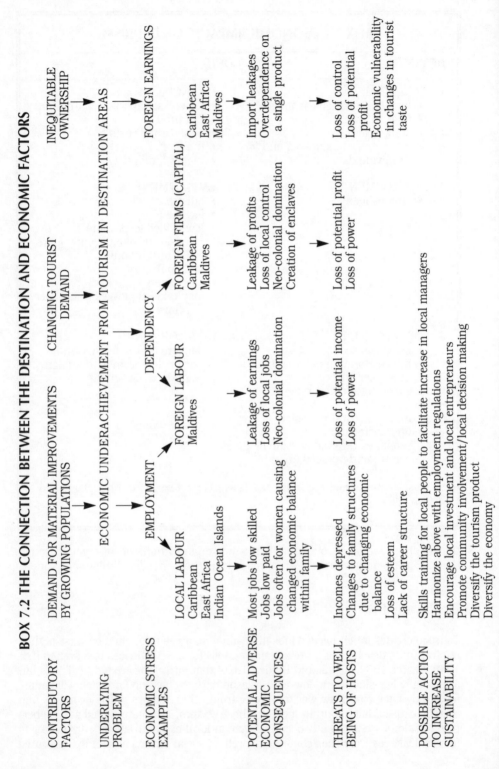

BOX 7.2 THE CONNECTION BETWEEN THE DESTINATION AND ECONOMIC FACTORS

CONTRIBUTORY FACTORS	DEMAND FOR MATERIAL IMPROVEMENTS BY GROWING POPULATIONS	CHANGING TOURIST DEMAND	INEQUITABLE OWNERSHIP
UNDERLYING PROBLEM	ECONOMIC UNDERACHIEVEMENT FROM TOURISM IN DESTINATION AREAS		
ECONOMIC STRESS EXAMPLES	EMPLOYMENT	DEPENDENCY	FOREIGN EARNINGS
	LOCAL LABOUR Caribbean East Africa Indian Ocean Islands	FOREIGN LABOUR Maldives	FOREIGN FIRMS (CAPITAL) Caribbean Maldives	Caribbean East Africa Maldives
POTENTIAL ADVERSE ECONOMIC CONSEQUENCES	Most jobs low skilled Jobs low paid Jobs often for women causing changed economic balance within family	Leakage of earnings Loss of local jobs Neo-colonial domination	Leakage of profits Loss of local control Neo-colonial domination Creation of enclaves	Import leakages Overdependence on a single product
THREATS TO WELL BEING OF HOSTS	Incomes depressed Changes to family structures due to changing economic balance Loss of esteem Lack of career structure	Loss of potential income Loss of power	Loss of potential profit Loss of power	Loss of control Loss of potential profit Economic vulnerability in changes in tourist taste
POSSIBLE ACTION TO INCREASE SUSTAINABILITY	Skills training for local people to facilitate increase in local managers Harmonize above with employment regulations Encourage local investment and local entrepreneurs Promote community involvement/local decision making Diversify the tourism product Diversify the economy		

166

workers. Skill acquisition may be encouraged, but the opportunity to practise these skills and receive commensurate reward for them is not always available.

Economic development

Tourism may be criticized as a strategy for improving the material wellbeing of people living in a destination area, but all too often other possibilities are simply not available (Ferguson 1990, Shaw and Williams 1994). It is perceived as a valuable and viable option for the transformation of the economy at the destination (Lea 1988) and its secondary and tertiary effects, through the multiplier, are important, although often inaccurately calculated (Lea 1988, Shaw and Williams 1994)

The economic costs and benefits of tourism are summarized in a balanced way in the reading from Lea (1988). In the earlier stages of post-war mass tourism the benefits of the industry were generally considered to outweigh the costs. However, by the early 1980s academics like Marfurt were beginning to recognize that costs could be very significant. Her paper (1983) is included here and these costs are also shown in Box 7.2, which incorporates suggestions for ways in which these costs can be reduced and sustainability increased. This reader does not intend to focus on methods of impact measurement. A range of examples illustrate the variety of situations in which tourism can increase economic sustainability complete the readings.

REFERENCES

Britton, S G (1980) 'The spatial organisation of tourism in a neo-colonial economy: a Fiji case study', *Pacific Viewpoint* 21 (2) pp144–65

Burns, P M and Holden, A (1995) *Tourism A New Perspective*, Prentice Hall International (UK) Limited, Hemel Hempstead

Ferguson, J (1990) *Far From Paradise. An Introduction to Caribbean Development*, Latin America Bureau Ltd, London

Lea, J (1988) *Tourism and Development in the Third World*, Routledge, London

Marfurt, E (1983) 'Tourism and the third world: dream or nightmare?', *Swiss Review of World Affairs* July 14–21

Mathieson, A and Wall, G (1982) *Tourism. Economic, Physical and Social Impacts*, Longman, Harlow

O'Grady, A (ed) (1990) *The Challenge of Tourism*, Ecumenical Coalition on Third World Tourism, Bangkok

Pearce, D (1989) *Tourist Development* 2nd edition, Longman, Harlow

Ryan, C (1991) *Recreational Tourism*, Routledge, London

Shaw, G and Williams, A M (1994) *Critical Issues in Tourism. A Geographical Perspective*, Blackwell, Oxford

Van Doorn, J W M (1979) 'The Developing Countries: Are they Really Affected by Tourism? Some Critical Notes on Socio-cultural Impact Studies' Paper presented at Seminar on Leisure Studies and Tourism, 7–8 December, Warsaw (mimeo) Quoted in Pearce (1989)

Tourism's Economic Impacts

John Lea

ECONOMIC ANALYSIS

Economic impacts outweigh other considerations in most assessments of tourism development in the Third World. However, the extensive literature has tended to be much more specific about expected benefits than costs, and extends from the discussion of broad effects on the whole economy to detailed impacts of a single new project. The unifying feature is a focus on things capable of being measured and evaluated by the tools of economic analysis. [...]

The balance of payments

The search by most Third World countries for hard currency with which to pay for modern industrial imports like machinery and motor cars puts international tourism high on the list of development priorities. Tourist spending gives rise to inward and outward currency flows which are generally thought to balance out in favour of Third World destinations, although there is evidence to show that few studies really investigate what happens in sufficient depth. These fiscal effects are generally categorized as follows:

Primary effects arising out of currency inflows from foreign visitor expenditure in a host country and outflows coming from the spending abroad by residents. They are recorded in various ways by banks and businesses and are fairly easy to measure.

Secondary effects arise as the direct expenditure is gradually felt in other sectors of the economy. They are divided into three categories: direct secondary effects (such as travel agent's commissions); indirect secondary effects as the tourist service industry passes some of its earnings on to other businesses (such as when an airline contracts a local company to supply on-board meals which, in turn, means importing some of the food); and induced secondary effects relating to the wages of those employed producing tourist goods and services. A proportion of this income may be remitted abroad by foreign employees.

Tertiary effects are the currency flows which do not come from direct tourist expenditure and relate to things like investment opportunities stimulated by tourist activity. Thus when Japanese tourists in New Zealand began buying large quantities of sheepskin products it led to the growth of an export industry.

A failure to investigate the secondary and tertiary effects of tourism spending makes it very difficult to discover where spending goes and the effects of its circulation. Net foreign exchange receipts are a good deal lower than gross earnings and reckoned to be as low as 50 to 60 per cent for countries in the Caribbean and the Pacific. One study found that the proportion of expatriates (non-nationals) in senior positions in the Caribbean tourist industry has been as high as 65 per cent (Cayman Islands) and accounted for over 48 per cent of all hotel and guesthouse workers in the British Virgin Islands. A considerable but unknown amount of the income received by these workers was remitted to their homes abroad, reducing the net benefit to the host countries.

Employment

The effect of tourist expenditure on employment generation is also widely discussed in the economic literature but has been limited to answering only some of the chief questions involved. Little is known, for example, about the skills required and the returns and benefits expected; the geographical distribution of employment; the overall contribution to national, regional, and local economies; and the future significance of the travel industry as an employment generator. Three types of employment are generally recognized: first, direct employment from expenditure on tourism facilities like hotels; second, indirect employment in businesses affected by tourism in a secondary way like local transport, handicrafts, and banks; and finally, induced employment arising from the spending of money by local residents from their tourist incomes.

Once again a failure to consider all these categories has resulted in rather crude analyses of the real employment situation in Third World countries. It is possible to make several generalizations about tourism and employment from existing studies.

- There is a close but not perfect correlation between the income-generating effects of tourism and the creation of employment, meaning that high returns from the industry do not translate directly into proportionately more jobs.
- The kind of tourist activity will influence employment because some types are more labour intensive. Jobs in restaurants and bars in Mexico for example, have been shown to provide almost 40 per cent more employment than jobs in hotels and motels.
- The types of work skills available locally also have an effect on employment, as illustrated by the high demand for unskilled labour. This has meant a preponderance of female employees in some Caribbean islands and the filling of senior jobs by expatriates.
- Tourism may actually take employees away from other sectors of the economy or offer part-time jobs, both of which will have little effect in reducing overall unemployment figures.
- Much tourism employment is seasonal. In the Caribbean, for example, the number of hotel employees per room varies from an in season high of 1.4 to 0.9 out of season.

Entrepreneurial activity

It is generally believed that tourism will develop backward linkages in an economy resulting in the creation of cost savings called external economies. This happens, for example, when an improvement to local services like transport or electricity is a result of tourism but additionally provides a benefit to everyone in the area. The extent to which such improvements can actually promote business activity in a Third World country has not received much attention and the factors involved are more complex than might at first be supposed. Linkages between the hotel sector and local businesses will depend upon factors like the types of suppliers required (foodstuffs, maintenance and repairs, and so on); the capacity of local suppliers; the historical development of tourism in the area; and the type of tourist development.

When hotels are built gradually over time, the supply of local produce will keep pace with demand for a while but demand may eventually outstrip capacity and lead to a dependence on imported food. In the case of large new urban hotels which have been rapidly developed, there is a huge and immediate requirement for agricultural produce which can be met only from imports. It is hard for locals to break into this system of reliance on foreign suppliers and the dependence on imports remains. Unfortunately there is no tradition of providing the foodstuffs involved in many small island societies, in ensuring reliable supplies, or in seeking the entrepreneurial opportunities which make such businesses flourish elsewhere. An example of this problem can be seen in the two small Southern African countries of Swaziland and Lesotho where the Taiwanese government has developed demonstration farms. The vegetables produced are of show quality but are scarcely noticed by most local people who, consider the whole exercise to be foreign to their own culture and of no application to themselves.

ECONOMIC COSTS OF TOURISM

Several authors maintain that over-optimistic claims about the benefits of tourism twenty years ago have damaged the economies of some developing countries. Although this is probably true, modern feasibility studies are much more competent than the early examples, and it is possible to identify the main sources of economic cost.

Opportunity costs

The relative economic benefits to be gained from investing in tourism rather than some other industry is a comparison known in economics as the 'opportunity cost' of an investment. There are few studies which have been able to measure the values of the opportunities forgone as far as tourism is concerned. Young (1973) mentions the case of the Caribbean island of St Lucia, where the coming of tourism resulted in a flight of labour from the local banana industry which was then the main source of foreign income. Those left on the land could not cope with the labour requirements of the banana crop with a consequent loss of productivity and earnings. Tourism led to a great increase in food imports as well and a great strain on the balance of payments. The net benefit to the island of the new industry was therefore marginal.

Over-dependence on tourism

Small Third World economies tend towards dependence on a single primary product and are badly affected by changes in commodity prices. In these circumstances the introduction of tourism appears initially as a welcome form of diversification. A problem arises (as in the case of St Lucia above) when tourism earnings supplant traditional activities and open the country's economy to instability of a different kind. Changes in tourism fashion, often dictated by transnational travel groups, can devastate such destinations and soon lead to a downward spiral of diminishing standards and poor publicity. This is all too evident in Jamaica where competition from new coastal resorts in Mexico's Cancun Peninsula is one factor which appears to have damaged a formerly buoyant industry.

As Young (1973) points out, the degree of acceptable reliance on tourism is also related to the structure of the economy.

> *Where there is high unemployment, a relatively unskilled labour-force and few alternative sources of employment ... then stimulation of the tourist industry may well be a correct course of action. The danger appears to be at the next stage of economic development, where unemployment and underemployment have been reduced, the labour-force is better educated and an infrastructure exists which might support other industries. Continuing dependence and emphasis on tourism may no longer be economically justifiable.*

Inflation

Although there are very few documented studies of how inflation due to tourism affects a host population, there is plenty of conventional wisdom to suggest that some price rises are linked to this cause. The more obvious instances involve increases in retail prices in shops during the tourist season, and steeply rising land values leading to a general rise in home costs and property taxes. Huge increases in land values in Swaziland's Ezulweni Valley tourist centre in the early 1970s are generally considered to have been due to pressure from South African investors and speculative buying from outside the country. The Swazi government countered this with a land speculation control act requiring all property to be first offered for sale to local buyers before permission could be granted by a review board for foreign purchase. The effect was to reduce land prices considerably and bring them back in reach of some local residents.

REFERENCES

Young, G (1973) *Tourism: Blessing or Blight?* Harmondsworth, Penguin

Tourism and the Third World: Dream or Nightmare?

Edith Marfurt

For masses of people in the industrialized world, booking a charter flight to some idyllic, sunny, exotic, seaside vacation spot has become almost as common-place as shopping in a discount store. But for years a discussion has been going on behind the scenes about the benefits that mass tourism brings to the countries involved, most of them in the Third World. This debate, which has gone through various phases during the years of expanding international tourism, continues to revolve largely around divergent views of its actual and potential effects in the sociocultural and economic realms.

In a euphoric phase during the second half of the 1960s, long-distance tourism was widely regarded as an essential component of Third World economic development because of its presumably large contribution to employment, income and the acquisition of foreign currency. By the start of the 1970s the tide of opinion had changed, as it was observed that the effects could vary greatly from country to country and were often much less positive than expected. In addition, attention began to be paid to the undesirable side-effects of intercultural encounter. Long-distance mass tourism, so went the new criticism, promotes the downfall of traditional social structures and value systems and the rise of criminality and prostitution around tourist centres, while generating a beggarly and tip-cadging mentality and encouraging the commercialization of hospitality and art. [...]

The fact that calls to abandon Third World tourism have come up at all among critics is probably due in part to the rather sobering experience of so-called alternative tourism. As early as 1978 G Armanski, a member of the alternative New Travel Group, in his book *Die kostbarsten Tage des Jahres* (*The Most Precious Days of the Year*), criticized what he called the 'anti-tourists' who, as he put it 'set out, with rucksacks on their backs and noble ideals in their heads, always looking for the last remnants of Paradise, which they promptly begin to destroy'.

According to R Jaisli of the Student Travel Service it is generally acknowledged today that even those forms of adventure and educational travel known as alternative tourism, including observation trips to development projects, do not hold the answer. On the contrary, experience has shown that even under these altered conditions tourists tend to maintain their consumer attitudes. As participants in organized tours, even 'enlightened' tourists may become burdensome to local populations. Participants in alternative educational tours often develop the arrogant and deceptive feeling that they have become quite knowledgeable, something in the nature of development experts. Ueli Mäder, Secretary of the previously cited Working Group, confirms this on the basis of his own experience. 'On one study trip in which I participated as well as observed, all participants were spontaneously prepared to make a concrete evaluation of development projects which they had examined for only about an hour each. Their very superficial impressions did not prevent any of them from venturing a final opinion.

Most participants found that what they had seen only served to confirm their prior views and prejudices about development policy.'

A notorious shortage of foreign exchange motivates many developing countries to promote tourism strongly. At 10 per cent, journeys to the 'poorhouse of the world' still occupy only a relatively modest slice of international tourism, but they have enjoyed unbroken growth since 1960. The subject of the economic value of long-distance tourism is a focal point of attention for many interest groups, sometimes opposing ones – governments of developing countries, investors and travel organizers, even institutions concerned with bilateral and multilateral development aid. This is particularly evident in the evaluation of foreign-exchange profitability. Depending on the source, projections for the selfsame region may vary considerably.

At an international conference on 'Church and Tourism' held in Stockholm at the end of 1981 the view was expressed that the material hopes which had been invested in the development of tourism have not been fulfilled. According to figures presented at the Stockholm meeting, because tourist centres are often owned by local elites or by multinational hotel chains and airlines, 80–90 per cent of the money spent by tourists on their vacations remain in Europe or North America. Other sources of information indicate that there is a broad range of foreign-exchange profitability. An international comparative study published in 1979 by R Cleverdon reached the conclusion that an island such as Mauritius, which is totally dependent on imports for the establishment and maintenance of its tourist industry, will enjoy net foreign-exchange earnings of only about 10 per cent. The situation is quite different in countries like Tunisia or Kenya, which can have net earnings of 70–90 per cent because they only need to import luxury items.

It is never sufficiently clear on what basis such studies arrive at their conclusions – which is a crucial failing. Some studies by UN organizations, for example, point to net foreign-exchange losses from tourism as a result of transfers of interest and profits to foreign investors as well as travel agency commissions and expenditures for promotion abroad. There are yet other factors to be considered: in the field of air transport, for example, the airlines of the developing countries are in an economically unfavourable, peripheral position. Wages for foreign management personnel and for the training of skilled domestic tourist industry personnel abroad, illegal black market transactions and even the so-called 'demonstration effect' (which stimulates a greater need for imports in a developing country) – all these factors can have a negative influence on the foreign-exchange balance.

Against the background of their often dramatic unemployment problems, many developing countries hope that tourism will provide lasting economic impetus and, partly through the multiplier effect, will create many new jobs. But whether the appearance of swarms of foreign tourists in the Caribbean, in East Africa or Sri Lanka also serves to generate swarms of new jobs, is at least open to question.

It is a safe basic assumption that the tourist would like to spend as little as possible for his holiday trip and, in order to make the best possible use of his two or three weeks, wants to get an idea of the main local points of interest as quickly as he can. Western efficiency in tourism has assumed some grotesque forms.

According to a recently passed law in West Germany, if during a package tour the featured dance troupe in the Congo fails to appear on schedule, if a bus driver is late in a country where time has little meaning, if the Indian porter in the Amazon has neglected to bring the canned meat for lunch, the tourist can now file charges against the travel agency. As Mrs G Castiello of the Hotelplan Travel

Service knows only too well from long experience, in the final analysis the average tourist wants to eat and drink just as he does at home. His willingness to engage in exotic culinary escapades is very slight. And in terms of the living standards of the host country, his demands for comfort are luxurious, though they may not entail any more than such 'ordinary' matters as 'room with bath'.

Because of the high quality standards of the international hotel industry and the low technical level of small industry and handicrafts in most developing countries, the local artisans and businessmen generally do not benefit much during the construction phase. Far more employment is generated by the operation of a tourist hotel. The number of new jobs created per hotel bed varies from 0.3 to 1.5, with locals usually providing the mass of low-paid employees, such as waiters and chambermaids. Much of the time it is foreign management personnel who run the hotels, which must be operated according to modern management principles and therefore require specialized knowledge. In Tunisia, half the total wage volume reportedly is accounted for by (generally European) management personnel.

Another dilemma which dramatically highlights tourism's limited potential as a stimulus for the precarious employment situation in Third World countries is the concentration of this economic sector in major centres and a few particularly attractive outlying spots. How can tourism help to halt the almost universal flight from the land when, in a country like Peru, most brief trips are limited to Lima and one of two 'musts' – Iquitos-Amazonas or Cuzco-Macchu Picchu? Or in Puerto Rico, where fully 78 per cent of all hotel rooms are situated in San Juan and its immediate environs?

Unemployment and underemployment in rural areas often result in an explosive growth of urban agglomerations. Yet the backward hinterlands, which most urgently need development, lack the basic features which would permit the creation of the infrastructure demanded by international tourism. This is a vicious cycle which serves only to heighten the fatal attraction of the cities and accelerates the desertion of rural areas by the more youthful segments of the populace. In the Seychelles the lucrative, expansive tourism industry has siphoned so many people away from fishing that the islands now import fish from Japan.

Too little attention has been paid thus far to the frequently observed price increases for mass consumer goods in the wake of a tourism boom. Policy makers are trying to hold back the tourist industry's high rate of imports by pressing for the widest possible assortment of domestic products. Essentially quite sensible, this strategy leads to supply bottlenecks and price increases wherever tourist facilities are concentrated in regions with inadequate self-supply capacity. In some cases expansive tourism gives rise to land speculation, the main beneficiaries of which are large landowners. On the Caribbean island of San Agustin the price of a parcel of land in touristically interesting areas rose by no less than 700 per cent in eight years. It is an open question how the local population copes with the resulting inflation in such cases.

In the overall view, then, the economic value of tourism for the Third World is highly variable, depending on a given economy's level of development, its structure, the kind of tourism emphasized (luxury, beach or round-trip tours) and whether growth takes place at a comfortable or an overheated pace. It would be undifferentiated to simply condemn all promotion of tourism and to try and blame all problems upon this one area of activity. By the same token a judgement of its value should not be based exclusively on the quoting of economic statistics. [...]

In many places an uncritical faith in economic growth has opened the door wide to mass tourism, with a large proportion of available national financial resources being invested in that sector. Some host countries have built expensive airports, hotels and freeways at a dizzying pace. There is no denying that considerations of prestige and a fascination with large figures animate some Third World governments to such action. It is rare indeed to come upon a case like that of the Kingdom of Bhutan, which is pursuing a careful, well-rationed policy of promoting tourism in a manner appropriate to local conditions and with care for maintaining its cultural and geographic charms.

But the Third World tourist infrastructure oriented toward international standards has almost always been created with the cooperation of the industrialized nations. Conditions of ownership are rather opaque, since, as R Jaisli of the Student Travel Service says, 'It is a simple matter to mobilize a pressure group in a country'. Solomon Aderi, an official of a church-run information service in Kenya, points out that a partnership between a financially powerful foreigner and a native Kenyan often consists of little more than the latter lending his name in order to demonstrate the 'Kenyan ownership' of some hotel.

Foreign travel organizations and hotel investors generally demand special investment incentives, such as high depreciation rates, free transfer of profits and extensive infrastructure work in advance. Not infrequently they are also granted partial tax exemptions. Under these circumstances how could a large percentage of the earnings from tourism fail to find its way back to the industrial nations?

Developing countries with excessively expansive tourism create for themselves the constraints which later plague them. Once the capital-intensive infrastructure has been built, it must be used at all costs. This can result in a situation verging on blackmail. Tunisia experienced something like this in 1972, when it refused to grant a bigger profit margin to a large German travel organization, whereupon the company reduced Tunisia's quota of tourists to one-fifth its former size. Developing countries are seldom in a position to defend themselves against this kind of economic coercion from abroad. Such a large, sudden loss of revenues can have catastrophic consequences for a country's economy. But it is not only such arbitrary acts which must be anticipated. Shifts in economic cycles, currency fluctuations, political unrest, epidemics, water shortages, massive pollution of sea and beaches, even sudden reversals of fashion trends, can shake the foundations of a country's existence, especially in nations with economies that depend entirely on tourism.

In an official position paper delivered at the 1980 conference of the World Tourism Organization (WTO) in Manila, the idea was launched of a sensible channelling of additional streams of tourists toward those developing countries best suited to receive them. The organization also lent its support to having the theme of tourism made an integral part of the North-South dialogue, so that both sides can recognize the problems and act accordingly.

In the intervening years the moves proposed by the WTO have not advanced beyond the stage of rhetoric. And it will doubtless take considerable time yet before the problems of tourism are acknowledged as constituting a subject of joint concern to all the developing nations. In the meantime their dream of tourism as a carrier of the blessings of progress may become a nightmare.

Strategies for Alternative Tourism: the Case of Tourism in Sagarmatha (Everest) National Park, Nepal

D W Robinson

The past decade has witnessed the appearance of alternative tourism designs that both recognize tourism's negative impacts and portray a more positive role for tourism linked to sustainable development. Often grouped under the title of alternative or appropriate tourism (Smith and Eadington 1992), these forms of tourism include ecotourism (Boo 1990), nature travel (Durst and Ingram 1988), ethnic tourism (McKean 1989) and adventure travel (Kutay 1990, Zurick 1992). Common to all of these is the tourist's desire for a participatory experience in a distinctive and often remote natural and/or cultural environment.

With a combined annual growth rate estimated at 20 to 27 per cent, these alternative models of tourism are the fastest-growing segment of the world travel market (Passoff 1991). Much of this growth has been associated with Third World destinations, such as the Himalaya regions of Tibet, Nepal and Bhutan, the coastal and rainforest regions of Central and South America, and the savannah regions of Africa. Currently, however, conflicting opinions abound on the role of alternative tourism in Third World development. Those who champion its core principle of sustainability argue that alternative tourism can help solve difficult Third World dilemmas about conservation and economic development, as well as promote a more equitable distribution of tourism earnings (Adams 1992, Gonsalves 1987, Harrison 1992, Healy 1992). Others suggest that the discussion on alternative tourism may be distorted, and argue that it may merely be an initial phase in an evolving system of conventional tourism which is more likely to be the ruin of ecologically and culturally sensitive areas of the Third World (Butler 1990, Cohen 1987, Greenwood 1989, Machlis and Bacci 1992, McKercher 1993, Wight 1993).

A destination which has come to typify the intense debate over the role of tourism in conservation and economic development is that of Sagarmatha (Everest) National Park in Nepal. While adventure travellers continue to be graciously welcomed to this area, and massive increases in visitors have generated a variety of economic and social benefits at both the local and national levels (Robinson 1992), there has also been increasing international concern expressed about tourism's negative impacts on this fragile mountain environment and its indigenous Sherpa population. Although a large body of literature exists that has portrayed Sagarmatha National Park as both a cultural and ecological catastrophe in the making, more recent reports (eg Fisher 1990, Stevens and Sherpa 1992a, 1992b, 1992c) suggest that these criticisms are premature and have ignored the adaptive strategies which have been developed to reconcile the stresses of tourism with local capabilities and needs.

The purpose of this paper is to describe and reappraise the economic, socio-cultural, and environmental changes that have been associated with the rapid growth of adventure travel in Sagarmatha National Park. In this context, the paper examines both the benefits and contradictions that tourism poses for sustainable development in Sagarmatha National Park, and outlines adaptive strategies that have been formulated to limit negative impacts on the local culture and environment. In seeking to further the discussion on the role of tourism in Third World development, the case study of Sagarmatha National Park illuminates the processes that underlie the expansion of tourism into frontier regions of the world (Zurick 1992) that would not otherwise be expected to develop mass tourism, and offers lessons to guide the development of policies to promote locally directed rural development and natural resource protection in other remote and sensitive tourism destinations.

The information presented in this paper draws on the author's research experiences during two periods (five months in total) of fieldwork in Sagarmatha National Park and Kathmandu, Nepal, in the fall of 1990 and the spring of 1992. This fieldwork involved meetings with Ministry of Tourism officials in Kathmandu, general field observations in both the popular and less frequented trekking districts of the national park, discussions with the national park wardens, and interviews with Sherpas residing in the national park. This information is set against recent reports of change in the region from the tourism research literature.

BACKGROUND ON ADVENTURE TOURISM IN NEPAL

In a manner similar to many other Third World countries that have large external debts, poverty, and scarce natural resources, Nepal has increasingly embraced tourism as a source of easily generated revenue. Having experienced unprecedented tourism growth in the past 25 years, Nepal is now among the more popular of the international tourism destinations. Today, tourism is Nepal's foremost source of foreign income and its major industry (Robinson 1992). Nepal's fame lies primarily in trekking and mountaineering, and it was here in the 1960s that the world's first commercial treks took place. Trekking and mountaineering visits to the Himalaya region of Nepal (which includes the protected national parks of Sagarmatha, Langtang, Shey Phksumdo and Rara, and the Annapurna Conservation Area) currently account for approximately 25 per cent of all tourist visits to this country. This represents an increase from a mere 650 trekkers and mountaineers in 1966 to over 46,000 in 1989 (although this number fell to 35,750 in 1990 owing to major political uprisings in Nepal during 1990 and the impact of the Gulf War on international travel). Hoping to maintain the growth of high mountain visitation, the Nepal Ministry of Tourism is planning infrastructure development in existing mountain parks, and plans to open up new trekking areas (such as Mustang, opened in March 1992) where they hope to divert some of the growing number of adventure travellers.

The most renowned tourist destination in Nepal is Sagarmatha National Park. Established in 1976 and declared a World Heritage Site in 1980, the park is famous for both its towering mountains, including Mount Everest, and the culture of its Sherpa people. The park is home to approximately 3000 Sherpas who live within its 1243 km^2 borders and is associated with the Sherpa culture more than any other Nepalese park. Migrating from Tibet in the early sixteenth century, the lives of the Sherpa are interwoven with teachings of Buddhism, and their communities have traditionally been based on agropastoralism and trade with Tibet. The

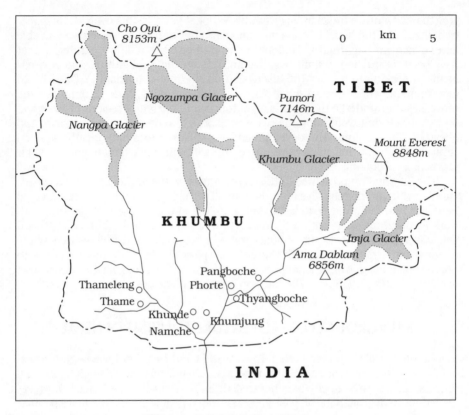

Figure 7.1 *Khumbu Region*

main trekking area in the park consists of four valleys near Mount Everest which are known as the Khumbu region (Figure 7.1). Within Khumbu are eight Sherpa villages and over 100 seasonal herding and secondary crop sites. These villages and secondary settlements are not part of the park proper, although all Sherpa grazing and forest lands are administered by the national park (Stevens and Sherpa 1992a).

TOURISM-RELATED CHANGES IN SAGARMATHA NATIONAL PARK

Since Nepal opened its borders to foreigners in 1951, Sagarmatha National Park has experienced a rapid increase in visitor numbers. The opening of the region's only commercial airstrip at Lukla (9000 feet) in 1964 reduced the travel time from Kathmandu to 40 minutes (as opposed to a walk in of one week from Jiri or two weeks from Kathmandu) and significantly boosted visitor numbers to the park. This region annually hosts mountaineering and trekking tourists numbering approximately twice the local population: in 1988 11,366 individual trekking permits were issued for the park, although the Ministry of Tourism's most recently available statistics indicate a decline to 5144 in 1990 (which was associated with domestic political problems and the impact of the Gulf War on international travel).

The changing economy

With tourism as the driving force during the past 20 years, the Khumbu has undergone a rapid transition from a subsistence to a cash economy and has experienced a rapid expansion of its local economy. An increasing dependency on tourism-generated income has brought considerable local economic benefits, and the Sherpas now enjoy a standard of living which is as high as any of the country's ethnic minorities.

Although Sherpas have a reputation for mountaineering skill, mountain-climbing was not a traditional Sherpa occupation. Sherpa involvement with mountaineering began inauspiciously in the 1920s when the British hired Sherpas for the servile work of portering (load-carrying) and guiding in the pioneering explorations both to Everest and Himalayan expeditions in North India. When trade between Khumbu and Tibet was severely impacted by the Chinese annexation of Tibet in 1959, trekking and mountaineering emerged as a new and lucrative financial opportunity. When commercial trekking began in Khumbu in the 1960s, entire Sherpa households were able to get involved in the industry. Sherpas were hired as high-status guides and later as office personnel in charge of hiring in foreign-owned trekking agencies in Kathmandu. These Sherpas, in turn, ensured high employment rates for their family and friends in Khumbu villages as porters, cook staff, and camping staff (Adams 1992).

In the 1970s, many young Sherpa men and families began to move to Kathmandu where greater employment opportunities existed in the trekking and mountaineering industry. Those with enough capital opened their own trekking agencies and hired villagers to work for them. Sherpa entrepreneurship has continued, and of the 100 trekking and travel agencies in Kathmandu in 1989, 26 of the 56 larger agencies registered with the Nepal Trekking Agent Association were controlled by Sherpas. Five of these larger agencies employed a total of 94 permanent salaried staff, 70 employees during part of the year, and 670 at peak season (Adams 1992, Kunwar, cited in Fisher 1990, 115).

Employment in the mountaineering and trekking industry in Khumbu itself has flourished at a number of levels. In the villages, many Sherpas have converted their homes into teashops and lodges to accommodate the growing number of foreign visitors, and today most households earn income from providing food, lodging, clothing, equipment or handicrafts. Khumbu Sherpas control most of the region's highly profitable tourist lodges, inns and teahouses, and have virtually monopolized tourism employment in the region. Young men and boys often gain low-paying jobs as porters, kitchen assistants or mail-runners on treks or expeditions. Those with more experience tend to gain salaried positions with an established trekking agency as cook or *sherpa* (a kind of general assistant to a trekking party). The most experienced Sherpas who possess leadership abilities may secure positions as trek or expedition leader (*sirdar*), which enables them to hire other villagers for daily wage work on a trek or expedition. Overall, the economic benefits appear to have been spread quite extensively throughout Khumbu; Adams (1992) reports that 80 per cent of the 141 village households and 92 per cent of the urban Sherpa households from Khumbu currently earn income from tourism.

It is typical for Sherpas to earn cash wages only during the high tourism seasons of autumn and spring, and although this is only four or five months per year, their incomes are nevertheless high by Nepalese standards. The owner of a popular lodge may gross over US$10,000 a year, and many are now among the wealthiest families in the region. In 1992, even a kitchen boy could earn more than 1500 rupees (US$50) per month, which is the equivalent to the salary of many office workers in Kathmandu. *Sirdars* may earn more than five times as much, for besides their base-salary they often make considerable extra money by making use of their own family members, servants, and packstock on treks and by over-reporting porter costs and other trail charges to their companies (Stevens and Sherpa 1992a). Since young Sherpas contribute to their parents' household until they marry in their mid- to late-twenties and establish their own households, several members of a Sherpa household will often earn income from trekking. While women from poor households have often earned some income from portering, trekking employment to date has been male-dominated, and it is only recently that women have begun to work as members of kitchen and camp crews. There are today only one or two examples of women *sirdars* in the Khumbu (Stevens and Sherpa 1992a).

A frequent criticism of tourism in Third World areas, and one that has been applied to this region, is the often exploitative nature of the tourist–host financial–labour relationship. Although Sherpas have been involved in tourism through traditional wage relationships, Adam's (1992) examination of the Sherpa economy indicates that the Sherpas have become neither 'commoditized' nor 'domesticated' as part of a subordinate local economy serving a Western-dominated tourism industry. Rather, increasing Sherpa ownership of trekking companies and unique tourist–Sherpa relationships have provided the Sherpas with opportunities to reconstitute their traditional social relationships, which were mixtures of both reciprocity and wage labour based on the Sherpa ideals of individualism and independence.

Today, tourism is extremely popular with the Khumbu Sherpas. Although some disaffection with tourism does exist, the Sherpas know that most of the region's inhabitants have gained substantially in financial terms, in standards of living, and through improved medical and educational facilities. Sherpa ownership of a substantial proportion of tourism businesses means that 'financial leakage' has undoubtedly been less than in many other Third World tourism areas. Primarily through tourism, this somewhat remote and poor rural society has rapidly become comparatively affluent – a situation which Stevens and Sherpa (1992a) and Adams (1992) have characterized as representing one of the world's foremost examples of successful local economic development through tourism.

Notwithstanding the Khumbu's current positive economic situation, however, the course of subsequent events will require careful attention. Not all Sherpa families have benefited equally from tourism, and neither have all Khumbu villages benefited from tourism. Related to the increasing demands from trekking and mountaineering groups, the inflation of the price of food and supplies in Khumbu has financially burdened those poorer families not involved in tourism. Also, while the region's tourism centre of Namche (11,000 feet) has experienced massive economic benefits, those villages remote from the main trekking routes, such as Thame, have changed very little.

Despite the aims of the government, there would appear to be little scope for further growth of tourism in Khumbu. This is primarily because the two airlines that fly into Lukla are severely limited in the number of tourists they can transport. Lukla's rudimentary landing strip, as well as the frequently turbulent flying conditions between Kathmandu and Lukla, have generated – for better or worse – a significant transportation bottleneck. Trekkers, however, will always have the option of a one-to-two-week walk in, and helicopter charters from Kathmandu are becoming popular. Yet even though the number of tourists is likely to remain fairly constant, new lodges continue to be built in Namche and along the lower Khumbu trekking route leading to Namche. As Fisher (1990) has noted, should the number of lodges proliferate too rapidly in this region, then earnings will be divided into an increasing number of shares, with average incomes diminishing or some businesses prospering at the expense of others. Khumbu Sherpas are also facing increased competition for trekking and mountaineering employment from neighbouring Solu Sherpas and other ethnic groups, such as Rais, Gurungs and Tamangs, who migrate seasonally into Khumbu in increasing numbers to seek employment (primarily portering). A new trend of foreign ownership of accommodation facilities, such as the newly reopened Japanese-owned luxury Everest View Hotel near Namche, also threatens Sherpa domination of the lodge industry.

The greatest apparent risk for large-scale tourism employment in the region is that tourism itself is susceptible to many events that can cause a major decline in the industry. The ramifications of such events as domestic political problems (as occurred in Nepal in both 1990 and the spring of 1992), a change in the government's tourism policy (Nepal establishes new tourism goals and policies every five years), economic recession, or another international oil crisis could be financially catastrophic to the region's newly monetarized economy. However, given that many 'tourist Sherpa' still return to their traditional lifestyles in the summer monsoon and winter seasons, most Sherpas do not as yet appear to have severed either their traditional economic or psychological ties to customary village life. As both Adams (1992) and Fisher (1990) have suggested, unlike inhabitants of other parts of the world who are heavily involved in tourism, most Sherpas would still be capable of returning to their customary ecological niche, and those who have been sufficiently educated would have the option of obtaining office jobs in Kathmandu and elsewhere. [...]

LESSONS FOR ALTERNATIVE TOURISM

The foregoing reappraisal of the nature and extent of tourism-related change in Sagarmatha National Park suggests that while the region is not without notable detrimental impacts, its characterization as an ecological and cultural catastrophe in the making has been premature. Some reports of adverse environmental impacts appear to have been overstated, and many of the worst impacts are being alleviated through both local and international efforts. Sherpas have also become highly affluent by Nepalese standards and, despite a changing economy and some social restructuring, their culture is strong and in many ways appears to have been intensified rather than adulterated by the presence of tourism. Other impacts, however, especially those of forest degradation and loss of ground-cover, remain serious problems, despite efforts to address them.

Many remote alternative tourism destinations in the Third World operate in tourism development contexts that are not dissimilar to that of Sagarmatha National Park: most have a sizeable indigenous population that possess strong cultural ties with past traditions and evolving ties to a land and renewable resource base; the indigenous population recognizes that their region, traditions and culture are of interest to the modern tourist; and, most have a limited but evolving infrastructure to cope with increasing tourist numbers. So the

Sagarmatha National Park case study offers the following lessons to guide the successful development of alternative forms of tourism in other remote, ecologically and culturally sensitive areas of the world.

The need for regional tourism planning

Having lacked a tourism development plan, Sagarmatha National Park is now responding in ad hoc fashion to counter the undesirable impacts of uncontrolled tourism development. The Sagarmatha experience indicates the necessity of establishing *a priori* a regional tourism development plan which considers the region's natural and social carrying capacities, and which encompasses a clear vision of what constitutes development that is *appropriate* to maintaining an area as a viable alternative tourism destination. Further environmental and cultural change, or the overdevelopment of services and facilities, could sufficiently change the tourism product provided by this region to cause the park to be abandoned as a destination for the true adventure traveller (Zurick 1992). The growth of adventure tourism in Sagarmatha has in many respects paralleled the stages of Butler's (1980) tourist area cycle model. Having passed quickly through the early stages of 'exploration' (few visitors and meagre facilities) and 'involvement' (residents provide services to increasing numbers of visitors), the region appears to be in the stage of 'development' (commercial and national agencies become involved in developing the area, the destination is advertized internationally, and visitor numbers peak). However, should tourism planning (or a lack of it) take the region beyond the 'development' stage, into 'consolidation' (development focuses almost exclusively on tourist services) and 'stagnation' (serious and long-term impacts occur), then Sagarmatha National Park may lose its niche in the international adventure travel market.

The measure of appropriate tourism development ultimately rests in the measure of its sustainability (Zurick 1992), which is determined by how successfully it protects the region's natural resources and environmental quality, minimizes adverse cultural impacts, and preserves the kind of experience which is important to its visitors. In seeking to achieve these outcomes, a regional tourism plan may regulate visitor ceilings and visitor user fees, set visitor quotas where necessary, authorize tourist access to given areas and guide tourist behaviour/activities, direct the development of infrastructure and services, generate taxation policies to equitably distribute tourism income, and regulate the use of the region's natural resources. Management planning must also be an on-going process involving periodic reviews to allow for changing regional objectives and adjustment to existing regulations (Robinson 1992).

For example, given that volume of tourists is closely tied to regional change (Butler 1990), a strong case can be made for reducing tourist numbers in Sagarmatha National Park while increasing their per capita expenditures. The park entry fee (about US$10) and trekking permits (about US$5/week) are currently so low as to be inconsequential to the majority of park visitors. Reducing visitors would not necessarily hurt the local economy if trekking fees were increased and the revenues put toward park improvement, or used for local subsidies (for alternative fuels for example) or local community development programmes. Gurung (cited in Wells (1992, p5) has further suggested that, in order to spread tourists more evenly through Nepal's parks, trekking or park entry fees could be set at different levels with relatively high fees for overcrowded areas and low fees for rarely visited areas. From this perspective, alternative tourism development would be selective and small in scale, which, while generating only modest economic returns, would better safeguard the local culture and protect natural resources (Wallace 1992).

Protected area management

Essential to the coordination of regional tourism planning is a protected area authority that has real decision and policy making clout and adequate funding to service its programmes. Sagarmatha National Park managers have been criticized for focusing their efforts on forest protection at the expense of providing a direction for tourism development, especially with regard to regulating visitor numbers, the proliferation of lodges, overgrazing by packstock and dealing with waste disposal (Stevens and Sherpa 1992b). In reality, however, the park authorities have been in the difficult position of having quite limited political power and insufficient funding to effectively run conservation or development projects. The park authority is required to run its programmes on whatever budget it is allocated by the government, it has no legal authority to intervene in village affairs, and it has at present minimal jurisdiction over visitors. For example, while the park authorities regard excessive visitations as contributing to substantial environmental degradation, a complex system beyond their influence dictates the level of visitation, with the Department of Immigration issuing all visas and trekking permits, the Nepal Mountaineering Association issuing trekking peak (below 6000m) permits, and the Ministry of Tourism authorizing expeditions to the higher peaks.

Successful tourism planning requires the expertise of individuals who are familiar with the region's social, cultural and ecological underpinnings, and who share a commitment to maintaining the region's long-term vitality. Protected area managers in the Third World are often native to the area or have resided for long periods in the area, and therefore tend to be knowledgeable of the area's successes and problems. Furthermore, since they can also provide the security of long-term planning, park managers should have real decision making influence when it comes to where, when and what kind of tourism should be permitted when the principal attraction is a protected area (Boo 1990, Wallace 1992).

Local involvement

The experience at Sagarmatha National Park demonstrates that local people can benefit economically from tourism development while maintaining their cultural integrity and major control of their local land and resource base. Although some of the processes that have shaped this balance may be unique to the region, others have wider applicability. The seasonality of tourism has allowed the Sherpas to maintain subsistence agriculture as a major part of their lifestyle and to not become entirely dependent on tourism revenues. Their close-knit society and strong culture have also been helped by distinctly supportive host–client relations. Perhaps of most significance, tourism development in Khumbu has been shaped first and foremost by the Sherpa themselves, with relatively little direction from the national park or local governments. Through their entrepreneurial efforts and support by foreign loans, the Sherpa have been able to dominate lodge ownership and regional tourism employment. The integration of *panchayat* (village government) in Khumbu has also enhanced community involvement in directing aspects of tourism development, and the reintroduction of the traditional forest guardian system has seemingly led the local people to see the forests again as their resource and responsibility, and has increased their concern for forest protection (Stevens and Sherpa 1992c). Although Sherpa access for forest and grazing resources has been restricted by park regulations, these costs appear relatively minor in comparison to their economic gains from tourism.

While the accomplishments in Sagarmatha National Park may be difficult to realize in other tourism places of the Third World, there are valuable lessons to be learned on the involvement of local communities. Since local people must live with the long-term consequences of tourism development, local communities must at the outset be educated to develop an understanding of what tourism means as a concept (Wray 1989), and be made aware not only of its potential economic benefits but also of both the positive and negative changes that tourism may bring to their lifestyles and social structures. Tourism must also be developed within the traditions of existing communities, essential to which is the involvement of local communities in decision making processes that directly influence their lifestyles, affect their community development, or use the locality's natural resources. The more aware local people are made of the potential rewards and pitfalls of tourism, and the more they are involved in and benefit from tourism development, then the greater the likelihood that they will accept the tourism industry and commit to preserve the natural and cultural values upon which tourism is based (Robinson 1992).

CONCLUSIONS

In conclusion, the experience of Sagarmatha National Park demonstrates that the longevity and prosperity of tourism in culturally and ecologically fragile areas depends not only on the tourism industry's ability to identify and develop tourism opportunities, but also on the industry's ability to conserve a region's natural and cultural assets (Val 1990). Although the region is not without outstanding environmental and socio-cultural issues, the new approaches which are at present being implemented in the park offer optimism for its long-term prospects as a viable adventure tourism destination. Alternative tourism brings with it the potential to inflict both beneficial and detrimental impacts, and for other remote tourism destinations in the Third World which offer exciting opportunities for the development of alternative forms of tourism, Sagarmatha National Park offers encouragement that alternative tourism designs can exist that effectively balance local economic development with ecological and cultural conservation.

REFERENCES

Adams, V (1992) 'Tourism and Sherpas, Nepal: reconstruction and reciprocity', *Annals of Tourism Research*, 19, pp534–54

Boo, E (1990) *Ecotourism: the Potentials and Pitfalls*, Vols 1 and 2, World Wildlife Fund, Washington, DC

Butler, R W (1980) 'The concept of the tourist area cycle of evolution: implications for managers of resources', *Canadian Geographer*, 14: pp5–12

Butler, R W (1990) 'Alternative tourism: pious hope or Trojan horse?', *Journal of Travel Research*, 28, pp40–45

Cohen, E (1987) 'Tourism – A critique', *Tourism Recreation Research*, 12, pp13–18

Durst, P B and Ingram,C D (1988) 'Nature oriented tourism promotion by developing countries', *Tourism Management*, March, pp39–43

Fisher, J (1990) *The Sherpas: Reflections on Change in Himalayan Nepal*, University of California Press, Berkeley, CA

Gonsalves, P S (1987) 'Alternative tourism – the evolution of a concept and establishment of a network', *Tourism Recreation Research*, 12, pp9–12

Greenwood, D J (1989) 'Culture by the pound: An anthropological perspective on tourism as cultural commoditization', in Smith, V (ed), *Hosts and Guests: The Anthropology of Tourism*, University of Pennsylvania Press, Philadelphia, PA, pp171–86

Harrison, D (ed) (1992) *Tourism and the Less Developed Countries*, Halsted Press, New York

Healy, R G (1992) 'The role of tourism in sustainable development', Paper presented at the IVth World Congress on National Parks and Protected Areas, February 1992, Caracas, Venezuela

Kutay, K (1990) 'The new ethic in adventure travel', *Buzzworm: The Environmental Journal*, 1, pp31–6

Machlis, G E and Bacci, M E (1992) 'Is ecotourism ideologically biased, elitist, short-sighted, anti-democratic and unsustainable?', Paper presented at the IVth World Congress on National Parks and Protected Areas, February 1992, Caracas, Venezuela

McKean, P F (1989) 'Towards a theoretical analysis of tourism: economic dualism and cultural involution', in Smith, V (ed), *Hosts and Guests: The Anthropology of Tourism*, University of Pennsylvania Press, Philadelphia, PA, pp119–38

McKercher, B (1993) 'Some fundamental truths about tourism: Understanding tourism's social and environmental impacts', *The Journal of Sustainable Tourism*, 1, pp6–16

Passoff, M (1991) 'Ecotourism re-examined', *Earth Island Journal*, Spring, pp28–9

Robinson, D W (1992) 'Socio-cultural impacts of mountain tourism in Nepal's Sagarmatha (Everest) National Park: Implications for sustainable tourism', in J Thorsell (ed), *World Heritage Twenty Years Later*: IVth World Congress on National Parks and Protected Areas, IUCN, Gland, Switzerland, pp123–31

Smith, V L and Eadington, W R (1992) *Tourism alternatives*, University of Pennsylvania Press, Philadelphia, PA

Stevens, S F and Sherpa, M Norbu (1992a) 'Tourism development in Sagarmatha (Mount Everest) National Park, Nepal', Paper presented at the IVth World Congress on National Parks and Protected Areas, February 1992, Caracas, Venezuela

Stevens, S F and Sherpa, M Norbu (1992b) 'Tourism impacts and protected area management in highland Nepal: Lessons from Sagarmatha National Park and Annapurna Conservation Area', Paper presented at the IVth World Congress on National Parks and Protected Areas, February 1992, Caracas, Venezuela

Stevens, S F and Sherpa, M Norbu (1992c) 'Indigenous peoples and protected area management: New approaches to conservation in Highland Nepal', Paper presented at the IVth World Congress on National Parks and Protected Areas, February 1992, Caracas, Venezuela

Val, E (1990) 'Parks, aboriginal peoples, and sustainable tourism in developing regions: The international experience and Canada's Northwest Territories', in J Vinning (ed), *Social Science and Natural Resource Recreation Management*, Westview, San Francisco, CA

Wallace, G N (1992) 'Real ecotourism: assisting protected area managers and getting benefits to local people', Paper presented at the IVth World Congress on National Parks and Protected Areas, February 1992, Caracas, Venezuela

Wells, M P (1992) 'Economic benefits and costs of protected areas in Nepal', Paper presented at the IVth World Congress on National Parks and Protected Areas, February 1992, Caracas, Venezuela

Wight, P (1993) 'Ecotourism: Ethics or eco-sell?', *Journal of Travel Research*, 31, pp3–9

Wray, G W (1989) 'Tourism initiatives in Canada's Northwest Territories: The Pangnirtung experience – a partnership for sustainable development', Paper presented at the World Conference on the Environment, October 1989, Canary Islands, Spain

Zurick, D N (1992) 'Adventure travel and sustainable tourism in the peripheral economy of Nepal', *Annals of the Association of American Geographers*, 8, pp608–28

Integrating Tourism and Agricultural Development

Albert J Gomes

INTRODUCTION

This chapter examines the scope for improving the impact of the tourism industry on Caribbean economies, especially the agricultural sector. However, while there is a tremendous amount of interest in the subject, there are very few hard facts available concerning the 'leakages' of tourist receipts, when foreign exchange earned from tourism is used immediately (often prior to visitor arrivals) for food imports and other tourist consumption items. This chapter, therefore, attempts to estimate the magnitude of purchases made by hotels and other tourist enterprises on food and beverage procurement to support their guests. It then discusses the demand/supply constraints on local production of food and other consumables. The final portion of the chapter is devoted to actions that a country might take to define its own import substitution opportunities and hence reduce its food dependency, not only for tourists but also for the resident population.

BACKGROUND

There is a widely perceived problem in the Caribbean regarding the lack of integration between tourism and agricultural development. This problem and its solutions have been debated in the Caribbean for at least three decades, but little in the way of a viable approach to integrating tourism with agricultural development has emerged from these deliberations. In the mean time, those destinations in the Caribbean that have developed a significant tourism industry continue to import more food products, not only to feed more tourists but also the satisfy increased demand for certain food items from the local population. The increase in food imports to satisfy new local demand is due to at least two factors. The first is the so-called 'demonstration effect' of locals changing their food preferences in line with the pattern of tourist consumption (Bryden 1973). The second is the increase in domestic purchasing power at least partly brought about by tourism itself. Riegert (1982) observes that the role of tourism has been to stimulate the local market, generate new demands and introduce more exacting quality standards, thus prompting increased food impact, while identifying product possibilities for local producers.

In other words, tourism's impact on the economies of the Caribbean has been to make them proportionately more dependent on food imports than in the past. The challenge is to reverse the mechanism and use the market expansion effect of increased demand for agricultural products from temporary residents to work towards greater import substitution.

THE NATURE AND MAGNITUDE OF THE DEMAND

The Caribbean Tourism Organization (CTO) (1991) reports that the thirty-two countries/destinations that comprise the region received a total of 11.84 million tourists in 1990. In addition, there were 7.45 million cruise-ship passengers and other excursionists, yielding a total of 19.29 million visitors in 1990. Gross expenditure by all categories of visitor (tourist, cruise-ship passengers and other excursionists) to the Caribbean were estimated at $8.9 billion in 1990 or a per capita expenditure of $461.38 per tourist.

Assuming an average length of stay of about eight days, the modal daily expenditure works out to be $57.29 in 1990 on all items including accommodation, food and beverages, entertainment, souvenirs and local transportation. Some authorities (Belisle 1983) estimate that food accounts for approximately one-third of tourist expenditure, which puts the total expenditure on food at about $19 per day per visitor on average. Even if this figure were accurate it would only indicate the sale price of meals purchased by tourists, which includes not only the pure ingredient cost but the cost of labour in the kitchen, back-of-the house and restaurant floor, as well as imputed facility cost, utilities, enterprise profit and other elements.

A more accurate way of estimating the agricultural component of tourism expenditure is to use hotel statistics as a basis. For instance, the annual publication of Pannell Kerr Forster (PKF) (1991) provides detailed information on hotel revenues and expenses in certain Caribbean countries and overall Caribbean averages for the year 1990. The PKF data is, however, not based on a predictable sample and is weighted towards large upscale hotels, resorts and chain-affiliated properties in the region which voluntarily supply information on their operations. The data may, therefore, be somewhat biased towards the larger and more upscale segments of the hospitality industry in the region, but is still considered valid for the purpose of this analysis.

The PKF data for the Caribbean as a whole shows the array of income and expenses relating to food and beverage operations per available room, per year, based on its 1990 sample of hotels, depicted in Table 7.1. it should be noted that while revenues are earned from occupied rooms, the PKF data in Table 7.1 relates total revenues and expenses to the total inventory of available rooms.

The net food cost in the PKF statistics includes the cost of employee meals but is still a fraction of the retail price of meals sold through hotels. The mark-up between the net cost of food and beverages and the revenues accruing to the hotels from this department is accounted for by other expenses such as salaries and wages, including payroll-related items (45.1 per cent of food and beverage revenues). The remaining 13.2 per cent of food and beverage revenues is the contribution from the food and beverage department to the hotel to defray the cost of administrative and general expenses, heat, light and power, marketing, property operation and maintenance, plus management/franchise fees, taxes on income and entrepreneurial profit.

As the PKF statistics provide information on food and beverage cost per available room, it is possible to gross up the figure to include all available hotel rooms in the Caribbean. Thus, according the CTO's latest statistics, there were 124,191 hotel rooms in the Caribbean during 1990. This means that hotels in the Caribbean accounted for total purchases of food and beverages amounting to $780 million, as computed in Table 7.2. However, not all tourists stay in hotels or

Table 7.1 *Cost of food and beverages per available room purchased by hotels in the Caribbean 1990*

Category	Revenues per available room (US$)	Net cost per available room (US$)	Percentage of revenue
Food	14,544	5,054	34.75
Beverage	5,558	1,220	21.95
Total	20,102	6,274	56.70

Source: Pannell Kerr Forster (1991) p45

other commercial establishments. Many stay in private accommodation, either with relatives or friends, or in rented facilities, or in their villas or apartments. Table 7.3 summarizes place-of-stay information for 1990 in terms of percentage mix. Based on this, it can be estimated that, for the Caribbean as a whole, roughly 51 per cent of all tourists stay in hotels, 11 per cent stay in guest-houses and self-catering apartments, 33 per cent stay in private homes or unregistered accommodation, and the balance stay in other types of facilities.

A question that needs to be addressed at the outset is whether the food purchase patterns of hotels revealed by the PKF statistics should be significantly different from those of other establishments. Starting with guest-houses, which are generally smaller than the hotels in the PKF sample and many of which operate restaurants and bars, or offer food to residents under a meal plan, there is no reasons to believe that their costs of food should be any different from those of hotels. Any 'quality premium' applicable to large hotels and upscale resorts could be offset by the larger hotels availing themselves of quantity discounts or cheaper direct importation of certain food items. Tourists staying in self-catering apartments and preparing all their meals would have to buy food and beverage items from supermarkets and other retailers. A typical daily market basket of food purchased for a North American diet – 61.4 per cent of all visitors to the Caribbean in 1990 were from the United States or Canada – at the retail level would probably cost more than that bought by hotels and guest-houses from wholesalers or other purveyors serving the hospitality industry. Similarly, the base cost of food and beverages purchased by local restaurants, some of which cater to tourists, is likely to follow the same pattern as the hotels. Based on these assumptions, it is possible to project the total food and beverages consumed by tourists in 1990 as computed in Table 7.4 for all classes of accommodation.

Table 7.2 *Total purchases of food and beverages by Caribbean hotels, 1990*

Category	Purchases per available room	Total available rooms (US$)	Total purchases (US$)
Food	5,054	124,191	627.66
Beverage	1,220	124,191	151.51
Total	6,274	124,191	779.17

Source: Pannell Kerr Forster 1991, CTO 1991

Table 7.3 *Tourist arrivals by place of stay*

Country	Hotels %	Percentage distribution			
		Guest-houses/ apartments %	Private/ unregistered %	Other %	Total %
Angilla[*]	47	23	28	2	100
Aruba	77	7	16	–	100
Barbados[1]	51	24	25	–	100
Bahamas[*]	84	–	16	–	100
Bermuda	68	14	1	17	100
British Virgin Islands[**2]	25	11	6	58	100
Cayman Islands	61	25	14	–	100
Curacao[*]	53	3	44	–	100
Dominica	23	14	56	7	100
Dominican Republic[*]	85	3	9	3	100
Grenada[2]	38	3	56	3	100
Guadeloupe	85	9	3	3	100
Haiti[****]	25	53	22	–	100
Jamaica	67	10	22	1	100
Martinique[**]	59	10	25	6	100
Montserrat[****]	25	26	49	–	100
Puerto Rico	38	–	62	–	100
St Kitts and Nevis	55	27	16	2	100
St Lucia	66	16	12	6	100
St Maarten[****]	66	–	34	–	100
St Vincent and the Grenadines	30	32	32	6	100
Suriname[****]	10	4	86	–	100
Trinidad and Tobago	36	5	59	–	100
US Virgin Islands	56	14	13	17	100

Source: CTO 1991, p75

Notes:
1 Apartment hotels included under hotels
2 Boats and yacht charters included in 'other'
* 1989 ** 1988 *** 1987 **** 1986

Some food and beverage purchases, amounting to 10 per cent of the total, are made by free-standing restaurants. This percentage accounts for those hotel guests who do not eat all their meals at their place of residence, as well as food patronage by cruise-ship and transit passengers, food purchased for airline meals and other food vendors who sell to tourists, as well as local customers.

The magnitude of the total purchases of food and beverages, estimated in Table 7.4 at $1.7 billion in 1990, can be assessed by relating it to the following parameters:

Table 7.4 *Estimated total food and beverages purchased to support tourist industry in the Caribbean, 1990*

Purchaser category	Percentage of total	Food purchases (US$ million)	Beverage purchases (US$ million)	Total purchases (US$ million)
Accommodation				
Hotels	51	627.66	151.51	779.17
Guest houses/private apartments	11	135.38	32.68	168.06
Private homes/ unregistered accommodation	33	406.13	98.04	504.17
Other accommodation	5	61.54	14.85	76.39
Total accommodation	100	1,230.71	297.08	1,527.79
Restaurants and other food vendors	10	123.07	29.71	152.78
Grand total	–	1,353.78	326.79	1,680.57

1. total purchases of food and beverages in 1990 amounted to almost $142 per tourist based on a total of 11,841,500 tourists visiting the Caribbean during that year;
2. food and beverage purchases to support the tourist industry in the Caribbean amounted to almost 19 per cent of total expenditure of $8.9 billion by tourists in 1990; and
3. food and beverage purchases to support the tourist industry of $1.7 billion in 1990 were higher than the gross domestic product (GDP) of all but three countries in the Caribbean.

Notwithstanding the enormous size of the demand for food and beverage items from tourists visiting the Caribbean, there are certain demand factors that are cited to explain the lack of local production. These can be summarized as follows.

Tourists demand food items that are not normally grown in the Caribbean

There is some justification for this comment but very few proponents of greater agricultural self-sufficiency have recommended total import substitution. New York strip sirloin, caviar or Scotch whisky cannot be produced in the Caribbean but there are other products, such as local fish, chicken, fresh fruit and vegetables, that are readily accepted by tourists. If selected high-value local food products were grown using the best available techniques, the present food import bill of many Caribbean countries could be significantly reduced.

Hotels and resorts demand the very best in quality, appearance and uniformity in what they buy

Better use of technology, seeds and cultural practices will improve quality and, consequently, the yield to the producer from higher prices. Lesser quality products can be sold in the local market.

Tourists will not try local foods or local cuisine

Food preferences have changed tremendously in North America in recent years. Hotel chefs are always looking for new menu items and can convince tourists that consuming local foods is part of the holiday experience. There are also greater health concerns among North American consumers, moving them away from high cholesterol red meat towards the use of more complex carbohydrates and fibres that are typical of indigenous Caribbean food. These sentiments can be capitalized on by promoting certain locally available lean meat, as well as fruit and vegetables.

In summary, the demand for food by tourists visiting the Caribbean is not only large but it also poses no insuperable demand constraints on many countries in seeking to increase their agricultural output and thus substantially reduce their import bill for a wide variety of food items.

SUPPLY CONSTRAINTS

It is ironic that the Caribbean islands, which were colonized principally because of their agricultural potential, should continue to depend on imported food to feed their resident population, as well as their temporary visitors. Two observations must be made in this context. First, because of the wide diversity of islands included among the thirty-two Caribbean destinations involved, in terms of physical size, population, agricultural endowments, soil quality, rainfall and irrigation, and other cultural factors, any generalization about the Caribbean may be subject to specific exceptions. Second, there is no comparable, longitudinal data base from which to draw meaningful conclusions about the region as a whole.

Information published by the World Bank on agriculture's share of the gross domestic product (GDP) in selected Caribbean countries is shown in Table 7.5. Generally speaking, the poorer countries in the Caribbean Basin have a greater dependence on agriculture. Also, there appears to be a negative correlation between the number of tourists and the share of GDP accounted for by agriculture. A country-by-country analysis of the tourist destinations listed in Table 7.5 indicates that all these countries are both exporters and importers of agricultural products.

They export certain plantation products (for example, coffee, bananas and sugar) originally introduced in the colonial era for consumption in Europe and North America, and import a great deal of the food staples required to feed the plantation workers. The Organization of American States and the CTRC held a workshop on tourism and agricultural links in the Caribbean in 1984 (OAS/CTRC 1984). The final report of the workshop observed:

On the current situation, the paper identified the three studies commissioned

Extract 4: *Integrating Tourism and Agricultural Development*

Table 7.5 *Agriculture's share of GDP in selected Caribbean countries (1989 data)*

Country	GDP per capita 1989 (US$)	No of tourists (thousands) 1990	Agriculture's share of GDP %
OECS countries			
Antigua and Bardbuda	3880	205.7	6
Dominica	1670	45.0	31
Grenada	1900	82.0	21
St Kitts and Nevis	2860	75.7	10
St Lucia	1810	138.4	16
St Vincent and the			
Grenadines	1200	53.9	20
Other CARICOM			
Barbados	6370	432.1	7
Belize	1600	221.8	19
Guyana	310	67.0	25
Jamaica	1260	840.8	6
Trinidad and Tobago	3160	194.0	3
US Territories			
Puerto Rico	6010	2645.4	2
Other countries			
Dominican Republic	790	1533.2	15
Haiti	400	120.0	31
Suriname	3020	28.5	11

Source: The World Bank Atlas; CTO 1991

by and undertaken for the CTRC. These studies were carried out for the Dominican Republic, the Commonwealth of the Bahamas, and the Southern Windward Islands. All three studies agreed essentially in their perception of the constraints affecting the development of linkages between tourism and local food production. In all the countires examined, problems that surfaced were:

* high cost of local produce
* variable standard of local food products
* poor communication between producers and catering establishments on the need for and availability of local food
* poor production planning
* little, if any, promotion of local foods to tourists or the local population
* hardly any development of new local cuisine
* extreme seasonality of local food production
* a generally underdeveloped food farming sector in the economies.

The OAS/CTRC workshop, which was attended by fifteen regional agencies, recommended the adoption of a model for creating links between the various identified components of an agricultural production and distribution system, and highlighted the roles and functions to be performed by various entities and interest groups in the process of creating links. As sufficient time has already passed since the mid-1980s, an evaluation should be undertaken to determine whether this type of regional approach is likely to produce any meaningful results in achieving integration between tourism and agricultural development.

CONCLUSIONS AND RECOMMENDATIONS

The fundamental problem in integrating tourism and agricultural development in the Caribbean is that a 'peasant' food production system is being asked to meet the needs of some of the most sophisticated consumers in the world. Also, because of the wide diversity of agricultural resource endowments and cultural conditions, as well as sociocultural attitudes towards agricultural work among the islands that make up the Caribbean, a uniform regional approach is not likely to be very productive.

Instead, each country should estimate the quantity and value of different types of food and beverage items consumed by the tourist industry. This can be started through a sample survey of hotels during a representative week. Information on quantities used and the source of supplies – direct import, local wholesaler/retailer/market contract with grower/processor, door-to-door vendors – should be determined. The list of items could illustratively consist of the dummy tabulation provided in Table 7.6. The focus of the survey should be on what is being imported directly by the hotels or indirectly through local wholesalers or sole distributors.

These purchases by the sample survey of hotels can then be grossed up to annual volumes for all accommodation facilities, as well as other food service establishments, using the methodology employed in Table 7.4.

An evaluation could then be made of what items are being imported that could be produced locally, given local agricultural endowments, cultural conditions and other factors. The initial choice of items selected for import substitution should be restricted to those with a high probability of success. The actual agency chosen to do this evaluation and implement the pilot project would depend on the administrative structure in the particular country, but a ministry of agriculture or university extension service would seem to be the most appropriate. The pilot project should involve private growers or land owners, and have the dual purpose of meeting most, if not all, of the demand from tourists for the items selected for import substitution, as well as actual or latent demand from the resident population. Focused governmental assistance in terms of price support, marketing and technical assistance to individual farmers/growers selected for the pilot project should be considered, along with subsidized credit and other farm inputs, such as seeds, fertilizer and insecticide for the trial period.

This approach, with a modest goal of encouraging larger domestic production of certain food items currently being imported but which have a relatively high comparative advantage for import substitution, has the potential for slow but steady success.

REFERENCES

Belisle, F J (1983) 'Tourism and Food Production in the Caribbean', *Annals of Tourism Research*, Vol 10, pp497 and 573

Bryden, J M (1973) *Tourism and Development: Case Study of the Commonwealth Caribbean*, p14, Cambridge University Press, New York

Caribbean Tourism Organization, (1991) *Caribbean Tourism Statistical Report 1990*, July, Christ Church, Barbados

Pannell Kerr Forster, (1991) *Trends in the Hotel Industry*, International Edition, Houston, Texas

Extract 4: *Integrating Tourism and Agricultural Development*

Table 7.6 *Hotel purchases, prices and sources of supply (Dummy table)*

Commodity	Average Price	Quantity per week	Source of supply
Meat			
Beef			
Chicken			
Pork			
Canned/processed			
Shortening/oils			
Fish			
Snapper/grouper			
Lobster			
Shrimp			
Other fish			
Dairy and Eggs			
Milk (fresh)			
Butter			
Cheeses			
Canned milk			
Eggs			

Vegetables and Fruit

Lettuce	Bananas
Tomatoes	Plantains
Potatoes	Pumpkin
Carrots	Onions
Cabbages	Mangoes
Citrus	Papayas
Dasheen	Limes
Sweet potatoes	Pineapple
Cucumbers	Yams
Sweet peppers	Watermelon
Other melon	

Beverages
Rum
Beer
Liquor
Non-alcoholic

Ornamentals
Cut flowers
Potted plants
Other nursery items

Organization of American States/Caribbean Tourism Research and Development Centre, (1984) *Final Report of OAS/CTRC Workshop on Tourism and Agricultural Linkages in the Caribbean*, Christ Church, Barbados

Riegert, T J (1982) 'The Impact of Tourism on Economic Development in The Caribbean 1960–1980', unpublished report, General Secretariat, Organization of American States

The Economics of Nature Tourism: Determining if it Pays

Paul B Sherman and John A Dixon

NATURE TOURISM AND ECONOMIC DEVELOPMENT

Properly implemented, nature tourism can integrate conservation and rural development by helping to protect valuable natural areas by providing revenues for planning and management, stimulating economic development through tourism expenditures, and providing jobs and markets for local goods.

Nature tourism has the potential to help economic development at both the local and the national level. Depending on the scale of the nature tourism industry relative to the size of the local economy, the effect on the local level can be anywhere from minimal to substantial. At the national level, nature tourism is likely to have less impact, but it still may have significant influence in countries with small economies or where the potential size of the industry is very large. In Kenya, for example, the safari industry generates foreign exchange earnings of some $350 million to $400 million per year and is Kenya's largest source of foreign exchange.

In this section, we will first look at how national and local governments can maximize the revenues they receive from nature tourism. Then we will discuss how to maximize benefits for local residents.

MAXIMIZING GOVERNMENT REVENUES

While nature tourism has the potential to provide substantial benefits to countries with outstanding nature tourism sites, this will not always be the case. Too often the majority of benefits accrue to the tour operator and little remains in-country. Boo (1990) cites a World Bank study (Frueh 1988) that estimates that over one-half of gross tourism revenues in the developing countries leak back to developed countries. This is hypothesized to be even higher in the least-developed countries, where most of the goods used by tourists are imported (Mathieson and Wall 1982). Nevertheless, there are a number of mechanisms governments can put in place to increase the benefits their country receives from nature tourism.

User fees

The easiest method of capturing benefits from nature tourism is to charge a fee to use the area. Though many countries already charge small fees at cultural sites and in national parks, few countries have instituted fee schedules that reflect consumers' willingness to pay. While a small, token payment is clearly better than a no fee at all, there is no reason for a country, especially a developing country, to subsidize the cost of foreigners' visits.

Developing countries should consider adopting a two-tier fee system, with a lower charge for domestic residents and a higher charge for international visitors. Some countries have already instituted such a system; China, for example, uses a two-tiered fee structure for most cultural and historic sites. Given the expense of international travel, even a relatively high fee of US$10 or more per day would probably have a negligible effect on the total number of visitors. This is especially true for unique areas that can handle only a limited number of visitors. In the Mountain Gorilla Project (MGP) in Rwanda, for example, foreigners are charged an entrance fee of $170 per day and yet demand has remained strong. It has been noted that this is among the highest such fee charged anywhere in the world and may be near the upper limit of visitor willingness-to-pay (Lindberg 1989).

User fees help to support the Saba Marine Park in the Netherland Antilles. Since the main attraction of the park is its scuba diving and snorkelling, divers are charged $1 per dive, paid through the dive boat operators, to support conservation activities. This modest fee provides valuable revenue and is unnoticed in the overall costs of diving (van't Hof 1989).

Fees for government-owned accommodations near nature tourism sites should be priced at levels comparable to privately owned accommodations. Camping fees could also be set on a two-tier system as suggested for entrance fees. At present, many national parks charge very low accommodation or camping fees, resulting in excess demand for these facilities and insufficient funds for operation and maintenance. Businesslike behavior can be as beneficial to public operations as it is to private ones.

Concession fees

In addition to charging fees directly to visitors, fees can also be charged to individuals or firms who provide services to these visitors. This would include licensing of concessions for food, lodging, transportation, guide services, and retail stores. By auctioning or leasing the rights to operate such concessions, governments can control the types of development in and nearby nature tourism sites and simultaneously raise revenues to help maintain the area. Governments also can impose conditions on concession leases to address other objectives such as hiring local employees or selling locally produced goods.

Royalties

Establishment of royalty systems on activities and products in tourist areas is another potential source of revenue. For example, permission for books, photos, or films to be made at tourism sites could be exchanged for some percentage of the revenues made on these items. In the Saba Marine Park, sales of T-shirts and guidebooks are a major source of revenue. Such souvenir sales, either direct or via licensing, can be major revenue producers.

Tax policies

Governments can enact tax policies to increase the revenues they receive from nature tourism. Perhaps the most common type of tax is a hotel room tax, which is also relatively popular among residents since it falls primarily on visitors. Hotel room taxes of 5 to 10 per cent are found in many areas.

Special taxes also can be enacted near popular tourist sites. In pre-war Cambodia, for example, the famous complex of ruins associated with Angkor Wat was maintained by the government but was completely open to visitors without any formal payment. This enhanced the visitors' enjoyment of the site and allowed casual exploration. The government, however, collected a special tax on all hotel rooms in the nearby town of Siemréap to support its conservation and preservation efforts. Since virtually all visitors to Angkor stayed in these hotels (and the ruins were the main reason for people coming to the town), this was an effective and unobtrusive means of revenue collection.

Other forms of taxes include sales or excise taxes on tourist-related goods and services. These might be levied on food bought in restaurants, specialized equipment, and tour guide services.

Donation programmes

Governments can take advantage of the increasing international awareness of the problems faced by important natural areas by establishing and promoting donation programmes. Such programmes can be geared toward both tourists and nontourists. For tourists, guides can point out the problems of protecting the area, and encourage donations to help alleviate these pressures. To reach nontourists (and potential tourists), governments might join with conservation groups in a campaign to raise funds from interested individuals.

MAXIMIZING LOCAL BENEFITS

One of the critical issues concerning nature tourism is its impact on local residents, and especially rural villagers, in developing countries. Since much of the growth in nature tourism will take place in such areas, it is important that steps are taken at an early stage to ensure that local residents benefit from the tourist industry.

The most direct way of benefiting local communities is to employ as many residents as possible in tourism-related services. This includes jobs in restaurants, accommodation facilities, and as guides. Other employment possibilities include construction activities, helping to build trails, providing daily maintenance, and retail sales. If local workers do not possess the skills needed, training programmes should be considered before bringing in workers from other areas.

Use of locally produced goods will also benefit the community. Governments and/or NGOs can help farmers grow crops and livestock to supply tourist facilities. Promotion of local handicrafts also provides income-earning opportunities.

Local residents also will benefit if a portion of fees collected from nature tourism is earmarked for them. This is especially important if local residents have had to give up use of an area to ensure its continued existence for tourism. For example, in many countries, collection of firewood, food, timber, or other products is not allowed in national parks. This loss of income may be devastating to people already living at or near subsistence levels.

Using a portion of the fees collected to compensate local residents provides a means of offsetting these losses. In the Chitwan National Park in Nepal, for example, conservation of this important rhino habitat is promoted by allowing villagers to harvest elephant grass periodically, thereby helping to meet their needs for income from this valuable thatch material while discouraging illegal harvest of park resources (MacKinnon et al 1986).

Compensation can be provided in a number of ways. One possibility is to develop alternative supplies of the resource outside the tourist destination. Woodlots for firewood, captive breeding for wildlife, and farms or plantations for plant species are examples.

Developing a substitute for the lost resource is another form of compensation. If the resource was used for food, for example, a different food crop could be substituted. If it was used to generate income, other types of income-generating activities can be used to offset losses to local residents.

Fees collected from nature tourism also can be used for community development activities. Construction of schools, sanitation facilities, electricity, water systems, and health clinics are potential forms of compensation. Residents must be made aware, however, that the provision of these facilities are, at least in part, compensation for losses associated with tourism.

Compensation is also warranted in cases where there are indirect costs to local residents from nature tourism, for example, damage from wildlife. One example of compensation is the case of traditional Masai herders and Kenya's Amboseli National Park. Both the Masai cattle and the area's wildlife depend on water and pasturelands located within and outside the park; the needs and range of both cattle and wildlife change during the year depending on the amount of rainfall and pasture availability. Restricting wildlife to the park's boundaries and excluding all cattle would result in a decreased population of both.

A compromise solution between the local Masai and the park authorities resulted in substantial economic gains to both parties. The solution included payment of a grazing compensation to the Masai to cover their livestock losses to wildlife migrants. According to Western (1984), the net monetary gain to the park from use of Masai lands is about $500,000 per year and the benefits from the park to the Masai result in an income 85 per cent greater than from cattle herding alone. (There remain, however, significant conflicts between the park and the Masai; see Chapter 2).

Schemes such as those described in this section are vital if nature tourism is to benefit, rather than hurt, local communities. They also help to discourage activities that may damage tourism by providing alternatives. An International Union for the Conservation of Nature (IUCN) report discusses a number of such schemes that have been successful at both benefiting local communities and protecting natural resources (McNeely 1988).

EXAMPLES OF ECONOMIC ANALYSES OF NATURE TOURISM

Khao Yai National Park, Thailand

KhaoYai, Thailand's first national park, is located about 160 kilometres northeast of Bangkok (see Figure 7.2). Covering 2168 square kilometres, Khao Yai has been one of Thailand's most popular parks since its establishment in 1962 and is one of ten ASEAN Heritage Parks and Reserves (NPD 1986).

Khao Yai provides a number of benefits both to the surrounding region and to the nation. It is a premier tourist destination in the region, with between 250,000 and 400,000 visits per year. Since it contains most of the remaining forest in the area, it is of critical importance for wildlife and also profoundly affects the hydrology of the region. Four river basins have their headwaters in Khao Yai, and two major reservoirs are dependent on water from the park.

In addition to being the oldest national park in Thailand, Khao Yai is also one of the most popular and well-developed parks for recreation. Located approximately three hours away from Bangkok by car, Khao Yai attracts large numbers of both Thais and foreigners. Visits to Khao Yai more than tripled between 1977 and 1987.

A recent survey of Khao Yai visitors designed by the authors and members of the World Wide Fund for Nature Beneficial Use Project, and undertaken by the latter group between March and May 1988, found that the site was visited mainly as a nature tourism destination. For foreigners visiting the park, more than 62 per cent stated that wildlife viewing was one of their three main reasons for coming to Khao Yai. This was followed by scenery (58 per cent), relaxation (43 per cent), and hiking (41 per cent).

Thai nationals overwhelmingly said that enjoying the scenery (54 per cent) was their main reason for visiting Khao Yai. (Note that relaxation was not given as a separate choice in the Thai-language version of the survey, so percentages are not directly comparable). Adding the percentage of people indicating any specific activity as one of their top three reasons for coming to Khao Yai showed that viewing scenery was still number one (86 per cent), followed by seeing the waterfalls (58 per cent), wildlife viewing (36 per cent), picnicking (29 per cent), and overnight camping (25 per cent). (More detailed responses from this survey can be found in Dobias et al 1988).

Financial benefits

Both the National Parks Division (NPD) and Tourist Authority of Thailand (TAT) operate lodging facilities in Khao Yai. Revenues from NPD-operated accommodations were almost 1.5 million baht in 1987 (approximately 26 baht equals US $1). Dobias et al (1988) report that the TAT income from lodging in 1987 was almost 5 million baht, while TAT-run restaurants received 4.2 million baht in income. TAT also received 400,000 baht from golf course fees, 318,000 baht from their souvenir shop, and 230,000 baht from nighttime excursions to view wildlife with spotlights. Thus, TAT's gross income was more than 10 million baht in 1987, while its expenditures during that year were approximately 3.3 million baht. While these figures do not include prior capital expenditures to build facilities, it is nonetheless clear that TAT's operations are profitable. Unfortunately, all profits from TAT's operations go to TAT and not to the NPD and, therefore, they do not contribute to the

Figure 7.1 *Khao Yai National Park, Thailand*

management and preservation of the park.

Gate fees from admission to the park in recent years ranged from 1.6 to 2.4 million baht per year. Adding the gate fees and NPD-operated accommodation charges, tourism directly contributed approximately 3 million baht in 1987. In addition, NPD received 150,000 baht in concession fees from the four restaurants/food stalls within park boundaries.

The Beneficial Use Project (Dobias 1988; Dobias et al 1988) has generated some interesting data on the expenditures of both Thai and foreign visitors to the park. In general, foreign visitors spend more per person than do Thai visitors. Based on data from organized bus tours, average daily per person expenses for foreign visitors range from 500 to 800 baht, of which the formal admission fee is less than 1 per cent. Clearly, gate receipts are only a very small fraction of people's willingness-to-pay to visit Khao Yai.

With more than 400,000 visitors per year, the total expenditures generated by Khao Yai tourism are large – from 40 million to 200 million baht ($1.5 to $7.7 million) if per capita expenditures are 100 to 500 baht. These expenditures, of course, are not an economic measure of the value of the park. To determine the true economic (ie social welfare) gain from visiting Khao Yai, we would need to measure consumer's surplus, that is, the maximum willingness-to-pay over and above the actual cash costs of visiting Khao Yai. This amount could be estimated by carrying out a travel-cost study, an approach widely used to value the nonpriced benefits enjoyed by visitors to parks and other recreational areas. By carefully controlling for origin, visitor background, and other variables, the pattern of recreational use of a park provides the data from which a demand curve and, in turn, consumer's surplus can be estimated (see Hufschmidt et al 1983 for a more detailed description).

In sum, the financial contribution of tourism is already substantial and can be expected to increase in the future. Bangkok is near Khao Yai and as incomes rise and fewer alternative open areas remain, Khao Yai will become increasingly valuable. Foreign tourism could also increase with improved facilities and promotion. Furthermore, virtually all Khao Yai tourism activities are restricted to a very small part of the park accessible from the one north-south road. More than 90 per cent of the park is completely undeveloped and inaccessible, other than on foot. Future expansion of facilities is likely. VALUE: Tourism-related expenditures are 100 to 200 million baht (roughly US\$4 to \$8 million) per year, and estimates of consumer's surplus (an economic measure) are from 10 to 25 million baht per year.

Biodiversity/ecological benefits

Maintaining Khao Yai as a national park for nature tourism and other uses provides benefits by protecting biological diversity and maintaining ecological processes. Khao Yai's rich diversity of plants and animals makes it an important reserve for many species. Although most famous for its elephants, numerous other species contribute to its biological diversity. In addition to the pure 'existence value' of species diversity, it also provides a powerful pull for tourists. We are not able, however, to place a monetary value on many aspects of the current and future values of the benefits of maintaining biodiversity. VALUE: Undetermined. Expenditures on research and education related to species in Khao Yai total 1 to 2 million baht per year. Option/existence value based on Khao Yai's role as an elephant sanctuary is estimated at more than 120 million baht per year (see Dixon and Sherman 1990 for more information on how this figure was determined).

Watershed protection

Khao Yai provides important watershed benefits in terms of the quantity, quality, and timing of water flows. The reservoirs located downstream depend on Khao Yai's watershed protection function. Maintaining Khao Yai in its current state for nature tourism and other uses will preserve these benefits as well. VALUE: Can be calculated but undetermined at present.

Management costs

The present annual management budget for Khao Yai is about 3.4 million baht. Implementation of the Khao Yai Management Plan (NPD 1986) to meet protection, interpretation, and development goals will result in increased annual budgets and large capital expenditures in the next few years. With its large area and closely settled borders, greater effort is needed to support programmes that help improve the standard of living of nearby residents, thereby reducing their dependence on illegal and unsustainable uses of the park. COST: Current government management costs are 3 to 4 million baht per year but will rise significantly over the next few years.

Opportunity costs

A variety of development benefits are lost because of protection. Foremost are water resource development, timber harvesting, and agriculture. The potential economic benefits from agriculture appear to be relatively small and high extraction costs for timber limit its profitability. Precise estimates of these opportunity costs require more data. Impacts on tourism, biodiversity, and ecological processes, if these activities were allowed, may be large.

Another major category of opportunity costs is the loss of income to local villagers due to prohibitions on the gathering and harvesting of plants and animals in the park. Note that the two categories are not cumulative since development of park resources would also result in a loss of opportunity to collect plants and animals. VALUE: A rough 'guesstimate' of the reduction in villager-derived income from park resources is 27 million baht per year, though this amount would probably not be sustainable and would result in significant damage to highly valued species (Dixon and Sherman 1990).

Overall, Khao Yai is a good example of a protected area that fits the socially beneficial category. It provides recreational, wildlife habitat, and watershed benefits that are quantifiable in physical, and in some cases economic, terms. It also provides less tangible benefits in terms of preservation of forest cover and associated biological diversity. Without government intervention, however, such a large area could not exist. The benefits are too diffuse and the financial returns from preservation would be outweighed by the direct benefits from exploitation of Khao Yai's timber, land, and animal resources.

Management issues

Many areas just inside the park are heavily degraded. These areas should be made into buffer zones and managed to provide benefits to nearby villagers. Programmes should be developed in these areas to promote production of plants that are currently being poached within the park or to establish other opportunities to supplement villager incomes. These programmes could be paid for, at least partially, with a percentage of tourism revenues. Once established, penalties for poaching beyond the buffer zone should be strictly enforced. However, limited hunting of certain species could be allowed in the buffer zones. Such a policy would have to be accompanied by a clear demarcation of park boundaries.

Certain tourist development activities could also have secondary benefits. Development of organized multiday hikes could provide employment opportunities for local villagers as guides and support staff. One programme of this type has already begun at Ban Sap Tai village under the auspices of a WWF project (Dobias et al 1988). These hikes could also be accompanied by guards who would help patrol forest areas currently not guarded effectively.

203

In 1987, fees from concessions, accommodations, and entrance were almost equal to the budget allocated to Khao Yai (3.18 million baht versus 3.38 million baht respectively). If the NPD were allowed to take over facilities currently run by the Tourist Authority of Thailand (TAT), it is likely that Khao Yai could more than pay for itself with direct revenues from tourism.

The NPD should also consider establishing a two-tier fee system. Current entrance fees, though reasonable for Thais, are extremely low by foreign standards. Fees probably could be raised to ten times their current levels without significantly reducing the number of foreign visitors.

REFERENCES

Boo, E (1990) *Ecotourism: The Potentials and Pitfalls*, World Wildlife Fund, Washington, DC

Dixon, J A and Sherman, P B (1990) *Economics of Protected Areas: A New Look at Benefits and Costs*, Island Press, Covelo, California

Dobias, R J (1988) 'WWF Contract 3757: Influencing Decision Makers About Providing Enhanced Support for Protected Areas in Thailand (Beneficial Use Project)' Interim report, mimeo

Dobias, R J, Wangwacharakul, V and Sangswang, N (1988) 'Beneficial Use Quantifications of Khao Yai National Park: Executive Summary and Main Report' Thorani Tech for World Wide Fund for Nature, Bangkok

Frueh, S (1988) 'Report to WWF on Tourism to Protected Areas' mimeo, World Wildlife Fund – US, Washington, DC

Hufschmidt, M M, James, D E, Meister, A D, Bower, B T and Dixon, J A (1983) *Environment, Natural Systems and Development: An Economic Valuation Guide*, Johns Hopkins University Press, Baltimore, MA

Lindberg, K (1989) 'Tourism as a Conservation Tool', mimeo, Johns Hopkins University (SAIS), Washington, DC

MacKinnon, J, MacKinnon, K, Child, G and Thorsell, J (1986) *Managing Protected Areas in the Tropics*, International Union for the Conservation of Nature, Gland, Switzerland

McNeely, J A (1988) *Economics and Biological Diversity: Developing and Using Incentives to Conserve Biological Resources*, International Union for the Conservation of Nature, Gland, Switzerland

Mathieson, A and Wall G (1982) *Tourism: Economic, Physical and Social Impacts*, Longman, London and New York

National Parks Division (NPD) (1986) 'Khao Yai National Park Management Plan 1987–1991', National Parks Division, Royal Forest Department, Bangkok

van't Hof, T (1989) 'Making Marine Parks Self-Sufficient: The Case of Saba' Paper presented at the Conference on Economics and the Environment, November 6–8, Barbados

Western, D (1984) 'Amboseli National Park: Human Values and the Conservation of a Savanna Ecosystem', in *National Parks, Conservation and Development: The Role of Protected Areas in Sustaining Society*, McNeely, J A and Miller, K R (ed), Smithsonian Institution Press, Washington, DC

Ecotourism in Costa Rica

David Weaver

ECOTOURISM IN COSTA RICA

Ecotourism remained virtually non-existent as an organized sector in Costa Rica until the late 1970s. Most of the 300,000 international tourists arriving in 1976 originated from within Central America and had San José, the capital, as their primary destination (Boo 1990). The first major ecotourism initiatives were under-taken by private sector entrepreneurs, capitalizing on the emerging reputation of the expanding park system (Fennell and Eagles 1990). Pioneering companies included the American-founded Costa Rica Expeditions Travel Agency (1979) and the Costa Rican-owned Takal (1983) and Horizontes (1984) groups (Boo 1990). Although the number of ecotourist arrivals did increase through the early 1980s, local entrepreneurs attributed the boom of the late 1980s to two specific high profile events: the awarding of the Nobel Peace Prize to President Oscar Arias in 1987 and the holding of the Seventeenth General Assembly of the World Conservation Union in San José during 1988 (Rovinski, 1991). These events followed the transfer of the National Parks Service from Agriculture to the newly created Ministry of Natural Resources in 1986, which was accompanied by a change in management philosophy from preservation to sustainable development. According to Rovinski (1991, p45), 'the use of protected areas for lucrative and non-destructive activities, such as ecotourism, became a priority'. This change in strategy reinforced the Tourism Development Strategy of 1984–90, which targeted nature and adventure tourism as one of four market niches to be pursued, along with 3S, cruise ship and business/convention tourism (Boo 1990). Not only did the number of international arrivals subsequently grow to over 500,000 by 1992 (when tourism emerged as the single largest earner of foreign exchange), but fully 50 per cent of these tourists paid at least one visit to a National Park, compared with about 20 per cent in 1986 (Wood 1993). As anticipated, many of these visits were undertaken as add-on ecotourism excursions by visitors whose primary motives were not nature-oriented. However, the significance of ecotourism among interna-tional tourists is apparent from a Board of Tourism Survey conducted in 1987, in which 36.1 per cent of arrivals cited ecotourism as a major motivation for their visit, whereas 72.3 per cent cited the natural beauty of Costa Rica (Boo 1990).

Other indicators corroborate the growth of ecotourism in Costa Rica while also providing evidence of its impacts. For example, one-third of the country's 30 travel agencies cater mainly to the ecotourism market, generating significant amounts of foreign exchange (Boo 1990). The Costa Rica Expeditions Travel Agency now attracts 20,000 clients annually, three-quarters of whom arrive for ecotourism purposes, with each visitor spending an average of US$148 each day (Rovinski 1991). In 1989, the 13,000 ecotourists who visited the privately owned

La Selva Biological Field Station spent US$29,000, whereas the nearby Rara Avis private reserve generates an annual income of US$80,000 in the adjacent settlement of Horquetas (Rovinski 1991).

Such revenues may not appear very large by national standards, but their economic impact on local communities is extremely important. Other evidence points to a more ambiguous impact. In an analysis of Tortuguero National Park's socio-economic impact on the adjacent community of the same name, Place (1988) found that the local population's traditional self-reliance, based on the exploitation of the area's biological resources (eg bush meat, fish, etc), has been replaced by a dependence on mainly part-time jobs generated by park visitors and other tourists. This transition from a largely subsistence to a market economy had, however, already begun before the park was created, and Place (1988) suggests that small-scale nature-based tourism has so far proved more benign than other modern economic alternatives which could have dominated instead. The key appears to be the retention of this type of tourism within the context of a village-based delivery system ensuring participation by the largest possible number of locals, some of whom still resent the confiscation of their traditional hunting and gathering areas to create the park.

The environmental impacts of ecotourism in Costa Rica are also ambiguous. Although the large number and size of protected areas could allow for the wide dispersal of park visitors, certain popular and/or readily accessible areas are experiencing visitation levels in excess of their environmental carrying capacities. Serious problems of overcrowding, water pollution, trail erosion and changes in wildlife behaviour have been noted in Manuel Antonio National Park (Rovinski 1991), though much of the disruption can be attributed to beach-oriented excursionists. Unfortunately, most parks still lack sustainable management plans, trained personnel and research into the carrying capacities of individual areas, while facing unregulated commercial development near and sometimes within the parks (Rovinski 1991). Some attempts have been made to harmonize visitation levels with carrying capacity. For example, no more than 25 visitors are allowed to view the sea turtle nesting sites each night at Nancite Beach, Santa Rose National Park (Clark 1991).

Noting the increase in international visits to the park system from 50,000 in 1986 to 250,000 in 1991, Wood (1993) warns that the parks are becoming the victims of their own success through overvisitation, and that the commitment of government funds to park maintenance has been highly irregular despite the revenue potential of protected areas. Wood therefore advocates a differential structure whereby foreigners would pay a higher park entrance fee than Costa Rican nationals, with the extra revenues being allocated toward the enhancement of the park system. Currently, entrance fee revenues are not necessarily used for this purpose. A differential fee structure could also serve to regulate visitation by allowing for the increase in entrance costs to a level where visitor numbers are in concordance with carrying capacity (Lindberg 1991). Certain private reserves have already raised their entrance fees as a means of controlling visitation and increasing their revenues. Monteverde, where visitation has risen from 500 in 1974 to 15,322 in 1988 (Fennell and Eagles 1990), charged an entrance fee of US$2.75 in 1989, compared with US$0.65 in the National Parks (Boo 1990).

A broader issue facing the park system is the continuing deforestation of the countryside, which threatens to eliminate virtually all natural habitat outside the protected areas within the next two decades. Not only does this belie the country's progressive environmental image, it suggests that high quality ecotourism opportunities will soon be available only within the increasingly stressed parks and reserves.

REFERENCES

Boo, E (1990) *Ecotourism: the Potentials and Pitfalls*, Vol 2 – Country Case Studies, World Wildlife Fund, Washington, DC

Clark, J R (1991) 'Carrying capacity and tourism in coastal and marine areas', *Parks*, 2(3), pp13–17

Fennell, D A and Eagles, P F (1990) 'Ecotourism in Costa Rica: a conceptual framework', *Journal of Park and Recreation Administration*, 8(1), pp 23–34

Lindberg, K (1991) *Policies for Maximizing Nature Tourism's Ecological and Economic Benefits*, World Resources Institute, Washington, DC

Place, S (1988) The impact of National Park development in Tortuguero, Costa Rica, *Journal of Cultural Geography*, 9(1), pp37–52

Rovinski, Y (1991) 'Private reserves, parks and ecotourism in Costa Rica', pp39–57 in Whelan, T (ed) *Nature Tourism: Managing for the Environment*, Island Press, Washington, DC

Wood, M E (1993) 'Costa Rican parks threatened by tourism boom: Society launches letter-writing campaign', *The Ecotourism Society Newsletter*, 3(1), pp1–2

Tourism in Difficult Areas
Case studies of Bradford, Bristol, Glasgow and Hamm

Peter J Buckley and Stephen F Witt

Tourism development in four difficult areas (Bradford, Bristol, Glasgow and Hamm) is analysed, and set against the national picture of tourism in the UK and FR Germany. Difficult areas are described as having small visitor receipts, unfavourable social or economic conditions, and a lack of tourism infrastructure. The potential of each area for tourism development is analysed, and strategies maximizing the unique features of each area are suggested. It is concluded that tourism development from a low base is feasible provided a definite target market segment is chosen. The limited resources put into tourism development so far have paid dividends in attracting revenue and creating employment.

Keywords: UK; FR Germany; tourism maximizing strategies

ORGANIZATION OF TOURISM AND TOURISM RESOURCES

Organization of tourist development

Tourism management as a nascent activity in the four centres of study is undergoing organizational changes.[*] In Bradford, tourism is organized under a Marketing Manager as part of Bradford Metropolitan District Council's Economic Development Unit. The budget is fixed at £100,000 in 1980 prices, index linked for inflation. The 1984 budget was £125,000. Only recently in 1984 Bristol has launched the Bristol Marketing Board as a joint venture between Bristol City Council and private sector interests. It has no fixed budget as yet, operating on project-based funding. Glasgow's tourism effort is organized under the Greater Glasgow Tourist Board with a 1984 budget of £500,000. The numbers of staff in each of the British authorities are: Bradford 5, Bristol 4 and Glasgow (maximum) 18.

Tourism resources

Bradford

The success of tourism development in Bradford is shown by the growth of the

---

[*] For a critical view see H L Hughes, 'A note on local authorities and tourism', *The Service Industries Journal*, Vol 3 No 1, March 1983, pp87–92

Table 7.7 *The four study areas: tourism budget and staff*

Town	Budget (1984)	Staff
Bradford	£125,000	5
Bristol	Project based	4
Glasgow	£500,000	18
Hamm	na	na

Source: Author's survey

Bradford Metropolitan District Council backed package holidays, which began in 1980. In 1981–82 2000 were sold; in 1982–83 15,000; in 1983–84 25,000; and this is expected to rise to over 30,000 in the near future. Over 80 tour operators feature Bradford.

In terms of built resources, Bradford has a good array of museums, including the National Museum of Photography, Film and Television (which recently attracted 6,000 visitors in one weekend) and a unique industrial heritage centred on the wool textile industry, as well as the Worth Valley Steam Railway. In cultural resources, the outstanding attraction is the connection with the Brontë Sisters, making Haworth the second most popular destination for literary pilgrimages after Stratford. Also, recent film and television programmes have directed attention to the natural resources of the area, centred on the moorlands of Ilkley and Haworth, and attracted stop-over visitors to North Yorkshire and Scotland.

The marketing of these attractions has been very successful as demonstrated by the rapid increase in tourism business and increased market share of the short-break holiday market, and by the receipt of awards for tourism marketing. Under the banner 'Bradford: A Surprising Place' an attractive campaign has been mounted, including a 'tourism hotline' telephone service guide to 'what's on'. Awards include the Sir Mark Henig Award for Tourism Development 1982 and the Travel GBI/Consort Hotels UK Tourism Awards.

Private capital has been attracted into tourism development. New hotels have been built and one large redundant hotel refurbished and reopened.

Council-backed investment has encouraged private development, eg £1x10^6 council money has been invested in St George's Hall for concerts and meetings; the Delius Festival in May 1985 will benefit as a result. The World Speedway Finals in August 1985 have been attracted to Odsal Stadium, in which £1.5x10^6 has been invested. The Alhambra music hall and theatre is being refurbished at a total cost of £7x10^6 including £2.3x10^6 from European Community's funds. Infrastructural investments are badly needed but the extension of the Leeds/Bradford airport runway should attract more visitors.

Major threats to Bradford's tourist development include:

- poor economic and social conditions in inner city areas (many of which have a high immigrant population);
- a poor image of the city despite the improvements and marketing efforts;
- declining regional income;
- lack of resources for tourist development; and
- increased competition for short-break holidays.

Bristol: docklands area

The inclusion of Bristol in a study of difficult areas may seem unfair until it is remembered that Bristol has a huge area of redundant dockland (six miles of waterfront) centred on the 'floating harbour' requiring regeneration. Bristol's historic harbour was chosen as the pilot project for the Tourism Development Action Programme (TDAP), a partnership between the English Tourist Board, the City Council and Bristol Marketing Board. A strategy is being developed aimed at the key markets of overseas visitors, and short-break and special-interest holiday and day visitors. Entry into the Conference and Exhibition markets also supports this strategy. A shortage of four- and five-star hotel accommodation has been identified as a major constraint.

Current attractions of the docklands area include Brunel's rebuilt SS Great Britain and his Temple Meads station (a Grade I listed building in the course of restoration by the Brunel Engineering Centre Trust, a registered charity), refurbished warehouses as hotels, media and arts centres, speciality shopping, the Industrial Museum and National Lifeboat Museum, a water leisure centre and caravan site. Currently, a new Maritime Heritage Centre is being built alongside the SS Great Britain and moves are afoot to designate the Harbour as Britain's first Urban Heritage Park.

Only in 1984 was the Bristol Marketing Board launched to give impetus to tourism development. The slogan 'Br1stol' (Bristol First) has been adopted and initial marketing centres on the historic harbour and 'Bristol – birthplace of America'. A great deal of preliminary effort has been put into the attraction of private capital. Bristol is currently featured by 19 tour operators. Special events include speedboat and powerboat racing, an annual 'balloon fiesta', the World Wine Fair and a visit from the Orient Express.

Problems facing Bristol are its non-image (rather than a negative image), local competition from Bath as an established tourist destination and the lack so far of a firm organization backing tourism with a definite budget. The lack of top quality hotels and budget hotels is a crucial bottleneck.

Glasgow

As Scotland's largest city, Glasgow is well placed to attract both local national tourists and foreign visitors, particularly North Americans with 'heritage' connections. In terms of buildings resources, Glasgow has a wealth of Victorian architecture, the special buildings of Charles Rennie Mackintosh, a wide array of museums (Transport, Art Galleries, the Hunterian in Glasgow University), the magnificent Burrell Collection and Botanic Gardens. It has an excellent cultural tradition and claims (pace Edinburgh) to be the cultural capital of Scotland with a 50-week festival! A campaign in 1983 'Welcome Home to Glasgow' was a trial run for a more intensive programme to attract ex-Glaswegians back. This has been followed by a widely reported promotion 'Glasgow's miles better'. The surrounding countryside of Greater Glasgow, notably Loch Lomond, is a major natural asset.

Glasgow's problem with respect to the tourism market is to attempt to get visitors to Scotland to stop off on the way, or to foster two-centre holidays. It appears that Glasgow only has a negative image (based on past violence and deprivation) within the UK and that stereotypical views are not held in the major overseas markets of the USA and Canada. Glasgow's task is thus to convince the people who have influence on volume tourist traffic that Glasgow has much to offer tourists. As foreign tourists spend three times per head as much as domestic tourists, a share of Scotland's tourist trade can pay large local dividends for Glasgow. Like Bristol, Glasgow also hopes to attract Conference traffic and the Scottish Exhibition Centre costing £36x10⁶ is being built in Glasgow's Queen's Dock.

The problems facing tourism development in Glasgow are centred on its image (60 per cent unemployment is recorded in areas of the city), the fact that it is still bypassed by major tourist routes, and competition from Edinburgh. Major opportunities exist in marketing the city's attractions in key foreign markets and for major developments, such as the third National Garden Festival, which is to be held in the city in 1988.

Hamm

Tourism in Hamm has been in decline with the number of visitors in registered accommodation falling from 32,000 in 1975 to 22,000 in 1982. Although the average length of stay has increased over the period from 1.5 nights to 1.9 nights, the total number of bed-nights has also fallen from 47,000 in 1975 to 42,000 in 1982. However, with the staging of the *Landesgartenschau* – the country garden exhibition – in Hamm in 1984, a substantial increase in tourist visits took place.

Until recently Hamm had little in the way of buildings resources to attract tourists – mainly the Gustav-Lübcke museum. But in order to host the county garden exhibition from April to September 1984, considerable investment took place (approximately 50x10⁶ DM), which resulted in a marked rise in visitor numbers. Over one million people visited the exhibition alone. The Hamm *Landesgartenschau* was unique in that it was the first time that the event had taken place on reclaimed industrial land – the area had previously been the site of a coal mine. A feature was therefore being made of the industrial heritage of the region. The cultural resources include a zoo, exhibition hall, theatre/concert hall and open-air stage. Furthermore, six million people live within 60 miles of Hamm, so the potential for tourist development is high.

Future development of tourist attractions in Hamm centres on the conversion of the garden exhibition site to other permanent uses. For example, a wildlife park is planned, as is an Energon (high-technology) museum analogous to Philips Evoluon in Eindhoven, Holland (to be financed by 50 per cent private and 50 per cent public capital) where exhibitions relating to solar energy, etc will be displayed. It is also intended that a large convention and leisure centre should open in 1986, again financed partly out of private and partly out of public funds. Private capital has already been attracted into tourist development; during the period 1975–82 only one new hotel was opened in Hamm and only small family hotels with a maximum of 60 bedrooms existed, but in 1983 the first large (220 bedroom) luxury hotel became operational and it has been highly successful.

The main problem facing Hamm has been its negative image – that of a coal-mining and steel-producing area. Although considerable progress has now been made in creating an attractive town, there has been little to encourage tourists directly, and hence tourism starts from a low base. The 1984 garden exhibition changed Hamm's image and the subsequent development of the site together with other planned tourist-attracting schemes should result in a substantial boost to tourism. Furthermore, the addition of a large luxury hotel to the town's stock of hotels has opened up the area of conference tourism. Improvement may be effected by additional investment in tourist-attracting projects and widely publicizing the tourist facilities offered.

CONCLUSIONS

- The development of tourism in difficult areas is a feasible strategy to increase employment and prosperity. It is not, however, a panacea and can be only one part of an economic and social programme. Bradford's package holidays are estimated to have created just over 200 jobs. Hamm's total tourist developments (including the one-off *Landesgartenshau*) have contributed 1000 jobs. Returns to the area are estimated as $£59 \times 10^6$ (all visitors) in Bristol and $£27 \times 10^6$ (holiday visitors only) in Glasgow.
- A concerted, targeted marketing effort is essential to the launch of tourist development and to sustaining its impact. Weekend packages are only one market segment. Foreign visitors, conference trade and specialist holidays are all to be exploited; but it is necessary to have a clear strategy, not a scattergun approach. An appraisal of strengths, weaknesses and opportunities is vital.
- Success cannot be achieved without the support and cooperation of the private sector. The impetus from local authorities will be lost unless the private sector is involved *ab initio* as a partner. Hotel owners and chains, tour operators and travel agents, operators of local facilities and the private sector in general must be involved in the development of tourism.
- Resources are necessary to mount a drive to attract tourists. With declining real local authority spending, priorities must be set and the opportunity cost of tourist development calculated. This necessitates keeping a better record of tourist expenditure, visits and costs, and a regular appraisal of policy achievements.
- From the diverse patterns and results in the four areas, it appears that an exchange of information would be beneficial for all concerned. National Tourist Authorities would do well to consider a conference of tourism development managers facing similar problems.

Chapter 8

The Role of Governments

INTRODUCTION

Sustainable development can only be achieved when tourism is managed in a controlled and integrated manner and is soundly based in careful and effective legislative restriction. Many examples exist of uncontrolled developments that may reap short-term benefits but which, in the longer term, have led to socio-cultural and environmental problems and to the emergence of poor quality destinations (Inskeep 1994). As in Majorca and Benidorm, strenuous attempts to improve such venues have been made that might have been unnecessary had strong planning measures been imposed from the beginning.

Planning and management can occur at many different scales. A piecemeal approach is inevitably less successful than a carefully structured policy that defines and applies appropriate principles at every level. Space forbids the inclusion of all relevant aspects of the planning and management process in this volume, although an outline of some important approaches is shown in Box 8.1. Instead, the focus will be upon planning at the national scale, because without an overarching national plan unsupported regional and local efforts are less likely to achieve a long-term solution to the damaging impacts unchecked tourism often generates. However, it is worth noting that in some countries regional devolution may increase the role of planning at the regional scale. The region of Catalonia, in Spain, is an appropriate example of such a situation.

The first of the readings, from Pearce (1989), examines some of the theory behind national planning, while the remaining extracts provide illustrations from a variety of environments. Malta and Bermuda, for example, both have well-developed tourism industries. The former sought to expand and diversify its tourism product, whereas the latter remains one of the few countries in which planning restrictions have constrained the number of tourist arrivals while retaining a relatively successful industry. Bhutan, with a very small tourism sector that was strictly controlled and aimed at high-spending adventure tourists, has begun to expand tourism in search of greater economic returns. It will be interesting to see if the hitherto rigid plan is still followed once the population begin to reap financial rewards and whether it can check any of the damaging effects of the industry.

BOX 8.1 APPROACHES TO THE PLANNING AND MANAGEMENT OF TOURISM ENVIRONMENTS

AIMS	TECHNIQUES	EXAMPLES
Build responsible tourism	• control capacity, eg via quotas, entry fees	• Bermuda; US National Parks
	• develop tourism with dignity, eg involving local people	• Lower Casamance Scheme in Senegal
	• plan for tourism – at national, regional and local levels	• Malta, Bhutan
Encourage conservation	• educate local people and tourists	• school-based tourism education in St. Lucia; attempts by media aimed at tourists in Britain
	• encourage pressure groups to take appropriate action	• ACAP scheme in Nepal; National Trust work in several countries
	• lead by example	• designation of National Parks worldwide
Develop an environmental focus	• solve environmental problems and export solutions	• quota restrictions on entrance to some National Parks and Wilderness Areas, as in the USA
	• develop ecotourism	• Belize; Dominica
	• move beyond ecotourism	• Campfire Project in Zimbabwe

Note: While techniques may prove successful when initially implemented, a change in circumstances, eg rapidly growing tourist numbers, a shift in government policy or changes in tastes or in fashion, may reduce their effectiveness and result in a search for still further new approaches.

Source: Poon 1993, p294

REFERENCES

Inskeep, E (1994) *National and Regional Tourism Planning. Methodologies and Case Studies*, Routledge, London

Pearce, D (1989) *Tourist Development*, 2nd edition, Longman, Harlow

Poon, A (1993) *Tourism, Technology and Competitive Strategies*, CAB International, Wallingford

Planning for Tourism

Douglas Pearce

PLANNING AT THE NATIONAL LEVEL

As Acerenza (1985) and others have argued, planning for tourism at the national level, as at other scales, should be undertaken in the light of broader national development goals and objectives. In some cases these may be stated explicitly or there may be firm government direction. Elsewhere they may not be clearly articulated and the tourism planner has little guidance as to what overall goals should be pursued through the development of tourism. In many instances tourism plans focus specifically on tourism goals with little direct reference to broader issues, thus lessening the likelihood that tourism will contribute effectively to national development.

Earlier chapters have shown tourism is frequently seen to further national development by improving the balance of payments situation, by generating employment, spreading growth and so on. Where tourism is related to broader goals this is often done in economic terms, although growing emphasis is placed on social and environmental goals. Planners in West Germany (Klöpper 1976, Romsa 1981) and Switzerland (Keller 1976), for instance, stress the need to provide recreational facilities for their urban populations and to protect the environment.

Ashworth and Bergsma (1987, p154) note that recent Dutch policy has stressed the need to mitigate the large adverse balance of international tourist payments by the stimulation of four aspects of the tourist industry:

- The capturing of a larger share of the high-spending intercontinental tourist trade to Western Europe...;
- The diversion of part of the Dutch market from foreign to domestic destinations, as a form of 'important substitution';
- The encouragement of 'near-neighbour holiday-making' especially from the West German market, in order to exploit trends either to more off-season holidays or summer holidays closer to home; and
- ... more profitable exploitation of European transit tourists.'

Cyprus tourism policy aims to attract tourists from the high and middle income groups (Andronicou 1983). Not only are the economic benefits from these groups perceived to be greater but a low-volume high-spending market is believed to be more in keeping with a small island where (p. 210) 'mass tourism would have had adverse effects both on the environment and the social fabric of the country with a consequential deterioration of all tourist attractions'.

Malaysia is one country where tourism planning has been tied directly to broader development goals (Din 1982). The 1975 tourism development plan was formulated, inter alia '... to provide a basis upon which Malaysia may develop her tourist potentials in an orderly and balanced manner within the framework of the national development plan and the New Economic Policy'. The New Economic Policy which emerged during the 1970s had national unity as its stated primary goal, national unity being sought by eradicating poverty irrespective of race and by eliminating racial and spatial imbalances in the economy. Thus the 1975 master tourism plan attempts to decentralize tourism from the urban areas of the west coast of Peninsular Malaysia by developing regions and tourist corridors on the east coast and in the states of Sabah and Sarawak. While this may reduce some of the spatial and associated regional imbalances, Din points out that the plan makes no specific suggestions as to how local or *bumiputra* (indigenous group) participation in tourism might be encouraged. He also notes the practical difficulties of reconciling the double tasks of promotion of growth, where the existing pattern of demand is centred on the established tourist centres of Kuala Lumpur and Penang, and the promotion of redistribution.

In his study of the Cook Islands, Milne (1987) highlights the tension which may exist between different development goals and the role of different strategies in attaining them. In Figure 8.1 the two major objectives of the Cook Islands Government with regard to tourism are shown to be maximizing gross tourist revenue generation on the one hand and maximizing local participation on the other. Intensification of the present pattern of development characterized by large foreign or European-owned establishments with minimal local linkages might enable the first objective to be met but local control would be sacrificed. Conversely, encouragement of alternative tourist development would enhance local participation and reduce leakages but at the expense of lower tourist expenditure per day. While not intending to prescribe a strategy for the expansion of tourism in the Cook Islands, Milne suggests that an optimal solution for future development continues to lie in a path between the two poles.

The total or partial incompatibility of different objectives was also recognized explicitly by the British Tourism Association (BTA 1976) in its 1976 strategic plan for overseas tourism. The BTA ranked its primary objectives (p2): 'in accordance with current government policy of giving preference to the earning of foreign exchange in cases where regional spread of traffic might compromise such earnings', and considered the interaction among various operational objectives which might achieve these (Table 8.1). Reconciliation of different tourist development goals may clearly be no easy matter but the task is facilitated if reference is made to broader national goals and the nature of the relationships between different objectives is examined at the outset.

Even where regional redistribution is not a primary aim, spatial considerations arise for planning cannot be done in a vacuum and national or regional goals must be translated into geographic terms.

Commenting on tourism planning in Turkey, Ersek and Düzgunoglu (1976, p69) note:

> *Significant problems in this field have been encountered during the implementation stages of the First Five-Year Plan and during the first two years of the Second Plan (1963–72) due to lack of policy decisions and tools to indicate the spatial distribution of resources and priority areas. The definition of priority areas and policy decisions concerning the geographical distribution of*

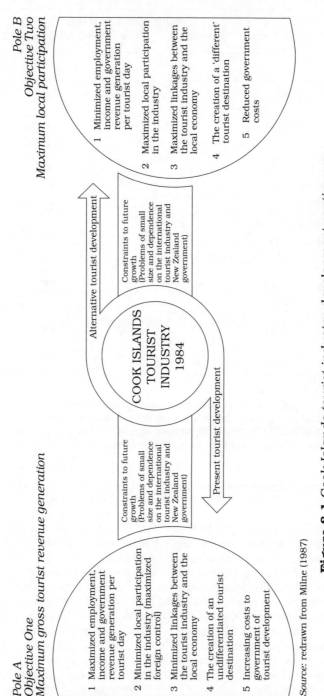

Pole A
Objective One
Maximum gross tourist revenue generation

1 Maximized employment, income and government revenue generation per tourist day

2 Minimized local participation in the industry (maximized foreign control)

3 Minimized linkages between the tourist industry and the local economy

4 The creation of an undifferentiated tourist destination

5 Increasing costs to government of tourist development

Pole B
Objective Two
Maximum local participation

1 Minimized employment, income and government revenue generation per tourist day

2 Maximized local participation in the industry

3 Maximized linkages between the tourist industry and the local economy

4 The creation of a 'different' tourist destination

5 Reduced government costs

Alternative tourist development

Constraints to future growth (Problems of small size and dependence on the international tourist industry and New Zealand government)

COOK ISLANDS TOURIST INDUSTRY 1984

Constraints to future growth (Problems of small size and dependence on the international tourist industry and New Zealand government)

Present tourist development

Source: redrawn from Milne (1987)

Figure 8.1 *Cook Islands tourist industry development continuum*

217

Table 8.1 *Possible Tourism Objectives*

Primary objectives	Possible operational objectives				
	Maximize in total	visitor per day	revenue per day	Maximize regional spread	Maximize seasonal spread
Improving foreign exchange earnings/ balance of payments	Y	(Y)	X	X	X
Raising incomes	Y	(Y)	X	X	(Y)
Redistributing incomes	X	X	X	Y	X
Maintaining employment	Y	(Y)	X	(Y)	XY
Conserving environment and heritage	XY	XY	XY	XY	(Y)
Fostering the arts, amenities and services	XY	XY	XY	XY	XY
Trade and goodwill	(Y)	X	X	(Y)	(Y)

Source: BTA 1976

Y = Operational makes major contribution toward primary objective
(Y) = Operational makes some contribution toward primary objective
XY = Operational partly contributes to primary objective but is partly at variance with it
X = Operational may be at variance with primary objective

> resources is of prime importance for a country like Turkey. This is especially
> so because of the scale and variety of Turkey's tourism resources.

A major concern at the national level therefore is to determine the most important regions to develop (United Nations 1970). For those nations with an as yet poorly developed tourist industry, this will involve an examination of the country's tourist resources along the lines discussed in Ch. 5, together with an assessment of likely demand (Ch. 4), and the delimitation of one or several areas to develop. In other nations where tourism is already a significant activity, resource evaluation and marketing techniques may need to be applied to the question of where or how to concentrate future growth. Elsewhere, the prime concern may be to identify and rectify bottle-necks and deficiencies in the national tourist system rather than to promote new areas. This is especially important in countries such as New Zealand where the emphasis for overseas visitors at least, is on touring rather than destina-tion-oriented tourism (Forer and Pearce 1984). Bottle-necks in one or two key places may effectively limit the growth of tourism throughout the country as a whole.

Where possible, selection of areas should be guided by national planning objectives. In Mexico, for example, specific planning criteria have been defined (Collins 1979, p345): 'New tourist centres should develop new sources of employment in areas with tourist potential. These areas should be located near important rural centres with low incomes and few alternatives to develop other productive activities in the near future. New resorts should spur regional development with new agricultural, industrial and handicraft activities in the zones.' These and other factors led to the development of Mexico's first planned tourism complex in economically depressed Quintana Roo (Cancun) in preference to other more developed areas such as Acapulco, or equally depressed regions like the Coast of Oaxaca which, however, lack infrastructure.

One of the objectives of Thai national planning has been to foster growth selectively throughout the country by designating key development areas. Elsewhere, for example in Bali (Rodenburg 1980) and Tanzania (Jenkins 1982), development has been geographically concentrated to limit some of the socially disruptive effects of tourism.

Spatial co-ordination with other sectors of the economy is also important at the national level. Development of major infrastructure such as roads, airports or ports, for example, should take into account not only the needs and demands of tourism but also those of other sectors such as agriculture or manufacturing. In some instances, multiple use of new infrastructure has been severely limited as Rodenburg (1980, p183) notes in Nusa Dua, Bali: 'Only $8.2 million (22.6 per cent) of the planned infrastructure budget of $36.1 million will be used for multipurpose roads and is the only item, with the exception of water and electrical supply lines to two local villages, that can be said to serve both the Balinese and the tourist industry.' Co-ordination is also necessary to ensure that valuable tourist resources are not destroyed by other activities. Ciaccio (1975), for instance, observes how the tourist development of much of the Sicilian coastline was seriously compromised by the installation of large oil refineries.

Structurally, one of the major concerns at a national level will be linking development areas with gateway cities. In many countries the majority of arrivals by air will be to a single city and links with the hinterland, particularly in developing countries, may not be strong. Even in economically advanced countries where such linkages exist, for example, Japan and the United Kingdom, international tourists may still be heavily concentrated in the capital city (Pearce 1987a). Selective development of a small number of key tourist regions will reduce the number of linkages to be developed and at the same time permit the promotion of a stronger, more coherent image of these regions enabling them to compete more effectively with the points of arrival. However, in large countries where the potential is for touring rather than resort development, promotion of a second major entry/exit point will help increase the flow of visitors throughout the country and obviate the need for them to backtrack. But where the concern is for social tourism and promoting the recreational opportunities of nationals, the emphasis will be towards developing more localized linkages between the major urban areas and their immediate hinterlands.

In most cases, development of domestic tourism and international tourism will be complementary. The Dubrovnik Seminar (United Nations 1970) noted:

> ...in some countries development of domestic tourism might lead to a development of foreign tourism, whilst in others, as yet undeveloped, but well

> endowed with tourist attractions, the encouragement of foreign tourism would lead in due course to growth in domestic tourism. In both cases, however, tourist development plans should provide from the start for both foreign and domestic tourists.

Many of these spatial elements were incorporated in a recent 10-year development plan for tourism in Belize (Pearce 1984). There, the resource evaluation, the analysis of existing demand and the marketing study suggested a developmental strategy focused on the main gateways, the northern cays and the southern coastal zone. Emphasis was given to facilitating access from the gateways to these coastal areas and to improving the distribution of information at the points of arrival in order to encourage longer visits amongst overland travellers by directing them out to the more attractive cays and along the coast. In these latter areas a prime concern was to upgrade the infrastructure.

REFERENCES

Acerenza, M A (1985) 'Planificación estratégica del turismo: esquema metodológico', *Estudios Turísticos*, 85, pp47–70

Andronicou, A (1983) 'Selecting and planning for tourists – The case of Cyprus', *Tourism Management*, 4(3), pp209–11

Ashworth, G J and Bergsma, J R (1987) 'New policies for tourism: Opportunities or problems?', *Tijdschrift voor Economische en Sociale Geografie* 78(2), pp151–5

BTA (1976) *International Tourism and Strategic Planning*, British Tourist Association, London

Ciaccio, C (1975) 'Développement touristique et groupes de pression en Sicile', *Travaux de l'Institut de Géographie de Reims*, 23–4, pp81–7

Collins, C O (1979) 'Site and situation strategy in tourism planning: A Mexican case study', *Annals of Tourism Research*, 6(3), pp351–66

Din, K H (1982) 'Tourism in Malaysia: competing needs in a plural society', *Annals of Tourism Research*, 9(3), pp453–80

Ersek, S and Düzgunoglu, E (1976) 'An approach to physical planning for tourism development in Turkey', pp68–76 in ECE, *Planning and Development of the Tourist Industry in the ECE Region*, United Nations, New York

Forer, P C and Pearce, D G (1984) 'Spatial patterns of package tourism in New Zealand', *New Zealand Geographer*, 40(1), pp34–42

Jenkins, C L (1982) 'The effects of scale in tourism projects in developing countries', *Annals of Tourism Research*, 9(2), pp229–49

Keller, P (1976) 'Objectives and measures for achieving planned tourist development', pp190–8, in ECE, *Planning and Development of the Tourist Industry in the ECE Region*, United Nations, New York

Klöpper, R (1976) 'Physical planning and tourism in the Federal Republic of Germany', pp50–6 in ECE, *Planning and Development of the Tourist Industry in the ECE Region*, United Nations, New York

Milne, S (1987) *The Economic Impact of Tourism in the Cook Islands*, Occasional Publication 21, Department of Geography, University of Auckland

Pearce, D G (1984) 'Planning for tourism in Belize', *Geographical Review*, 74(3), pp291–303

Pearce, D G (1987) *Tourism Daily: A Geographical Analysis*, Longman, Harlow and John Wiley, New York

Rodenburg, E E (1980) 'The effects of scale in economic development: tourism in Bali', *Annals of Tourism Research*, 7(2), pp177–96

Romsa, G (1981) 'An overview of tourism and planning in the Federal Republic of Germany', *Annals of Tourism Research*, 8(3), pp333–56

United Nations (1970) *Report of the Interregional Seminar on Physical Planning for Tourist Development*, Dubrovnik, Yugoslavia, 19 October–3 November 1970, ST/TAO/Serv C/131, United Nations, New York

Tourism Planning Approach of Malta

E Inskeep[*]

Tourism planning for the Republic of Malta represents an approach applied to an already established tourist destination. Planning is to shift the direction of the country's tourism development and to guide its future expansion.

BACKGROUND

The Republic of Malta is an independent country located in the central Mediterranean Sea south of Sicily. The country is composed of the islands of Malta, Gozo and Comino and encompasses 316 square kilometres. The population is about 350,000, most of which is concentrated on the island of Malta. The country has a long history reflected in highly interesting archaeological sites, medieval villages, old town districts and buildings and extensive fortifications. The historic area around the Grand Harbour at the capital city of Valletta is particularly interesting. Malta is the home of the Knights of the Order of St. John. Some major historical battles were fought in Malta.

For tourism, Malta offers a mild Mediterranean climate combined with good beaches and scenic views. In addition to major archaeological and historic places, the traditional village and lifestyles are important cultural attractions. The country is conveniently located near to major tourist market countries in nearby Europe. Access for virtually all tourists is by air.

Malta already has considerable development of tourism. Tourism is mostly focused on Malta Island, but there is also some tourism on Gozo. The country received almost 900,000 tourist arrivals in 1990. Most accommodation is small scale, including many self-catering units, with only a few larger hotels developed. Tourist arrivals are heavily skewed toward the British market, and generally are low spending types of tourists. In the late 1980s, the tourism development issues were identified by the government as the need to increase income and employment from tourism. At the same time, it wished to improve the quality of tourism, including attracting higher spending tourists. The government also wanted to reduce the impact of high seasonality by expanding tourism during the shoulder and off-peak periods.

THE TOURISM PLANNING APPROACH

The Maltese Islands Tourism Development Plan was prepared in 1989 (UNDP and WTO 1989). *The Maltese Islands Tourism Development Plan*. Madrid: WTO).

We should like to thank the World Tourism Organization for its permission to reproduce the articles: 'Tourism Planning Approach of Malta' and 'Tourism Planning in Bhutan'. Both studies were prepared within the framework of UNDP–WTO projects in Bhutan and Malta.

Although a separate project, the tourism plan was designed to be incorporated into the overall development plan and programme of the country. The overall planning was scheduled to be carried out subsequent to the tourism planning.

The tourism planning approach is a comprehensive one. The tourism development objectives are specified, based on the government's general objectives indicated above. A detailed environmental analysis was conducted. This is an especially important procedure because of Malta's small size and limited remaining natural areas. The environmental analysis identifies environmentally sensitive areas which should be preserved, as follows:

- Agricultural – lands of good agricultural capability that should be retained for agricultural use.
- Ecological – lands that contain important flora and fauna that should be preserved.
- Geological – areas of important geological features that should be preserved.
- Entomological – areas important as insect habitats.
- Ornithological – areas important as bird habitats, including stopover points for migratory birds.

Also identified is the location of underground water aquifers where any development permitted should have strict controls applied, so that groundwater recharging capability is not impaired nor the groundwater polluted. Because of limited water supply in the islands, maintenance of groundwater resources is essential.

Existing land use is surveyed and mapped, using the categories of:

- Development zone boundaries – areas which are zoned and mostly already developed with urban uses. These areas generally would not be available for new tourism development (except urban tourism).
- Industrial areas – areas which have been industrially developed and therefore are not compatible with tourism development.
- Airport – the airport area is one where tourism development would be adversely affected because of aircraft movements and noise.

The tourist attractions are surveyed in detail and categorized, as follows:

- Places of major historic interest – these particularly include entire historic urban districts and archaeological sites.
- Tower, forts and palaces – these are specific historic features of touristic interest.
- Traditional village cores and clusters – these are village areas of traditional architectural character and lifestyles.
- Major panoramic views – the Maltese islands are small scale but hilly, and an interesting aspect of island tours are the many scenic views offered.
- Beaches – these are specifically located, named and classified into rocky or sandy types.

The approach to surveying tourist attractions includes identification and evaluation of the coastal bay resources for tourism. The existing areas of intensive tourism development were also surveyed and mapped in order to graphically show the relationships of existing development to the various attraction features. The location of existing tourism development is also, of course, a consideration in planning for expansion. This survey includes evaluation of the quality of existing tourism development, and its environmental integration as related to the beaches and coastal areas.

All types of transportation are surveyed and evaluated. First, the organization of the transport sector is reviewed. Then, the major issues of air transport access to Malta are identified, with consideration given to travel facilitation procedures. The sea links to and among the islands are examined. Internal surface means of transportation, including bus, taxi and rent-a-car services, are evaluated. The short cruise boat tours offered by tour operators among the islands are also reviewed. Recommendations on improvement to all aspects of transportation are made in the plan.

All tourist accommodation is inventoried. A market analysis is conducted and market targets established based on the development objectives, evaluation of tourist attractions and other factors. These targets reflect the greater mix of types of tourist markets which the country wishes to attract and are realistic to accomplish. Based on the market targets, the number and type of future accommodation are projected. The institutional elements of tourism – organizational approaches and structures, investment incentives, legislation requirements and manpower planning – were investigated, with recommendations made for any improvements required. Economic, environmental and socio-cultural impacts are evaluated and recommendations made on these factors.

In preparing the plan, the major consideration was the need to improve and diversify the tourism product. This is necessary in order to upgrade and diversify the tourism markets, one of the plan objectives. Based on another plan objective, market and product improvements must be accomplished within the framework of expanding tourism as a major economic sector of the country.

For planning purposes, the two main islands of Malta and Gozo were divided into 12 zones, 10 on Malta and two on Gozo. This division provides for the systematic analysis of relatively homogeneous areas for which recommendations can be made. Within each zone, many recommendations are made on the specific policies that should be adopted and the actions that are required in order to improve the areas (as related to tourism development). TPUs (tourism planning units) are designated as specific 'no go' areas – places where no new tourism development should be allowed until detailed plans have been prepared and adopted to guide future development. Two of the tourism zones are designated as priority areas for improvements.

As part of the planning project, detailed planning and some urban design improvements were prepared for the two priority areas. Detailed planning, design and development programming were also prepared for visitor facilities at selected major archaeological and historic sites. In the implementation programme, the plan recommends an effective institutional approach for reviewing and taking action on future tourism development projects such as hotels and resorts, proposed by the private sector. This procedure is essential so that new development projects reflect the plan's recommendations, and do not generate any environmental or social problems. Also it allows for efficient processing of the project proposals. The implementation approach includes a specific action and project development programme.

A major element of the planning study is the marketing plan and related product improvement programme. The market planning approach reflects the close relationship between developing the tourism product and promoting tourist markets. The strategy recommended in the marketing plan comprises the three elements of: 1) market diversification; 2) quality improvement; and 3) lengthening the tourist season. Then, derived from the strategy, marketing policies are determined and the action plans set forth for 1990–94. The action plans recommend specific actions and activities, related to coordinated product development and promotion, that should be carried out.

The product development programme specifies various actions for the short- and medium-term periods. These include the following:

- Implementing the tourism area upgrading schemes.
- Promoting hotel and other facilities upgrading with an incentive package.
- Encouraging the development of high quality hotels and other facilities related to specific target markets.
- Promoting the development of leisure facilities, such as yacht marinas, sports complexes, entertainment facilities, an underwater national park, cultural heritage sites, more shopping, and a light and laser harbour show.

The plan states that sufficient time will be required to achieve the shifting of markets and the product improvement needed, and that progress can best be made on a step-by-step basis. But it anticipates that, if the policies and programme are followed on schedule, the desired changes will be well underway by 1995. Over the longer term, the plan envisages Malta as a quality 'good value-for-money' destination, appealing to diversified middle and higher income market groups.

CONCLUSIONS

The Malta plan is a good example of a substantially developed tourist destination that needs to expand tourism for economic reasons. At the same time, the country wishes to shift its tourist markets to more diversified and higher spending ones. Another objective is to have a better seasonal distribution of tourists throughout the year. A principle here is that, in addition to the greater expenditures of more tourists in total, the higher spending tourists visiting throughout the year will generate more income per tourist. The desired income will be generated by a fewer number of higher spending tourists rather than a large number of lower spending tourists. This reduces the negative environmental and social impacts of large-scale tourism.

To accomplish these objectives, the plan recognizes that the key issues are: 1) to improve and diversify (as well as expand) the tourism product of accommodation, other facilities and attraction features; and 2) to change the marketing strategy and promotion techniques. The plan rightfully emphasizes that tourism product improvements and market changes must proceed together, as a basic principle of tourism development. The plan also recognizes that these changes should take place within the framework of a comprehensive and specific physical plan, institutional improvements and development programming.

It is important to note that the planning includes a detailed environmental analysis which takes into account the scarce land and water resources of these small islands. This is an essential approach to achieve sustainable development.

The land use patterns are also very important to understand in deciding on location of tourism areas. It is noteworthy that the tourism plan is intended to be integrated into the overall development plan of the islands. This should achieve better integration of tourism into the total development patterns of the country.

Dividing the country into tourism zones of relatively homogeneous areas represents an important planning principle. These zones provide a geographically rational basis for analysis and formulation of specific development policies, and for which to prepare detailed physical plans.

The marketing plan approach is a logical one that proceeds from general objectives to strategy, policies and action plans, with each policy and action plan specified in detail. Product development is carefully programmed and promotional techniques identified. In its statement that some time will be required to accomplish the desired changes, the plan presents a cautionary note to Malta that it needs to be patient but persistent in achieving its tourism objectives.

REFERENCES

UNDP and WTO (1989) *The Maltese Islands Tourism Development Plan*, WTO, Madrid

Tourism Planning in Bhutan

E Inskeep[*]

Policy and planning for tourism in Bhutan are based on the concept of maintaining high value, special interest and adventure tourism, which is developed in a very controlled and staged manner. There is much involvement of the government and religious leaders in the planning and management process.

BACKGROUND

Located in the eastern Himalaya Mountains of South Asia, the Kingdom of Bhutan is mostly high and mountainous. Bordering India on the south are foothills with subtropical wildlife and vegetation. The country contains a population of about 1.5 million, most of which is agricultural. Only about 5 per cent of the people live in urban places. Nomadism is still practised by certain groups in the higher elevations. Many Bhutanese live a relatively secure and comfortable subsistence life style that is not, to a great extent, integrated into the modern cash economy.

Attractions for tourists are the spectacular mountain scenery and strongly traditional Buddhist cultural patterns. The distinctive Bhutanese architectural styles of monasteries, palaces, shops and homes are a major feature. The castle-monasteries called dzongs are particularly striking features of the cultural landscape. Handicrafts are available. Cultural tours and mountain trekking are the most popular activities of tourists. Access to the country for tourists is primarily by air to the international airport at Paro in western Bhutan. The airport is at a relatively short distance from the capital city of Thimpu, and connects to the country's road network. There is also one road access from India in the southwest.

Tourism in Bhutan commenced after the Royal Coronation of the present King in 1974, when it was realized that the hotels developed for that event could be utilized for tourists. The objectives of tourism at the time of its introduction were to:

- Generate revenue, especially foreign exchange.
- Publicize the culture and traditions of the country to the outside world.
- Play an active role in the country's socio-economic development.

However, the government was concerned that the unrestricted flow of tourists could lead to socio-cultural and environmental problems, and it applied a strict policy of controlling tourism development. Until the mid-1980s, the maximum number of international holiday tourist arrivals, excluding the neighbouring Indians, was maintained at 2000 annually. In 1986, 2500 arrivals were targeted. Arrivals have remained at about the 2500–3000 level into the early 1990s.

We should like to thank the World Tourism Organization for its permission to reproduce the articles: 'Tourism Planning Approach of Malta' and 'Tourism Planning in Bhutan'. Both studies were prepared within the framework of UNDP–WTO projects in Bhutan and Malta.

THE TOURISM PLAN

A national tourism development plan was completed in 1984 and, after long debate by the government, adopted in 1986 (UNDP and WTO 1986). The plan indicates that Bhutan's resources present potential for three types of tourism, each in a different geographical zone, as follows:

- Himalayan zone for mountaineering and high altitude trekking.
- Central zone for cultural tours, including trekking.
- Southern foothills zone for wildlife tourism in conjunction with Indian winter tourism.

The plan states that, 'The central cultural zone has unique attractions by world standards, and creates great potential as a focus for all aspects of Bhutanese tourism development.'

The plan recognizes the government's desire to continue the policy of controlled tourism development, gradually opening up new areas as infrastructure is developed. The overriding aim is to ensure that the type and rate of growth of tourism does not damage the natural environment nor degrade the cultural heritage. In fact, the tourism plan views controlled tourism as an important vehicle for conserving and enhancing the cultural assets of the country.

In the tourism plan, growth targets for international tourist arrivals were set at 3000 for 1990 and 5600 for 1995 under the preferred strategy. The National Seventh Five-Year Development Plan for 1992–96 closely follows and further refines these market targets.

The tourism development strategy set forth in the plan is to focus development around tourism service centres in the main potential areas, linked by tourist excursion routes. Eight such centres are recommended for the long-term period in the western, central, eastern and southern regions of the country. The strategy identifies three time phases, which are illustrated in Figure 8.2, and described as follows:

- Short-term (1986–90) – Continuation of the process of improving standards of tourist facilities and services with high utilization of existing infrastructure in the presently opened areas in the western and central regions.
- Medium-term (1991–95) – Expansion of tourism in the central region with development of some new facilities and infrastructure, and starting cultural safari tourism in the eastern region.
- Long-term (post-1995) – Further expansion of tourism development in the western and central regions, gradual expansion of development in the eastern region, and development of wildlife tourism in the southern region.

The plan reinforces that already established policy of the government that the architectural design of any new development, including tourist facilities, must utilize traditional design motifs and building materials to the greatest extent possible. This policy has been followed. Recently developed hotels and other buildings, especially in the rapidly growing capital city of Thimpu, incorporate the traditional architectural character and blend in well with older development and the natural environment.

Adequate sewage disposal systems for hotels are also required. Electric power is provided from the national grid in the more developed areas and on-site generation is used in other places. More generally, the country has adopted a policy, and has programmes underway, for strict conservation of the natural environment.

In order to provide trained tourism personnel, a training unit was set up at the Bhutan Hotel in Thimpu in the mid-1980s under the UNDP/WTO. This project also included overseas education in hotel and tourism management for several persons.

In the mid-1980s, some religious leaders objected to certain forms of tourist activities, particularly those that involve tourists visiting important religious sites. A special tourism commission was established and it investigated the situation. The commission reported to the National Assembly that tourism may have an adverse moral impact on young people, if they observe tourists' behaviour that might be interpreted as belittling the mystical power of the country's religious beliefs. This resulted in a Royal Command to the tourism office to designate certain monasteries and temples closed to tourists, effective in 1988. This seems to have been an acceptable arrangement to the parties involved.

In order to carry out the concept of controlled, high value tourism, certain approaches have been applied. All non-Indian tourists must come on pre-arranged, all-inclusive package tours, and no individual tourists are permitted entry into the country. These package tourists must obtain visas before arrival. Presumably, if the planned number of tourist arrivals is going to be exceeded in a particular year, no more tour groups would be allowed in during that period. Also, marketing of tourism for the country is kept very limited and targeted to special interest groups, so as not to encourage casually interested tourists. Minimum daily expenditures per tourist have been established. These vary depending on the season and type of tour and are periodically increased. These required minimum expenditures are much higher than the average expenditures of tourists elsewhere in South Asia.

Contacts are maintained with overseas tour operators who specialize in Bhutan tours. These operators handle the visa arrangements and receive the tourists' tour payments before arrival in the country. Approximately 80 per cent of the tourists come for cultural tours and most of the remainder for trekking, including cultural treks to visit monasteries and historic places. A very limited number of mountain climbing expeditions are allowed.

CONCLUSIONS

The Bhutan plan demonstrates the application of establishing tourism zones, in this case based on different geographical areas which are related to different types of tourist attractions and activities. The plan also applies the concept of establishing tourism centres. An important aspect of the plan is logical staging of development during successive five-year periods. Although specified by time periods, in fact, this staging can be carried out within a flexible time frame depending on future circumstances, especially development of infrastructure.

The plan reflects the strong government policy to control tourism so that any undesirable impacts on the natural and cultural environment are minimized. Controlling impacts is achieved primarily through limiting the number of tourist arrivals. In Bhutan, the limitation on tourist arrivals is maintained by requiring that all tourists come on package tours and obtain visas before arrival. This approach is in contrast to some countries which remove visa requirements, or

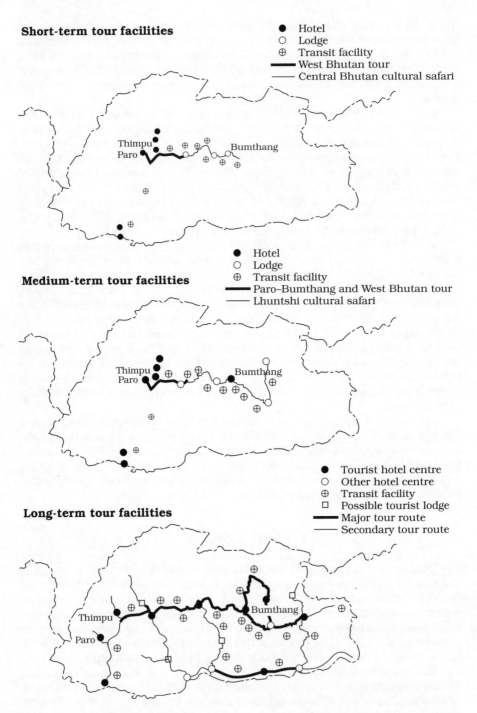

Figure 8.2 *Bhutan tourism development plan*

allow visas to be given on arrival, to many types of tourists, in order to encourage more tourism. The package tours also provide the opportunity to control the travel movements of all tourists. In order to receive substantial economic benefits from tourism, Bhutan somewhat compensates for the limited number of tourists by requiring a high level of tourist expenditures.

As another controlled tourism technique, the limited and targeted marketing – as well as the high spending levels required – will tend to attract only those tourists who have a serious interest in, and respect for, the country's culture and environment. Impacts are also controlled and tourism development environmentally integrated by requiring compatible architectural styles of tourist facilities and proper development of infrastructure. An important impact control measure is prohibition of entry of tourists to certain culturally sensitive religious monuments.

The tourism education and training programme and training unit were particularly important to develop in Bhutan because of the lack of tourism trained personnel in the country. This programme provides the skills and knowledge necessary to operate good quality tourist facilities and services, and to manage highly controlled development.

The approach in Bhutan includes the strong involvement of the government and religious leaders in the planning and management process. In this manner, the plan recommendations reflect government and religious policy, and the plan will receive good support. As should be done in any tourism area, continuous monitoring of tourism is maintained in Bhutan. When problems arise, as they did in 1987, the situation is investigated and remedial measures taken. Thus, tourism can be continuously responsive to local people's concerns while still generating benefits to the country.

REFERENCES

UNDP and WTO (1986) *Tourism Development Master Plan for Bhutan*, WTO, Madrid

Rejuvenation Planning for Island Tourism: the Bermuda Example

Michael V Conlin

BERMUDA TOURISM POLICY

During the 1960s and 1970s, Bermuda examined the type of tourist market it wished to continue attracting and concluded that it would be in the country's best interest to preserve its image as an upscale resort destination (Riley 1991). As a result of numerous studies, a number of policies which would preserve this image were adopted and continue to be the foundation of the country's tourism policy.

MORATORIUM ON DEVELOPMENT

The most important policy was one which directly limited growth in carrying capacity by imposing a moratorium on the construction of new hotels and the maintenance of a 10,000-bed ceiling. This policy still forms the basis of development for Bermuda's tourism industry and is enforced through a phasing scheme which maintains the 10,000-bed ceiling and allocates available space within the ceiling to the stronger properties which maintain high standards.

The policy has been overruled on two occasions. In the late 1970s, the government gave permission for Bermuda College to construct a 64-room resort hotel on the island's south shore. Named the Stonington Beach Hotel, the property is adjacent to the College's Hotel School and serves as the training facility for students in hospitality programmes. The government also agreed in 1989 to allow the Ritz-Carlton group to construct a 400-room resort property, also on the south shore. However, the deteriorating financial condition of the industry worldwide and the continuing objections of local residents have caused the project to be postponed indefinitely. Notwithstanding the above exceptions, the moratorium continues to be in effect, and its emphasis continues to be the strengthening of existing properties and the improvement of their occupancies.

GRADING POLICY

The emphasis on controlled, upscale development was further strengthened by the Department of Tourism's grading plan introduced in 1988 designed specifically to link the renewal of hotel licences with the maintenance of high-quality standards. Under this plan, properties are required to meet high standards of cleanliness, attractiveness and offer defined levels of amenities in order to ensure the renewal of their operating licence. Clearly, conventional mass tourism plays no part in Bermuda's tourism policy as to property development.

TIMESHARE POLICY

The conservative approach which the policies on development and standards attest to are mirrored by the country's policy with respect to timesharing properties. During the 1980s, two hotel properties received permission to convert to timesharing, and permission was granted in 1981 to York-Hannover, the Canadian developer, to construct a timesharing resort in the town of St George. Since then, a moratorium has been placed on any further timesharing development until the government can assess its role as a tourism product. This policy is contrary to that of many other island resort destinations which have embraced the timesharing concept, not always with positive results. In this sense, the policy is an indicator of the control which Bermuda exercises over innovative development in addition to traditional development.

CRUISESHIP POLICY

As indicated earlier, cruiseship arrivals have played a major part in Bermuda's tourism since its inception. This segment reached its high point in 1988 when arrivals totalled 158,368. However, concern about overcrowding on the part of hoteliers, and related impact to the island's image resulted in Bermuda adopting a restrictive policy in 1988. This policy limited cruiseship arrivals to 120,000 during the high season of May to October, and allowed only four scheduled cruiseships weekly between Monday and Friday. The policy also allowed for up to 12 additional occasional callers.

The rationale for such a restrictive policy was to reduce the pressure on Bermuda's tourism infrastructure and to maintain the image of the island as an upscale destination (Riley 1991). To further bolster these objectives, visits were only awarded to high-standard cruise operators such as the Royal Viking Line, Chandris Celebrity Cruises and Royal Caribbean.

In 1989, the year the restrictive policy began to take effect, cruiseship arivals fell to 131,322 and in 1990 actually fell below the 120,000 ceiling with a total of 113,000. As a result of this decrease and the deterioration in the tourism industry generally, the government raised the ceiling in the early 1990s to 150,000. This relaxing of the policy was designed to offset the drop in air arrivals which had been occurring since the 1987 high. This policy and its recent amendments again underscore the extent to which the maintenance of a narrow market approach form the basis of Bermuda tourism. Policies are flexible, striving always for a balance between arrivals and profitability. The focus is always on extracting the maximum return from the least number of visitors. [...]

THE SITUATION IN THE EARLY 1990S

By the end of the 1980s, an attitude pervaded Bermuda's tourism industry that it was unique, not really subject to competition or to the changes in the interna-

tional tourism market. This attitude led to complacency, an antipathy to innovation and a decreasing of service quality. This was accompanied by a significant
downturn in business which Table 8.2 illustrates. In 1991, the total number of
visitors to the island dropped by 32,700 from the 1990 total of 547,500. While
this represented only a 5.9 per cent decrease, the most significant drop was in the
number of hotel-based visitors. Whereas in 1990, 434,900 visitors stayed in
hotels, by 1991 the number dropped to 386,700, a decrease of 11.0 per cent.
Given that hotel-based visitors in 1991 represented an average daily expenditure
of $225 compared with cruise visitors whose average daily expenditure was $70,
the impact of the downturn in hotel-based visitors was catastrophic (*Commission
on Competitiveness* 1994, p54).

In 1992, the situation stabilized to some extent, but a small decrease of
11,500 in hotel-based visitors, representing a 2.9 per cent decline, was still experienced. Although the relaxed cruiseship policy saw a small increase in 1992 of
2800 visitors, the overall total in 1992 was still less than 1991, amounting to
506,200, the lowest annual visitor arrival since 1973. Perhaps most significantly,
the total tourism expenditures decreased from US$490.1 million in 1990 to
US$443.0 million in 1992.

The creation of the Commission on Competitiveness and the Tourism Planning
Committee can be understood in the light of these data. For the first time in recent
memory, Bermuda actually experienced a small level of unemployment in the
hospitality sector and allied economic areas such as retailing. This resulted in a
decrease in the granting of work permits, and the expatriate population of the
island dropped by approximately one-half during this period. While this alleviated
some of the employment concerns for Bermudians, it created other social consequences including a diminishing of rental revenues, a significant source of income
for a substantial number of Bermudians. [...]

Table 8.2 *Bermuda tourism arrivals and expenditure, 1990–93*

Year	Arrivals ('000s)			Expenditures ($ millions)		
	Air	Cruise	Total	Air	Cruise	Total
1990	434.9	112.6	547.5	467.9	22.2	490.1
1991	386.7	128.2	514.8	423.9	31.7	455.6
1992	375.2	131.0	506.2	410.5	32.5	443.0
1993	412.4	153.9	566.3	NA	NA	NA

Sources: *Commission on Competitiveness Final Report* 1994, p48 and *Bermuda in
Perspective*, 27 January 1994

CONCLUSIONS

As a result of its examination, the Tourism Planning Committee reached the
following conclusions:

• Bermuda has been a model for developing tourism as a basis for a prosper-
  ous economy. Its success in the past should provide confidence that
  Bermuda tourism can improve in the future.

- The economy and quality of life in Bermuda are dependent upon tourism. The current declines in tourism are serious and will not correct themselves without concerted effort. Nothing can adequately replace tourism in the island's economy, not even a greatly expanded international business sector.
- Changes in world tourism, including new products, choices and competition, will dictate many of the circumstances to which Bermuda will have to adapt.
- Bermuda is dependent upon the United States for its tourism market. It is losing its share of this market, and not primarily because of the US economy or international conflicts. The US market cannot be satisfactorily replaced with some other source market such as Europe or the Far East.
- Bermuda's essential tourism product, the large hotels, are losing business and this is the primary reason for the decline in tourism revenues. These declines have resulted in losses in jobs, income, and domestic business throughout Bermuda. The large hotels have not been profitable as a group since 1987 and have seen their occupancies drop on average from 68.0 per cent in 1987 to 55.9 per cent in 1992 (*Commission on Competitiveness* 1994, p62).
- The cruiseship visitor cannot replace the staying visitor for economic impact on the island. The data presented above attest to this.
- Seasonality is a problem in Bermuda, but its pattern has not changed significantly in recent years. It appears worse because all tourism has declined including the shoulder and off-season.
- There are concerns for the lack of tourism awareness and appreciation for tourism in Bermuda. Some Bermudians do not respect the need to accommodate tourists on the island.
- Management/labour problems on Bermuda, of serious concern in the tourism industry, exacerbate issues of hotel profitability, labour recruitment, costs and respect for the tourism industry.
- Bermuda has major deficiencies in providing shopping, dining, entertainment and recreational experiences to the tourist. These include inadequate product, information and access. Bermuda has not capitalized on its many assets like natural resources, marine environment, culture and heritage.
- Bermuda is overpriced in many respects and does not meet price/value expectations of visitors.
- Bermuda's problems are not the result of inadequate marketing or promotion but rather, inadequate product policies and price/value issues.
- Bermuda's source market is small, exclusive and affluent. It is a market sought after by much of Bermuda's competition, including destinations in the US. It is no longer valid to assume that Bermuda does not have any serious competition for this market niche.
- Bermuda must accept the need for fundamental change. It cannot dictate the terms of world tourism. This will require significant investment of resources and effort. There are no simple, single or quick fixes for improving the tourism industry in Bermuda (*Commission on Competitiveness* 1994, pp81–82).

Having reached these conclusions, the Tourism Planning Committee made the following major recommendations:

- The management of the tourism industry needed to be changed in a way which would result in more emphasis on product policy and development through a comprehensive planning process which would incorporate the input of various sectors of the industry. This recommendation included a consideration of the role which the Department of Tourism currently plays in the management of the tourism industry and suggestions for an expanded role to include some level of responsibility for strategic planning and product policy determination and implementation through a Policy Coordination Council appointed by the premier, Tourism Action Councils representing various sectors of the industry and a Tourism Education Council to co-ordinate education, training and tourism awareness activities. The Committee also presented various options for restructuring the Department including the QUANGO (Quasi-Autonomous Non-Governmental Organization) concept which would provide it with greater responsibility and more autonomy.

- The tourism product requires enhancement in terms of accommodation and eating facilities, events, transportation, amenities, retailing, development of public places and recreational activities. The Committee recommended the creation of the Bermuda Development Fund to attract domestic investment in the tourism industry and to provide capital for small business operators to enhance their services. The Committee also recommended that much of the enhancement co-ordination should utilize the services of national bodies such as the Bermuda Chamber of Commerce, whose membership has a direct stake in the improvement of the tourism industry.

- Recognizing that management/labour relations have bedevilled the industry for two decades, the Committee recommended that a Task Force on Employment be created to try and depolarize the two sides to this ongoing conflict through the greater dissemination of information, education and development of innovative human resource strategies including worker empowerment, involvement and recognition schemes.

- Given the importance of the large hotels to the continued viability of the industry, the Committee recommended that the profitability of the hotels be improved through efforts to expand the season including the use of innova-tive packaging based on emerging trends in the travel market such as cultural and ecotourism niches. It also recommended that the cost struc-tures for hotels be reviewed within the context of Bermuda's highly oligopolistic economy and that relief be sought to allow the hotels to become more competitive.

- Price/value considerations are critical for repeat visitation and the Committee recommended that value-added strategies including the offering of a greater range of no-cost or sponsored activities should be incorporated into the island's tourism product. It further emphasized the need for a review of the island's cost structures as mentioned above in order to bring costs in line with competing destinations, at least to the extent that this is possible.

- In its adoption of an inclusive planning process, the Committee recognized the fundamental role which the population of the island plays in the deter-mination of the quality of the product and the level of service provided for tourists. Accordingly, the Committee made a major recommendation relating to the issue of tourism appreciation including the creation of the Tourism Education Council and programmes of education, human resource develop-ment within the industry and the creation of national programmes of certification and recognition, all of which were considered to be part of enhancing the view which the population has of the industry and its value as a career choice.

* Although the Committee, along with the travel industry, recognized the superior reputation of the island for marketing, nonetheless the Committee recommended that greater use be made of database marketing techniques and co-operative advertising. The Committee also recommended that on-going research be conducted into the emerging niches in order to provide a basis for determining whether there are market opportunities which would fit with Bermuda's resources.

These recommendations were presented in detail with timelines and identified the organizations in the community which the Committee felt should have the respon-sibility for ensuring their implementation.

POSTSCRIPT

Given the underlying debate mentioned earlier between the economic cyclists and the structuralists, it is not surprising that implementation of the Committee's recommendations has been slow. Notwithstanding the broad community input which the Committee's recommendations reflect, their implementation in such a small community has implicit political consequences. Given that the government must consider the recommendations along with a plethora of other recommenda-tions relating to international business and new ventures, all within the political arena, it is inevitable that trade-offs will need to take place and compromises sought. This will take time.

In the meantime, the industry has enjoyed somewhat of a resurgence. Total arrivals in December 1993 amounted to 18,368, an increase of 17.2 per cent over the 1992 level of 15,674. Similarly, in January 1994, arrivals amounted to 9268, an 11.2 per cent increase over the 1993 level of 8331. For February, the compa-rable figures are 16,360 in 1994 compared with 14,841 in 1993 or an increase of 10.2 per cent. While these latest arrival levels are not quite back to those of the halcyon days of 1987, they are respectable and have given support to the economic cyclist position. Nonetheless, arrival data does not always translate into profits, and there is a suspicion within the industry that a number of properties have been discounting significantly in order to achieve occupancy. Data in support of this contention, however, is not available and it remains to be seen if the resur-gence will restore the profitability of the large hotels. What is clear is that the length of advance booking is becoming much shorter than in the past, indicating that the visitor's purchasing decision is more impulsive. It is also the case that the average length of stay is continuing to erode. In 1993, the average length of stay in registered commercial properties was 5.2 days which compared with 5.6 days for 1992. The member properties of the Bermuda Hotel Association reported a similar drop from 4.7 days in 1992 to 4.5 days in 1993 (*Bermuda In Perspective* 1994, p5).

This chapter has presented a model of inclusive, community-based planning for tourism in a small-island destination. The findings of the Tourism Planning Committee are probably indicative of those which any analysis of a mature desti-nation would uncover. The recommendations for improving the tourism product are reasonable yet innovative. They do not seek to reposition the destination but rather to build upon its existing strengths within a context of a changing tourism market. The recommendation calling for more industry participation in policy setting is consistent with a trend occurring in many jurisdictions. In that sense, the model is very contemporary and responds to the problems which mature destinations face in a manner which is not likely to lead to further erosion of the product for short-term gain. Rather, the aim is to rejuvenate the industry in a manner consistent with the community's wishes and the market's demands. The key will be the extent to which there is a will on the part of stakeholders and policy setters to make the necessary changes recommended by the Commission on Competitiveness.

NOTE

Pages 232–233 relating to Bermuda's tourism development are drawn substantially from Conlin (1993).

REFERENCES

Bermuda in Perspective: An Analysis of Monthly Visitor Statistics (1994) The Bermuda Department of Tourism, 27 January

Commission on Competitiveness. Final Report (1994) Available from the Centre for Tourism Research and Innovation, Bermuda College, P.O. Box DV356, Devonshire DV BX, Bermuda

Conlin, Michael V (1993) 'Bermuda Tourism: A Case Study in Single Segmentation', *Journal of Travel and Tourism Marketing*, 1(4), pp99–112

Riley, Cordell W (1991) 'Controlling Growth While Maintaining Your Customer Base', *Proceedings of the 22nd Travel and Tourism Research Association Conference*, Long Beach, California, pp65–73

Chapter 9

Conclusion

'In mass tourism, the tourist gaze is focused on the extraordinary' (Shaw and Williams 1994, 199). The 'extraordinary' has been packaged as sun or snow resorts that are usually situated at a distance from the urban industrial areas where the majority of consumers have traditionally lived. These destinations also generally differ, in terms of scenery, culture and/or climate, from the tourists' familiar home environments. In the era of postmodernism such resorts are often perceived as uncivilized and tasteless. They stand in contrast to new holiday venues where emphasis is placed upon natural rather than contrived settings. Specialist operators taking individual, more educated travellers to destinations unfrequented by the masses, highlight that part of postmodernism in which a desire to avoid the common herd predominates (Urry 1990). This apparently elitist and individual approach, typified by the appreciation of scenery or of nature, can occur indirectly through representations of reality such as postcards, guidebooks or travelogues, that allow a more widespread and often surrogate experience of pleasure (Urry 1990, Shaw and Williams 1994). As an ever greater variety of objects and places come to provide enjoyment, eg the media, theme parks, historic venues, so Urry's (1990) description of postmodernism in tourism is realized, as pleasure is found increasingly in home locations or through surrogate images. However a change of this nature does not necessarily mean the death of tourism in general, or of mass tourism in particular.

There are, indeed, a number of different trends that can be identified in international tourism. In the developed countries of Western Europe and North America, which are the traditional areas of high consumer demand, old-established tourism patterns continue to exist, albeit sometimes in a slightly different guise, alongside newly emergent forms. These strands appear to fall into three groups:

1. Second holidays, often taken in the form of short breaks, are not a new phenomenon but are becoming more widespread among the older, middle classes (Cater 1994). As many elderly people now experience a healthier and more active retirement so they, in particular, are able to use their disposable income to travel more frequently, thus expanding this sector of the market. Such tourists usually seek warm, sunny destinations, often of a specialist nature, where they can indulge in hobbies and pastimes like golf, painting, bird-watching, and visiting historical and cultural attractions.
2. Ecotourism and active holidays are frequently identified as the fastest growing type of tourism (Cater 1994). Tourists who opt for holidays like these are drawn from a variety of age groups and income levels, although surveys have shown that they are more likely to be older than conventional mass tourists (Boo 1990). They *may* choose to pursue their interests relatively close to home, but there is evidence of a growing demand for more distant venues as, for example, in the case of Britain, where long-haul

holidays have become increasingly popular (*The Times* 1996a). Potential destination countries with outstanding tourism resources, yet with troubled histories that have generated a bad image, like China, Vietnam and Haiti, have begun to promote tourism for the income it generates. In addition, regions like the Caribbean islands, with long-standing rivalries, have come to realise that cooperation is essential if they are to maintain and extend their tourism activities, thereby spreading benefits to the entire region. One of the ways in which they seek to achieve this aim is through the establishment of a model for attracting ecotourists (*The Times* 1996b).

3. Traditional, relaxing, sunshine holidays – particularly to more distant destinations – are also increasing in popularity. Research has shown (*The Times* 1996c) that high income groups, especially those in stressful occupations, are beginning to avoid active holidays and opt instead for those where they can relax and avoid mental and physical exertion. This accords with the popularity of all-inclusive resorts that remove pressure from more fragile locations by concentrating demand in areas able to cope with larger numbers of people. In contrast, such resorts are usually less acceptable, and less sustainable, for host economies and societies.

Although conflicting patterns appear to be emerging in the traditional tourist-originating countries, there is no doubt that the global distribution of originating countries is beginning to change. As incomes rise in newly-developing countries and political changes have given greater freedom of movement to a large number of people in areas like Eastern Europe, so more people have the ability to travel and enjoy holidays abroad. It is likely that many will select a 'sea, sun and sand' venue; for example, those from Eastern Europe may choose to patronize Mediterranean resorts like Torremolinos that are now regarded by many Western Europeans as past their fashionable heyday, while many tourists from the Pacific Rim countries seek heritage destinations, city shopping breaks or golf holidays. These growing numbers of Asian tourists can be divided into a number of distinct categories. There are those tourist movements that lie within Asia and encompass a variety of motivations for travel. The Japanese, for example, visit Nepal for its scenery and culture, and the Philippines, Malaysia and Thailand for their golf courses. Malays, along with other people from South and East Asia, go to Thailand for holidays involving sexual encounters, as well as for more traditional 'sea, sun and sand' and cultural reasons. Asian tourists also travel further afield, like the Japanese who visit Europe to experience a different culture and the heritage of a range of countries. It is quite possible, given global economic changes, that the future will see an increase in the proportion of international tourists from emerging tourist-originating countries: a highly visible manifestation of the process of globalization.

Amidst this changing pattern of tourism, what are the prospects for its increased sustainability? It is evident that the nature of the industry precludes the achievement of true sustainable development. Yet much *can* be done. New *types* of tourism can be encouraged that are capable of incorporating a greater measure of one or more aspects of sustainable development. Unfortunately alternative tourism with these characteristics is likely to involve relatively small numbers of tourists, while worldwide demand continues to rise. It is therefore important to encourage, persuade and coerce all the actors involved in mainstream mass tourism to incorporate a growing range of sustainable criteria into the industry. This is not the impossible task it might at first appear. The process of educating consumers and suppliers has begun and a greater awareness of the dangers of uncontrolled tourism is becoming widespread. Small, initial steps are taking place already, as many of the readings show. If 'best practice' can be widely disseminated, then its adoption can lead to a reduction in the costs and an increase in the benefits of tourism. This should, ultimately, lead to the realization of a far greater level of sustainability, resulting in a higher level of satisfaction for all those involved in the industry.

REFERENCES

Boo, E (1990) *Ecotourism: The Potentials and Pitfalls* Vol 1, World Wildlife Fund, Washington

Cater, E. (1994) 'Ecotourism in the Third World – Problems and Prospects for Sustainability', Chapter 5 in E Cater and G Lowman (eds) *Ecotourism. A Sustainable Option?*, Wiley, Chichester

Shaw, G and Williams, A M (1994) *Critical Issues in Tourism. A Geographical Perspective*, Blackwell, Oxford

The Times (1996a) 'Britons switch to long-haul holidays', Thursday 7 November, p39

The Times (1996b) 'Newcomers are keen to grab a slice of tourism', Thursday 14 November, p39

The Times (1996c) 'Executives tire of activity breaks', Thursday 31 October, p41

Urry, J (1990) *The Tourist Gaze. Leisure and Travel in Contemporary Societies*, Sage Publications, London

Sources of Information

CHAPTER 2: PRINCIPLES OF SUSTAINABLE TOURISM

Burns, P and Holden, A 'Alternative and sustainable tourism development – the way forward?' in P Burns and A Holden *Tourism. A New Perspective* Prentice-Hall: Hemel Hempstead, 1995, pp218–21

Muller, H 'The thorny path to sustainable tourism development' *The Journal of Sustainable Tourism* 1994, Vol 2, No 3, pp131–36

CHAPTER 3: CHANGING CONSUMPTION PATTERNS

Cater, E 'Ecotourism in the Third World – Problems and Prospects for sustainability' in E Cater and G Lowman *Ecotourism. A Sustainable Option?* Wiley, Chichester, 1994, pp69–86

Cooper, C and Jackson, S 'Destination Life Cycle. The Isle of Man Case Study', *Annals of Tourism Research* 1989, Vol 16, pp377–83

Krippendorf, H 'The motives of the mobile leisureman' and 'Behaviour and experiences while travelling', in J Krippendorf *The Holiday Makers* Butterworth and Heinemann: Oxford, 1989, pp22–9, 41–3

Poon, A 'Global transformation', in A Poon *Tourism, Technology and Competitive Strategies*, CAB International, Wallingford, 1993, pp85–92, 115

Wheeller, B 'Tourism's troubled times: responsible tourism is not the answer', *Tourism Management* 1991, June, pp91–6

CHAPTER 4: PROMOTING SUSTAINABLE DEVELOPMENT AND COMBATING POVERTY: ENVIRONMENTALLY SOUND PROGRAMMES

Cater, E and Goodall, B 'Must tourism destroy its resource base?', in S R Bowlby and A M Mannion *Environmental Issues in the 1990s* Wiley, Chichester, 1992, pp317–21

Munt, I and Higinio, E 'Belize – eco-tourism gone awry', *In Focus* 1993, Autumn, No 9, pp12–13. First printed in NACLA Report on the Americans, Vol XXVI, No 4 (February 1993), 475 Riverside Drive, Suite 454, New York, NY 10115.

Olindo, P 'The old man of nature tourism', in T Whelan *Nature Tourism*, Island Press, Washington DC, 1991, pp23–7, 30–8

CHAPTER 5: PROMOTING SUSTAINABLE DEVELOPMENT AND COMBATING POVERTY: SOCIO-CULTURALLY SENSITIVE PROGRAMMES

Hall, C M 'Sex tourism in S E Asia', in D Harrison *Tourism and the Less Developed Countries*, Belhaven Press, London, 1992, pp64–5, 66–9, 72–4

Patullo, P 'Reclaiming the heritage trail: culture and identity', in P Patullo *Last Resorts* LAB and Cassell, London, 1996, pp178–94

Reisinger, Y 'Social contact between tourists and hosts of different cultural backgrounds', in A Seaton et al *Tourism. The State of the Art*, Wiley, 1994, pp748–52

Shaw, G and Williams, A 'Individual consumption of tourism', in G Shaw and A Williams *Critical Issues in Tourism*, Blackwell, Oxford, 1994, pp87–93

Smith, V 'Introduction', in V Smith *Hosts and Guests: The Anthropology of Tourism*, 2nd ed University of Pennsylvania Press, Philadelphia 1989, pp9–17

CHAPTER 6: PROMOTING SUSTAINABLE DEVELOPMENT AND COMBATING POVERTY: EMPOWERING GROUPS AND COMMUNITIES

Bird, C 'Communal land, communal problems', *In Focus* 1995, Summer, No 16, pp7–8

Cammen, S van der 'Involving Maasi women', *In Focus* 1995, Summer, No 16, pp14–15

Hennessy, S 'Female employment in tourism development in South-west England', in V Kinnaird and D Hall *Tourism. A Gender Analysis*, Wiley, Chichester, 1994, pp39–47

CHAPTER 7: ECONOMIC PERSPECTIVES

Buckley, P J. and Witt, S F 'Tourism in difficult areas. Case studies of Bradford, Bristol, Glasgow and Hamm', *Tourism Management*, 1985, September, pp210–13

Gomes, A J 'Integrating tourism and agricultural development', in D J Gayle and J N Goodrich *Tourism Marketing and Management in the Caribbean*, Routledge, London, 1993, pp155–66

Lea, J 'Tourism's economic impacts', in J Lea *Tourism and Development in the Third World*, Routledge, London, 1988, pp44–50

Marfurt, E 'Tourism and the Third World: Dream or nightmare?', *Swiss Review of World Affairs*, 1983, July, pp14, 17–20

Robinson, D W 'Strategies for alternative tourism: The case of tourism in Sagarmatha (Everest) National Park, Nepal', in A Seaton et al *Tourism. The State of the Art*, Wiley, Chichester, 1994, pp691–5, 699–701

Sharman, P B and Dixon, J A 'The economics of nature tourism: Determining if it pays', in T Whelan *Nature Tourism*, Island Press, Washington DC, 1991, pp108–20

Weaver, D 'Ecotourism in the Caribbean Basin', in E Cater and G Lowman *Ecotourism. A Sustainable Option?*, Wiley, Chichester, 1994, pp171–3

CHAPTER 8: THE ROLE OF GOVERNMENTS

Conlin, M 'Rejuvenation planning for island tourism: The Bermuda example', in M Conlin and T Baum *Island Tourism*, Wiley, Chichester, 1995, pp181–2, 185–90, 192–4, 198–202

Inskeep, E 'Tourism planning approach of Malta' and 'Tourism planning in Bhutan', in E Inskeep *National and Regional Tourism Planning*, Routledge, London, 1994, pp81–5, 103–8

Pearce, D 'Planning for tourism', in D Pearce *Tourist Development*, 2nd ed Longman, Harlow, 1989, pp250–6

Index

Numbers in **bold** refer to figures in the text.

Index